I0817326

GEORGE F. PAUL

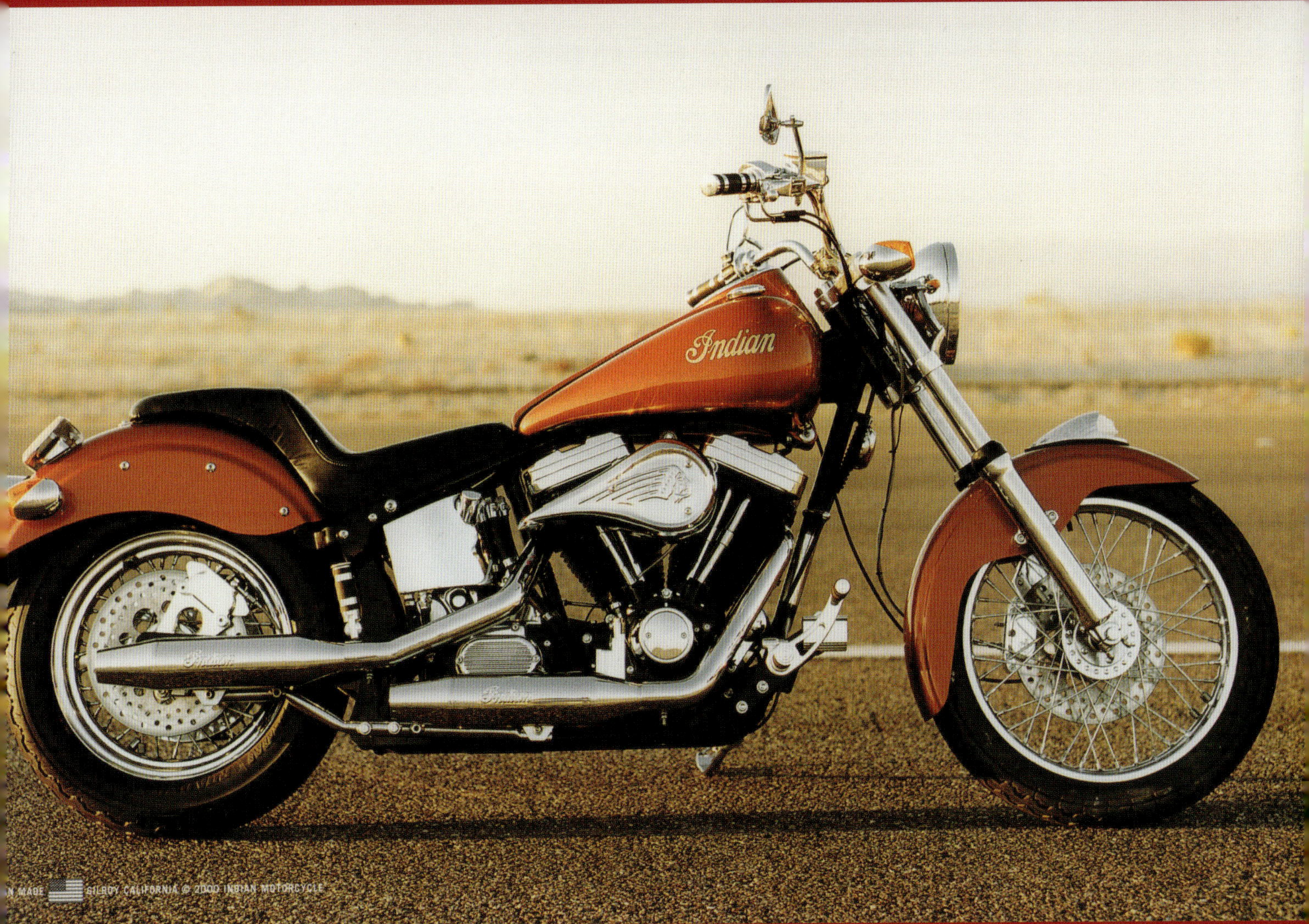

GILROY INDIANS

The Indian Motorcycle Company of America, 1999–2003

4880 Lower Valley Road • Atglen, PA 19310

DEDICATION

This book is dedicated to four people who contributed in significant ways to its conception and completion. To our son Tim's wife, Rachel, who (like my wife, Barbie) has no love of motorcycles but reluctantly supported Tim in acquiring his first one. To our son, Tim, whose request for a riding partner eventually launched me back into motorcycling after nearly thirty years. To Barbie, my wife of fifty years, whose love overcame her trepidation of my riding, and whose reluctant blessing eventually led to my discovery of Gilroy Indian motorcycles. To our daughter, Jess, who applied her considerable expertise to proofreading draft chapters and offered valuable suggestions. U dun reel good, huney. I love you all.

Library of Congress Control Number: 2025939984

Designed by Jack Chappell
Cover design by Jack Chappell
Type set in Sabon/Span/TT Norms/Times

ISBN: 978-0-7643-7105-9
ePub: 978-1-5073-0664-2
Printed in China

10 9 8 7 6 5 4 3 2 1

Published by Schiffer Publishing, Ltd.
4880 Lower Valley Road
Atglen, PA 19310
Phone: (610) 593-1777; Fax: (610) 593-2002
Email: info@schifferbooks.com
Web: www.schifferbooks.com

CONTENTS

FOREWORD

BY REY SOTELO

So, I got an email from George Paul asking me if I could give him some information on the Indian Motorcycle Company of America in Gilroy. George goes on to explain that he is writing a book on the history of the IMCOA. Well, before I respond to him, I do my research on George Paul and find out he is a very accomplished author and has had many books published over the years . . . now I am very curious, and I responded to him that I would be happy to talk to him about the Indian Motorcycle Company of America. In this book, George has captured what it was like to be part of history.

My relationship with motorcycles goes back further than I can remember. Motorcycles have not just been a passion; they've been the center of my life. Over the years, I've met some extraordinary people through my love for two wheels, including innovators, riders, and enthusiasts alike. Many of these connections were forged through a shared love of Indian motorcycles, a brand that has always held a special place in my heart.

I started my journey by opening my first motorcycle repair shop at twenty-two years old, and soon I found myself building custom motorcycles with my company, the California Motorcycle Company, producing over 1,500 custom bikes a year. In 1998, this passion led me to Indian motorcycles, when I sold my company to the Indian Motorcycle Company of America and became the new president.

That role changed my life and my association with motorcycles in ways I couldn't have imagined. Someone once said to me, "You must be living your dream." And I responded, "Who could dream this?" My time with Indian was a mix of adventure, education, and an opportunity to carry forward a brand I loved.

I am incredibly proud of our work to keep Indian alive during that time, despite the many challenges we faced. When I left in 2002, it was with a heavy heart. The company was heading in a direction I didn't believe in, and it was hard to walk away from something that had become such a huge part of me.

Years later, in 2013, while visiting an Indian Motorcycle dealership in Sydney, Australia, I met Steve Menneto, then the president of Indian. When I introduced myself, he knew who I was, and I told him something I deeply believed: "Had we not failed, you would not have succeeded, and this legendary motorcycle wouldn't be here." He agreed.

Today, I proudly carry forward that legacy as an Indian Motorcycle dealer in Hollister, California. My connection to Indian runs deep, and I'm grateful for the incredible people I've met along this journey, all connected through a shared love of motorcycles and this iconic brand.

This book is a great read. George captures the challenges, achievements, and heartaches of launching the company that finally revived the Indian Brand. The book chronicles the year-by-year development of the Gilroy-era motorcycle line, using original pictures and catalog pages. This book was written to garner the respect for the five-year production of IMCOA that it deserves, and George nailed it!

—Rey Sotelo, president of South County Motorcycles; California Motorcycle Company; Indian Motorcycle Company of America; Indian Motorcycles, Hollister California; and member of the Sturgis Motorcycle Hall of Fame Class of 2001

PREFACE

There's an old saying that goes "If I have to explain it, you wouldn't understand." I don't ascribe to that notion, because it's condescending and presumes the audience is incapable of appreciating the topic. Most people are better than that. I'm living that belief by attempting with this book to interest the uninitiated in a motorcycle company that existed for only five years and has been extinct for over two decades. The products it built are dinosaurs by today's standards. One might reasonably ask, "Why should any of this interest me?" Especially if one is not particularly interested in motorcycles.

The short answer is this: Americana, human interest, industrial design, noble ideals, lies, deceit, theft, high risk, heartbreaking failure, and mysterious infatuation—not necessarily in that order.

The Indian Motocycle Company (that's right—no "r") was once the largest motorcycle company in the world. Founded in 1901 in Springfield, Massachusetts, by the 1920s, Indian was *the* most recognized motorcycle brand—right up there with Ford, Chevrolet, Coca-Cola, Maxwell House, Brylcreem, A&W Root Beer, Land O'Lakes, and Sears, Roebuck. Indian motorcycles were as well known as Volkswagen Beetles would be in the 1960s. It seemed as though everybody knew somebody who had one. In addition, Indian motorcycles were legendary on racetracks and had a flair for style that equaled their technical excellence. Of the hundreds of American motorcycle brands, only two survived the Great Depression: Indian and Harley-Davidson. By 1953, a series of poor business decisions finally caused Indian to cease the manufacture of its famous steeds. The brand entered a long period of relative chaos.

You meet the nicest people on an Indian.

A decade or so after Indian's demise, many were nurturing fond memories of Indian motorcycles, and rather than becoming just old junk, they became collectors' items. Interest continued to grow, and the number of registered Indian motorcycles climbed from approximately 35,000 in the mid-1970s to over 50,000 in the 1990s (when these machines were forty to ninety-five years old). People just couldn't forget Indian. Finally, in 1999, after nearly a half century of being appropriated, sold, stolen, and defamed, the iconic Indian brand was saved and resurrected by the all-new Indian Motorcycle Company of America (IMCOA). No other motorcycle brand has experienced such resurgence. Why? Because Indian was and remains a *loved* brand, evoking a fondness that elevates a machine from a mere vehicle to an experiential joy.

I'm not exaggerating; I experienced it, albeit late in life. When I was a kid in the 1960s and 1970s, I thought those old Indian Chiefs with the skirted fenders were cool. In the 1980s and early 1990s, I owned a couple of Harleys, but for twenty years my office desk sported a model of an *Indian* motorcycle. At age sixty-seven, I bought my first Indian, and the experience eventually moved me to write this book about the company that manufactured it. Again, why? The human interest? The drama? The heartbreaking near misses? The distinctive motorcycles? History repeating itself?

I'd be obliged if, after reading this book, you would kindly explain it to me.

ACKNOWLEDGMENTS

A book is seldom the result of a single person's effort, and this book is no exception. I am deeply indebted to those responsible for the books and articles listed in the bibliography. Their efforts decades ago provided me with a foundational education of the brand. I learned much practical knowledge from several online sources, especially from members of the "Indian Motorcycle Community," the "Gilroy Era of Indian Motorcycles" Facebook group, and the "Gilroy Indian Motorcycles" Facebook group.

Very special thanks go out to Frank Aliano (former IMCOA consultant and owner of Blackhawk Motor Works), who provided much useful information on Blackhawk Powerplus 100 rebuilds and reviewed several draft chapters; to Guy Auyeung (former IMCOA logistics director and owner of American Moto Parts), who reviewed draft chapters and pointed out a couple of potentially embarrassing omissions; to Joe Malfa (owner of JAM Consulting, LLC), who reviewed draft chapters and offered helpful suggestions; to Bill Melvin (former CEO of National Equipment Retail Liquidators), who reviewed several draft chapters and provided many details surrounding the end of the Gilroy operation as well as kindly giving permission to publish descriptions and VINs of thirty-nine 2004 Indians sold after the factory closure; to Frank J. O'Connell (former president and CEO of IMCOA), who reviewed several draft chapters and offered much encouragement in addition to allowing me to quote extensively from his book, *Jump First, Think Fast*; to Mark Peterson (Gilroy Indian historian, restoration specialist, and collector extraordinaire), who opened his fabulous collection to my wife and me for photography and provided a gold mine of information on the 2004 models; and to Rey Sotelo (former president and CEO of IMCOA and current owner of Hollister Powersports), who reviewed draft chapters and offered information, insights, and passion. In addition, Rey kindly agreed to write the foreword to this book, for which I am honored. All of these generous people shared their knowledge and enthusiasm for this book, which means a lot. Their patience with my numerous emails and phone calls asking about arcane details is something for which I will always be grateful.

Ted Doering, Rob Taylor, and Lyn Conklin of the Motorcyclepedia Museum, 250 Lake Street, Newburgh, New York, very kindly opened their outstanding museum one sunny Wednesday morning for my wife and me, thus enabling a private photo shoot of their 2004 Chief Vintage.

Special thanks go to those who contributed images for the book, as acknowledged in the captions.

I'm in debt to Karla Rosenbusch, Editor, and Jack Chappell, Designer, (both of Schiffer Publishing, Ltd.) who endured my initial prodding and my subsequent niggling. I was lucky to get these two.

ACKNOWLEDGMENTS

I began writing this book two years before I realized it. My initial aim was simply to educate myself about Gilroy Indians, and as my knowledge grew, I outlined the history of IMCOA and its products into various Word documents purely for my own use. Over two years, those documents expanded into several "chapters," until it finally dawned on me that this was feeling familiar. I was writing a book. One problem with this sequence of events was that I hadn't kept a strict record of who contributed particular pieces of information. I remembered many sources, but for others I laboriously searched old posts in online groups and in my private messages. The following people kindly responded to my phone calls, emails, and online queries over the years: Chas Alan, James Bauer, Paul Baur, Cory Bear, Larry Bennett, Harry Best, Scout Bikerdog, Danny Blackburn, Tim Bonuccelli, Tom Borchardt, Bill Bowren, Shawn Brant, Rick Conway, Randall Cordell, Mat Costelloe, Bob Dalton, Steven Danford, Darrell Eilts, Tillman Estes, Danny Flucke, Vinny Fonderico, Steve Fortino, Dan Gagan, Terry Gibson, Brian Graham, Terry Greer, Paul Grice, Kevin Hanshew Sr., Chris Hester, Chris Hall, Tim Hall, Joe Howard, Tony Howell, Buzz Kanter, Michael Kuder, Sam Lees, Robert Lyons, Robert Majcherek, Kim and Joe Malfa, Wade Martin, Lou Michaud, Larry Long, Randall Jay Meier, Donovan Carl Moser, Mark Moses, Ken Netteberg, Kurt Patrick Noll, Julie Osadchey, Kent Palazzo, Nigel Peacock, Pete Peno, Polarn Per, Jimmy Pickett, Jamie Pickler, James Powell, Carey Roberts, Kevin Rose, Madeline Rose, Kurt Rosenberg Sr., Ken Ross, Gilbert Ruiz, Mark Ruiz, Landon Sanborn, Tim Scrivner, Mark Seefried, Ray Seidel, Hooman Skie, Ron Stoner, Scott Symons, Mike Tailford, Thomas Tarr, David Torres, Dan Troxel, Chris Wheeldon, and Norm Zabala. If I have overlooked anyone, please accept my apologies, but know that I truly appreciate your help. While all these kind people have assisted me in one way or another, either directly or indirectly, any inaccuracies in this book are my own, for which I am solely responsible.

CHAPTER 1

Phoenix Rising: The Birth of Gilroy Indian

Anyone who has explored, even casually, the storied history of the Indian Motocycle/Motorcycle Company of Springfield, Massachusetts (1901–1953) has encountered the charisma radiated by the brand. It seems nearly everyone has an Indian motorcycle story. A family member or friend had one. Sometimes a stranger will smile, a wistful look in his eye, and recall the Indian he once rode. Period advertisements stated, "There's Magic in the Name Indian." This was more than sales hype. Even during the darkest days of the brand (and there were many over the past 125 years), the memories and affection of millions—riders and nonriders alike—would not allow that magic to die. Despite everything that battered and bruised the legendary name and the various companies that sold it over the years, Indian refused to die. Magic indeed.

Rocky Road

Motorcycle manufacturing in the US has never been an easy business. The current owner of the Indian Motorcycle brand, Polaris Inc., didn't show a profit on the Indian Motorcycle business until twelve years after acquiring it. A new company usually cannot survive such conditions. Of the hundreds of American motorcycle brands that existed in the early twentieth century, only two (Indian and Harley-Davidson) survived the Great Depression. Unlike the latter firm, which was owned by the same family until 1969, Indian underwent several changes of ownership and management beginning in 1913. Over the years, some of those management teams proved competent, but others were grossly inept, even criminal, siphoning millions of dollars from the company coffers. Fortunately, E. Paul and Francis du Pont's purchase of Indian in 1930 saved the company during the Great Depression, despite its drain on the du Pont fortune. But by 1945, Indian had a worn-out plant, antiquated technology, a neglected dealer network, and very little capital to improve its situation in the postwar climate.

Ralph Rogers, who purchased Indian in late 1945, staked much of his fortune on reviving Indian with lightweight and middleweight bikes using modular engines. The idea was sound, but the execution was a disaster from which the company never recovered. In 1949, the Indian Motocycle Company

From Indian's 1941 catalog. The distinctive skirted fenders first appeared in 1940.

was split into two entities: the Indian Division of the Titeflex Corporation (the motorcycle-manufacturing arm) and the Indian Sales Corporation. At the time, no one could have guessed that the magical brand name "Indian" would not be legally owned by a single motorcycle manufacturing company again for fifty years.

During the 1960s, no entities took steps to protect Indian trademarks, so several people simply claimed to own them. Relative chaos gradually developed regarding the "Indian" brand, with the famous script being applied to metric motorcycles, minibikes, and mopeds built by various companies around the world. This state of affairs lasted for decades, and it sometimes seemed that the Indian magic might never be rekindled. (See the appendix, page 199, for a detailed account of the Indian brand history from 1949 to 1999.)

Retro Mania

By the late 1980s, many baby boomers who remembered the classic motorcycles of their youth were yearning for a "retro" motorcycle. Harley was doing very well with its Heritage Softail series (which even included a Springer Softail hearkening back to pre-1949 springer forks). Harley was, of course, an established company with a vibrant dealer network selling motorcycles by the hundreds of thousands each year (not to mention clothing and accessories). For a new company, it wasn't so easy.

For instance, Excelsior-Henderson had been a highly respected motorcycle firm of the early twentieth century that had ceased production in 1931. In 1993, a new Excelsior-Henderson Motorcycle Company emerged. Six years were spent in designing the new machine and building a factory.

In 1999, the company introduced its new Super-X heavy cruiser. But starting a new American motorcycle company proved to be a monumental and very expensive task. Ultimately, only 1,161 of these bikes were manufactured for 1999, and a further 720 for the 2000 model year. On December 21, 1999, the company filed for Chapter 11 reorganization. Excelsior-Henderson production never resumed. Shortly after the company's collapse, cofounder Dan Hanlon wrote,

> It is exceedingly strenuous to start a proprietary, independent, automobile or motorcycle manufacturing company. Most don't have the courage. What a tough Business Plan. Suffice it to say, there are significant barriers to entry, which is why in the last 75 years no independent start-up project in America even got as far as we did. And may never again.

A bad omen indeed for any proposed new Indian motorcycle production.

In addition to Harley-Davidson, other established companies had an easier time introducing "retro" machines. The 1997 Honda Shadow ACE was so similar to Harley-Davidson's retro cruisers that the Milwaukee firm brought suit. Harley complained that Honda's bike violated not only its visual design, but even its sound (eventually, Harley dropped the case).

Kawasaki, attempting to capture the enduring visual appeal of classic Indian motorcycles, introduced its Vulcan Drifter in 1999, which closely resembled a late 1940s–early 1950s Indian Chief. *Motorcycle Tour & Cruiser* magazine dubbed the bike "Cruiser of the Year." An article in *Rider* magazine quoted the creators as saying that "the object of the exercise had been to marry classic Indian styling with contemporary technology in order to create a motorcycle which one might have expected Indian to manufacture had it still been in existence at the time the project was launched." This goal would soon be echoed by others.

The Magic and Menace of the Indian Brand

The last Springfield-built Indian motorcycles rolled off the line in 1953, but the magic of the brand, unlike so many others, never died. In fact, over the years, thousands of old Indian motorcycles had been restored, resulting in the growth of Indian motorcycle registrations from approximately 35,000 in the mid-1970s to over 50,000 by the mid-1990s. Impressive growth from a brand that had ceased manufacture over forty years earlier! A lot of people wanted an Indian motorcycle, and unfortunately this demand resulted in some unsavory activity.

During the early 1990s, huckster Phillip Zanghi (who ultimately served seven and a half years in prison) lured investors into underwriting new "Indian" motorcycle companies, promising to manufacture modern versions of the classic Chiefs. Phony dealership franchises, IP licensing, and stock shares were offered to those who saw the rich investment opportunities. Not a single motorcycle was ever built by Zanghi. Eventually, investors were left with nothing more than worthless paper.

Wayne Baughman, an Albuquerque businessman, formed Indian Motorcycle Manufacturing Incorporated and promised production of a new "Century Chief." Again, franchises were sold and money collected in down payments for new motorcycles. Ultimately, only three prototypes were built, none of which were roadworthy. One had a wooden engine.

Such activities soured many people on the idea of ever reviving the Indian motorcycle brand. Numerous writers in various motorcycling magazines offered nothing more than skepticism for any possibility of a new US-built Indian motorcycle.

From *Indian Motorcycle Illustrated,* Vol. 1, no. 3 (Spring 1994)

From *Indian Motorcycle Illustrated,* Vol. 1, no. 4 (Summer 1994)

Introducing
The New
Century V-Twin Chief
All American
Motorcycle!

Wherever They Go
The Crowds Gather!
Only A Limited
Number Of Chiefs
Will Be Produced
In 1995.

Wayne Baughman's IMMI "Century Chief." Two-thirds of the total production is pictured in this flyer. Still, it was as close as anyone came to resurrecting an Indian motorcycle before 1999.

The Motorcycle

The IMMI Century V-Twin Chief is the most technically advanced sport touring motorcycle available today.

Century V-Twin Chief
Solo-rider-sport-touring motorcycle
Overall length: 100 in. - Weight, dry: 750 lbs. (est.)

Manufactured by:
Indian Motorcycle Manufacturing, Inc.
5154 Edith Blvd. N.E.
Albuquerque, NM 87107

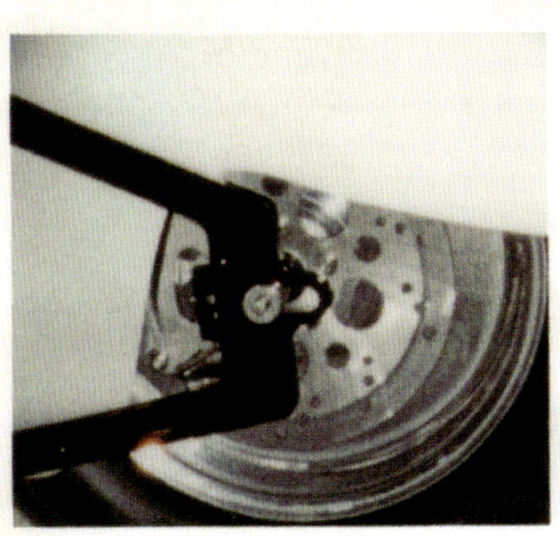

Suspension

Hydraulic clutch control
5-speed, constant-mesh transmission
Primary chain, "wet" clutch
Rear belt drive
Telescoping forks,
hydraulically damped
Articulating rear wheel cage
11.5-inch Disc brakes
Dual-action calipers
Traditional wire wheels
(optional billet aluminum)

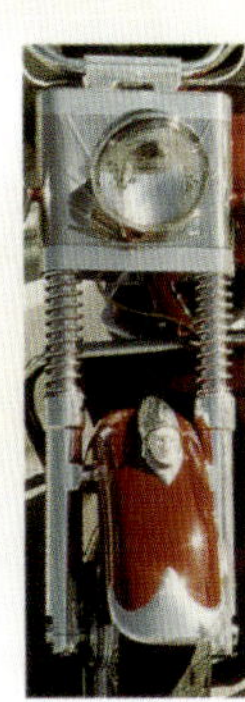

Engine

2-cylinder, 60-degree "V" wet-sleeve
Bore & Stroke: 4 in. x 4 in. (100 mm x 100 mm)
Displacement: 100.6 cu. in. (1667 cc)
85 HP+ at 5000 rpm (est.)
Torque (est.): 88 ft. lbs+ at 4800
Valves: 2 intake, 1 exhaust
Exhaust valve: 1.63-in diameter
Hydraulic valve lifters
Roller-tip rocker arms
Electronic, single fire ignition
Electronic fuel injection
Oil pressure: 60 psi cooling via heat exchanger

Design

Cursive lines flowing dramatically
from fender to handlebars to rear wheel,
a classic unity of form and function -
a styling exercise that holds the ground with security.

Tradition married to the best that modern materials and
computer analysis can offer to a sport touring motorcycle,
from the U.S. forks to the U.S. 100 cubic-inch engine
to the articulated, rear wheel cage,
a machine built with only two things in mind -
rider and road.

The New Indian: The Indian Motorcycle Company of America; Gilroy, California

Amid this craze for Indian motorcycles and the widespread mistrust of those seeking to manufacture new ones, in 1999 a consortium of nine corporate entities managed to secure the necessary manufacturing, financial, and legal resources to finally launch an honest-to-goodness resurrection of the US-built Indian motorcycle. This was the Indian Motorcycle Company of America (IMCOA), based in Gilroy, California. It was a gargantuan project, full of promise. It was the Gilroy-based Indian Motorcycle Company of America that finally consolidated all the Indian manufacturing rights, trademarks, designs, and other intellectual property under a single legal corporate owner (see chapter 4, "IMCOA Corporate History," for details). This momentous accomplishment enabled the resurrection and long-term survival of the Indian motorcycle brand.

The "Gilroy Indians" (as they became known) were initially the outgrowth of Rey Sotelo's California Motorcycle Company (CMC), one of the nine entities that composed the Indian Motorcycle Company of America. CMC custom-built popular bikes influenced by Harley-Davidson's Softail models. In 1998, CMC and Harley-Davidson were the only US motorcycle companies to be listed in the Kelly Blue Book as "Original Equipment Manufacturers." CMC was building approximately 2,100 motorcycles a year and distributing them through sixty dealers, so a fledgling manufacturing/sales network was already in place—a critical necessity in light of the US District Court's requirement for IMCOA to market its new Indian motorcycle within the first year.

The limited-edition (1,100 were built) 1999 Indian Chief utilized a CMC frame and an S&S 88-cubic-inch V-twin engine, plus the iconic full-skirted fenders and fuel tanks of the 1940–48 Chiefs. Hydraulic forks emulated those introduced on the 1950 Chiefs. The 39-inch-wide handlebars completed the machine's low, vintage vibe. In addition to overt nostalgia, the 1999 Indian catalog repeated the goal of other manufacturers: "If the Indian Chief had been around all these years, what would it be like today?"

Custom motorcycle designer Rick Doss developed a distinctive teardrop-shaped headlight and nacelle. These headlights mimicked the appearance of those found on classic Ford V8s of the late 1930s–1940s and were even reminiscent of the headlights seen on E. Paul du Pont's automobiles of the 1920s.

The inspiration: the 1948 Chief Roadmaster

A half century later: longer, lower, but with an unmistakable lineage. *From a 2001 catalog*

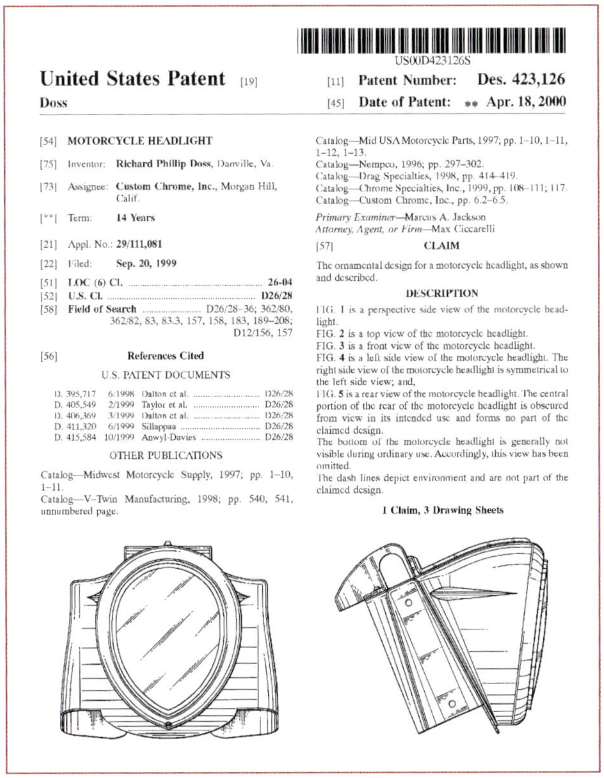

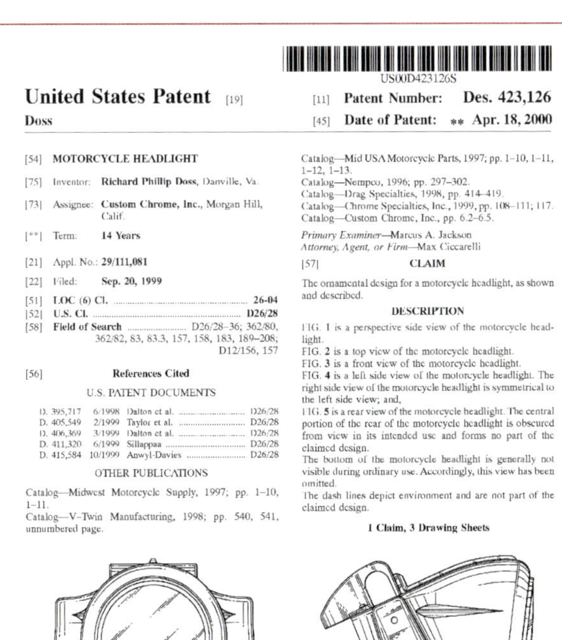

US00D423126S

United States Patent [19]
Doss

[11] **Patent Number: Des. 423,126**
[45] **Date of Patent: ** Apr. 18, 2000**

[54] **MOTORCYCLE HEADLIGHT**

[75] Inventor: **Richard Phillip Doss**, Danville, Va.

[73] Assignee: **Custom Chrome, Inc.**, Morgan Hill, Calif.

[**] Term: **14 Years**

[21] Appl. No.: **29/111,081**

[22] Filed: **Sep. 20, 1999**

[51] **LOC (6) Cl.** **26-04**
[52] **U.S. Cl.** **D26/28**
[58] **Field of Search** D26/28–36; 362/80, 362/82, 83, 83.3, 157, 158, 183, 189–208; D12/156, 157

[56] **References Cited**

U.S. PATENT DOCUMENTS

D. 395,717	6/1998	Dalton et al.	D26/28
D. 405,549	2/1999	Taylor et al.	D26/28
D. 406,369	3/1999	Dalton et al.	D26/28
D. 411,320	6/1999	Sillappaa	D26/28
D. 415,584	10/1999	Anwyl-Davies	D26/28

OTHER PUBLICATIONS

Catalog—Midwest Motorcycle Supply, 1997; pp. 1–10, 1–11.
Catalog—V–Twin Manufacturing, 1998; pp. 540, 541, unnumbered page.
Catalog—Mid USA Motorcycle Parts, 1997; pp. 1–10, 1–11, 1–12, 1–13.
Catalog—Nempco, 1996; pp. 297–302.
Catalog—Drag Specialties, 1998, pp. 414–419.
Catalog—Chrome Specialties, Inc., 1999, pp. 108–111; 117.
Catalog—Custom Chrome, Inc., pp. 6.2–6.5.

Primary Examiner—Marcus A. Jackson
Attorney, Agent, or Firm—Max Ciccarelli

[57] **CLAIM**

The ornamental design for a motorcycle headlight, as shown and described.

DESCRIPTION

FIG. **1** is a perspective side view of the motorcycle headlight.
FIG. **2** is a top view of the motorcycle headlight.
FIG. **3** is a front view of the motorcycle headlight.
FIG. **4** is a left side view of the motorcycle headlight. The right side view of the motorcycle headlight is symmetrical to the left side view; and,
FIG. **5** is a rear view of the motorcycle headlight. The central portion of the rear of the motorcycle headlight is obscured from view in its intended use and forms no part of the claimed design.
The bottom of the motorcycle headlight is generally not visible during ordinary use. Accordingly, this view has been omitted.
The dash lines depict environment and are not part of the claimed design.

1 Claim, 3 Drawing Sheets

The distinctive teardrop headlight of the IMCOA/Gilroy Indians. Note the interesting factory paper label on this 2004 Chief Vintage. *Courtesy of Motorcyclepedia Museum*

The "Aurora" taillight/signal assembly. *Courtesy of Motorcyclepedia Museum*

An elegant taillight/signal assembly called the "Aurora" (perhaps in homage to the Aurora Automatic Machinery Company, which manufactured Indian's early Hedstrom engines) was installed on the rear fender.

The front fender carried the classic "war bonnet" marker light, which first appeared on the 1947 Chiefs. With this mixture of the old and the new, the IMCOA/Gilroy Indian Chiefs looked like nothing else on the road.

Even the paint on the IMCOA/Gilroy Indians was furnished by Dupont—the same supplier of the vivid colors used on the classic Indian motorcycles of the 1930s and 1940s.

The workforce at Gilroy took their jobs seriously. Many were riders and regarded the resurrection of the Indian brand as something akin to a sacred act. As Frank J. O'Connell, former president and CEO of IMCOA, later recalled,

> Rey Sotelo had established the culture at Gilroy. . . . He had an interesting cast of characters and friends whom he had hired. Some were qualified people from the motorcycle business and others had come in from the automotive industry. . . . The culture defied precise definition. It was a combination of bad-boy Rey as the tribal chieftain . . . a motorcycle gang with professionals tossed in for good business measure, a huge customized motorcycle manufacturing operation, and the organizational silly putty that brought and held everyone together—the passion for the Indian brand. The Indian brand cast an aura that was more powerful than money or any individual. It truly felt like you were working toward the second coming of some mythological god.

Impossible Dream

Resurrecting the iconic brand and distinctive appearance aside, the Gilroy firm's goal from the first was to build all-Indian motorcycles. IMCOA's first CEO, Murray Smith, outlined three stages for the company's product development. Stage 1 was the building of "intro bikes" (CMC-built machines with skirted fenders, teardrop-shaped tanks, and the traditional Indian war bonnet on the front fender). Stage 2 was

After forty-six years, art deco fenders and war bonnet marker lights reappeared on Indian motorcycles. *From the 1999 catalog*

planned to occur in the 2000 model year (possibly beginning in August 1999), with a new Indian engine and 80 percent proprietary parts. A production of 11,000 motorcycles was projected for the 2000 model year (actual production was reportedly 3,616). Stage 3 was planned for 2001 and included a "Chief Classic," which would be "almost identical" to a 1947 Chief. Additional models being considered for 2001 were a Roadmaster, a Scout, and a Princess. The company expected to produce 25,000 motorcycles in 2001 (actual production was reportedly 3856).

It's rather heartbreaking to read contemporaneous accounts of what the Indian Motorcycle Company of America was planning in its early days, especially once one is familiar with what eventually occurred. Hopes and passion were high, experienced people were in key positions, the market was hot, and the financing appeared to be ample. IMCOA plowed full speed ahead into the frigid waters of the motorcycle industry, unaware of the icebergs ahead.e icebergs ahead.

CHAPTER 2

Return of the Native: The Gilroy Indians

A note regarding year-to-year changes outlined in this chapter:

Much of the information presented in this chapter was taken from original catalogs. However, keep in mind that many improvements and added features were "running changes" instituted after a production year was well underway. These disparities from catalog descriptions are occasionally seen on surviving machines. Running changes in production features may have been the result of changes in suppliers or using the remaining parts from a previous model year in the early stages of the next. Such variations–when known–have been noted in the text. However, it can be expected that other anomalies exist outside the catalog descriptions.

"The Past can't be repeated, imitated, or replicated. But the spark can be salvaged. The flame rekindled. The torch carried back to its rightful home."

–Indian advertisement from 2000

1999 Model Year

The impossible had finally happened: The Indian trademarks and designs were finally (and legally) in the hands of a bona fide motorcycle company. The promise of new Indian motorcycles was about to be fulfilled, but in order to meet the court-ordered mandate to offer them within one year, the Indian Motorcycle Company of America (IMCOA) had to move fast. Unlike the newly resurrected Excelsior-Henderson Motorcycle Company, which spent six years in development from incorporation to its first motorcycle, Indian had no time to complete the necessary research and design that precedes a new product. It would need to make use of as many existing components as possible. The California Motorcycle Company (one of the nine interests that composed the Indian Motorcycle Company of America) supplied the manufacturing facilities and the frames used on its popular custom bikes, as well as the distinctive sheet metal. S&S 88-cubic-inch Super Stock V-twin engines, Rev-Tech transmissions, Showa forks, Supertrapp exhausts, and other major components were outsourced. The first 150 or so machines were equipped with the inventoried electrical systems used by CMC (Thunder Heart electronic control units were soon substituted and remained standard equipment in Gilroy Indians for the balance of production). A belt-drive dry clutch with a belt final drive mated to a five-speed transmission was standard. The 1999–2001 Indian Chiefs featured a whopping 69-inch wheelbase—probably the longest of any production motorcycle. Despite being criticized by some as "kit bikes," the 1,100 Chiefs built in 1999 sold out quickly at $24,000 apiece.

Meanwhile, work immediately began on a new Indian wet primary, plus two new Indian models (the Scout and the Spirit) riding on Indian frames. In addition, a new Chief was already on the drawing board, complete with a new Indian frame and a new Indian V-twin engine.

Available in 6 × 6 in. as well as a deluxe 12 × 12 in. edition, the 1999 catalog emphasized the history of Indian motorcycles and the romance of riding the legendary brand built for the twenty-first century.

Any doubt concerning IMCOA's immediate intentions to build all-Indian motorcycles will be dispelled by this unique artifact.

This is a prototype outer primary drive housing for IMCOA's wet primary, which was introduced for the 2001 model year. *Courtesy of Mark Peterson*

Shown here is the inner face of the outer primary drive housing (clutch to left; stator to right). Note the engraved message. *Courtesy of Mark Peterson*

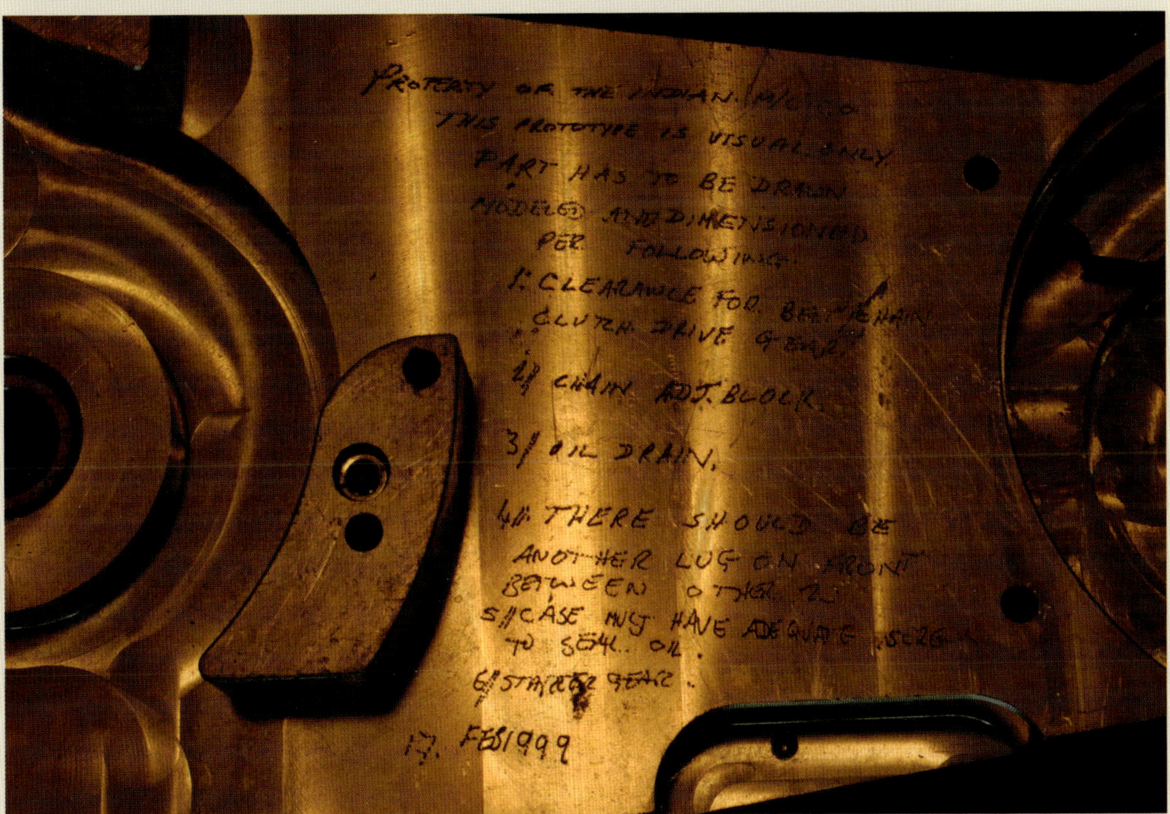

A tight shot of the engraving reveals this: "PROPERTY OF THE INDIAN M/C COMPANY; THIS PROTOTYPE IS VISUAL ONLY; PART HAS TO BE DRAWN, MODELED, AND DIMENSIONED PER FOLLOWING: 1: CLEARANCE FOR BELT/CHAIN CLUTCH DRIVE GEAR; 2: CHAIN ADJ. BLOCK; 3: OIL DRAIN; 4: THERE SHOULD BE ANOTHER LUG ON FRONT BETWEEN OTHER 2; 5: CASE MUST HAVE ADEQUATE SCREWS TO SEAL OIL; 6: STARTER GEAR; FEB 1999." *Courtesy of Mark Peterson*

Mighty Oaks from Little Acorns Grow

The clock was ticking, and, unavoidably, the first new US-built Indian motorcycles since 1953 would be comprised primarily of outsourced parts. This expediency was not entirely new to the Indian brand. In 1897, one of Indian's founders, George Hendee, reportedly used off-the-shelf parts extensively in his early production "Silver King" bicycles. From October 31, 1902, until March 5, 1907, the Hedstrom-designed Indian engines were manufactured by the Aurora Automatic Machinery Company in Aurora, Illinois. From mid-1916 onward, Indian's engine castings were made by Brown & Sharpe Company of Providence, Rhode Island. Frame and fork lugs were supplied by the Moore Drop Forge Company of Springfield, Massachusetts. Starting in January 1927, Indian sold the four-cylinder Ace as an "Indian Ace," although the bike carried no Indian-designed parts until August 1928. An additional number of small components were outsourced in 1932 (Albert Crocker supplied crankpin and lower bearing assemblies). And of course, in the early to mid-1950s, a number of British-built motorcycles were imported and badged as Indians, although they carried no Indian DNA whatsoever. For the new Indian Motorcycle Company of America, there was no other choice for the short term but to rely primarily on existing parts and components.

At an IMCOA board meeting in 1999, Rey Sotelo had concerns after hearing some members focusing on short-term returns rather than developing an all-Indian machine. For some investors unfamiliar with the motorcycling community, offering a bike that *looked* like an Indian seemed good enough. A common theme in the early years was to "sell the sizzle, not the steak." After sitting through a one-hour meeting where $10 million was allocated to marketing, but none to research and development, Sotelo was fuming. When asked for his opinion, Sotelo replied, "You guys don't know what the f**k you're doing. You don't know motorcycle manufacturing." Sotelo knew about motorcycle manufacturing, and he knew the motorcycling community. He was worried.

If the 1999 Indian motorcycles did not yet bring new machinery to the road, their distinctive appearance carried a dazzling resurrected heritage to the closing years of the twentieth century. The company could take pride in proclaiming, "The Indian Motorcycle logos, Indian Motorcycle, Chief, Scout, the skirted fender design and the war bonnet lamp design are trademarks of IMCOA Licensing America, Inc." Nothing else on the road looked quite like them, and there was promise ahead. The Indian was back on its feet.

The S&S Super Stock 88 V-Twin

"I don't want to build a Harley and call it Indian; I want to build an Indian. Let's build an Indian."

–Rey Sotelo, former president and CEO of IMCOA

The Indian Motorcycle Company of America had rescued the legendary brand, but now it had to build it. With no time to develop a new engine before mandated production, the company relied upon an established, proven design built by one of the most respected aftermarket engine manufacturers: S&S Cycle. Based on the outstanding Harley-Davidson Evolution V-twin of 1984–99, the S&S version increased the original H-D displacement from 82 to 88 cubic inches. Fitted with an S&S Super E carburetor and Thunder Heart electronic Ignition System, the S&S Super Stock 88 powered Indian Chiefs through the company's initial product development until 2002. The Indian Scouts and Spirits relied on the S&S 88 until nearly the end of production, when the new 92-cubic-inch Indian engines came online for the 2004 Scouts and Spirits.

From the 1999 catalog

If the resurrected Indian Motorcycle did not yet have an Indian engine, the company nevertheless did what it could to make its S&S 88 V-twins more distinctive. The engines were shipped disassembled to Gilroy, where IMCOA employees powder-coated them, polished the fins (for Chiefs), assembled them, and added a teardrop-shaped air box with an Indian head in full headdress embossed on the side. A 2001 catalog described the engine as "the specially modified S&S engine (1422cc) that is hand assembled by Indian." Unfortunately, this practice led to some unintended consequences. Bill Melvin, who bought and liquidated the contents of the factory after the company's failure, recalled:

> When an old, established company makes a motor, they fully understand that like a hospital, the place has to be spotless and temperature and humidity controlled. Gilroy was too new; not everyone knew the potential problems. I could see that the doors were often left open to cool the plant. Because they had supply and money problems, often parts set out for production, sat open and unprotected from humidity for too long. One tech told me that cases and heads that set out could gain a slight covering of oxidation. Then when automated torque wrenches were used for assembly, they would get false torque figures. Which led to damaged cases and blown head gaskets. —*Bill Melvin, former CEO of National Retail Equipment Liquidators*

Thus, the quality of the IMCOA S&S 88 builds was somewhat dependent upon the weather.

Above: Powder-coated S&S 88 V-twin components (polished fins at left for Chiefs) awaiting assembly at IMCOA in 2001

Right: Newly powder-coated S&S 88 V-twins being assembled at Gilroy. This practice was discontinued after the 2001 model year.

At first, IMCOA did not call much attention to the S&S 88 engines used in its motorcycles, but by 2002, their quality was being touted in the Spirit/Scout catalog.

As IMCOA's financial situation worsened during 2000, the company purchased certain less expensive engine components from Asian suppliers. Some of these parts functioned well, while others did not. Some owners, surprised at the failure of the usually bulletproof S&S mill, were outraged to discover lesser parts in their engines. The resultant problems added to IMCOA's growing warranty demands. Beginning with the 2002 model year, Scouts and Spirits, IMCOA bought the S&S 88 ready to run and with S&S warranties intact.

The S&S Super Stock 88 V-twin can be found in six variations as original equipment to IMCOA Indian motorcycles. The 1999 Chiefs sported black powder coating, polished fins, and a black band on the rocker boxes. The 2000 and 2001 Chiefs were equipped with black powder coating and polished fins. The 2001 Scouts and Spirits featured black powder coating. The 2002 Scout, Scout Deluxe, and Spirit featured engines with a "raw finish" (aluminum). The 2002 Spirit Deluxe was supplied with a "Black Finish" S&S. For 2003, the Scout, Scout Springfield, and Scout Deluxe retained engines with a "raw finish." The 2003 Spirit Deluxe, Spirit Springfield, and Spirit Roadmaster sported a raw finish with polished fins.

Although the S&S Super Stock 88 V-twin was not what the Indian Motorcycle Company of America or its customers originally envisioned for the resurrection of the iconic brand, it was nevertheless an excellent immediate expedient until the company could manufacture an all-Indian product. The S&S Super Stock 88 bears the distinction of powering the first US-built Indian motorcycles produced after nearly a half century, and some owners prefer it to the Indian-designed Powerplus 100 of 2002–03. Regardless of personal preferences, the S&S Super Stock 88 played a pivotal role in the resurrection of Indian motorcycles.

The 1999 Indian Chief, powered by the S&S 88-cubic-inch V-twin engine. Note the black band on the rocker boxes—seen only on the 1999 models. This was the first American-made Indian motorcycle in forty-six years. The staggered dual pipes were quickly replaced in production by a two-into-one exhaust.

INTRODUCING

THE LIMITED EDITION 1999 INDIAN CHIEF

ENGINE	
TYPE	S&S SUPER STOCK 45-DEGREE V-TWIN 4 CYCLE
DISPLACEMENT	88 CUBIC INCH-1442 CC
BORE X STROKE	4.25" X 3.625"
TRANSMISSION	CONSTANT MESH, FOOT SHIFT, 5-SPEED
FUEL SYSTEM	GRAVITY FEED NORMALLY ASPIRATED
EXHAUST SYSTEM	STAGGERED DUALS, FULLY INTEGRATED HEAT SHIELDS
PRIMARY DRIVE	PRIMO BELT DRIVE-DRY CLUTCH
FINAL DRIVE	BELT DRIVE
DIMENSIONS AND WEIGHTS	
LENGTH	102" / 259 CM
SEAT HEIGHT	24" / 60 CM
GROUND CLEARANCE	6" / 15 CM
WHEELBASE	69" / 175 CM
FUEL CAPACITY	5 GALLON U.S. / 18.9 LITRES
OIL CAPACITY	3.0 QUARTS W / FILTER / 2.8 LITRES
DRY WEIGHT	650 LBS.
WHEELS	
BRAKES	FRONT: LIVE 4 PISTON CALIPER, BILLET
	REAR: LIVE 4 PISTON CALIPER, BILLET
TIRES	FRONT: 130 / 90-16
	REAR: 130 / 90-16
WHEELS	FRONT: 60 SPOKE CHROME
	REAR: 60 SPOKE CHROME
FRONT SUSPENSION	SHOWA
REAR SUSPENSION	PROGRESSIVE SUSPENSION
GENERAL	
INSTRUMENTS	LED INDICATOR LIGHTS
SEAT	CUSTOM BY MIKE CORBIN
FRAME	STRETCHED AND RAKED
COLOR OPTIONS	SOLIDS: BLACK, RED, BLUE.
	TWO TONES: RED/BLACK, RED/CREAM, BLACK/GREY, MAROON/CREAM, BLUE/BLUE, BRIGHT YELLOW/WHITE, DOUBLE MOCHA.

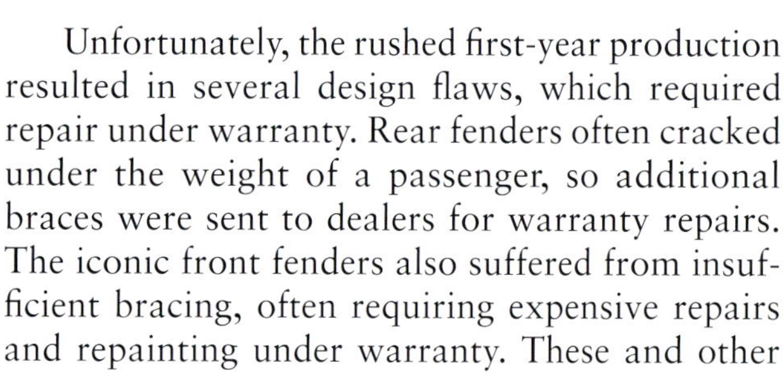

FOR INFORMATION CALL 1-800-350-7902
www.indianmotorcycleco.com

TM-INDIAN MOTORCYCLE AND INDIAN CHIEF ARE REGISTERED TRADEMARKS OF INDIAN MOTORCYCLE COMPANY INC. USED UNDER LICENSE. SPECIFICATIONS SUBJECT TO CHANGE.

Indian MOTORCYCLE

PRINTED IN CANADA

Although not specified on this spec sheet, the Chief's fork rake from 1999 through 2001 was 36 degrees, imparting what admirers call "the Gilroy Rake." The wheelbase was 69 inches.

Unfortunately, the rushed first-year production resulted in several design flaws, which required repair under warranty. Rear fenders often cracked under the weight of a passenger, so additional braces were sent to dealers for warranty repairs. The iconic front fenders also suffered from insufficient bracing, often requiring expensive repairs and repainting under warranty. These and other necessary fixes began to siphon resources from Indian's R&D, which was working on two new models (the Scout and the Spirit), a wet primary, plus a new 100-cubic-inch V-twin Indian engine and frame for the 2002 Chief. Despite the all-too-obvious growing pains, there was pride and optimism at Gilroy, and every 1999 Chief carried a numbered frame neck plate.

Left: Hearkening back to Indian's early days, the 1999 Chief was available in a variety of attractive colors. The paint was supplied by DuPont—the same supplier used by Indian from 1930 to 1953. *From the 1999 Indian catalog*

Right: These specifications printed in Indian's 1999 catalog include generous warranty protection, which would soon come back to haunt the new enterprise.

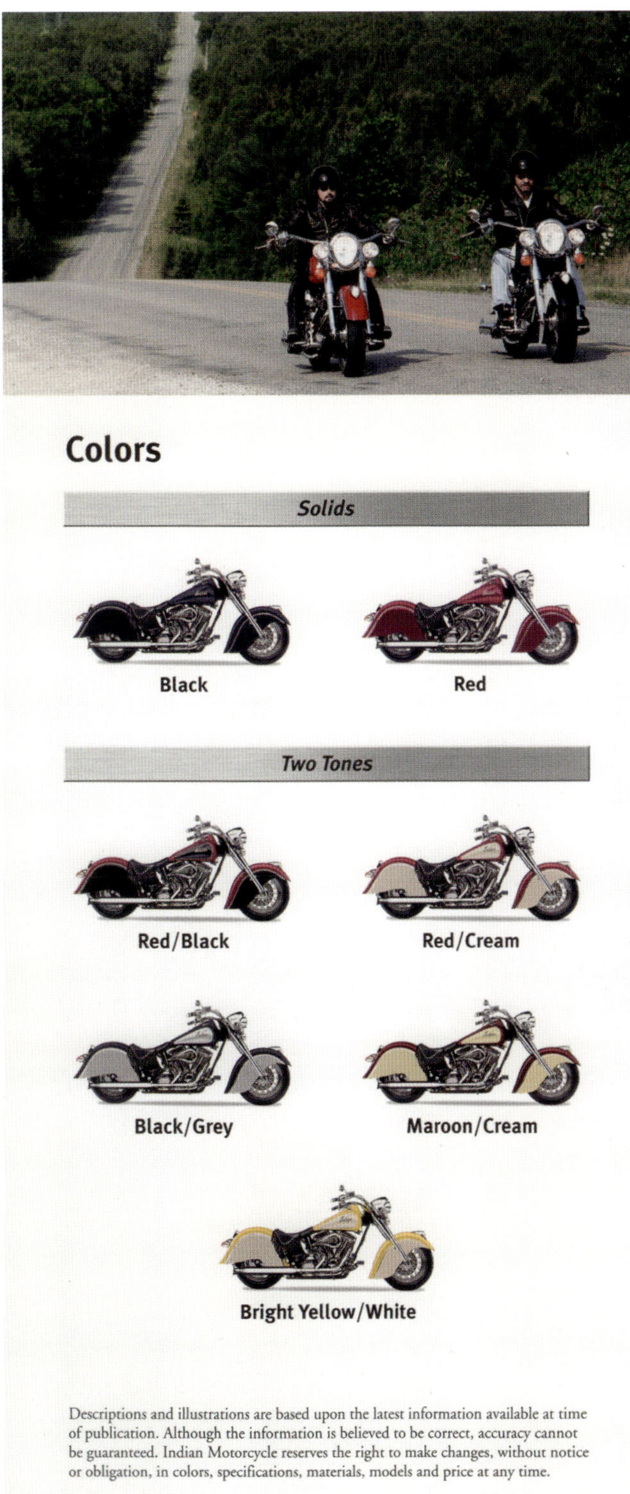

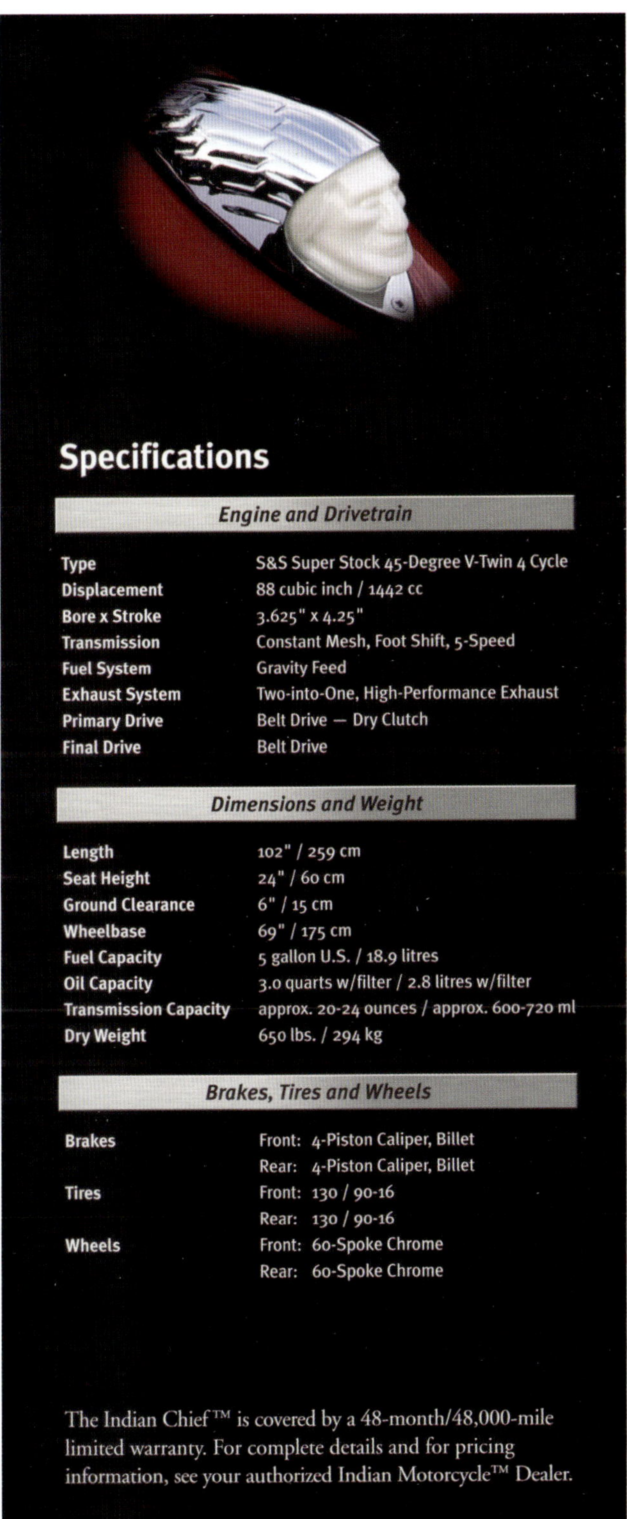

2000 Model Year
Holding Pattern

With the focus on developing the new Scout and Spirit models, along with a new Indian engine, the Chief remained the only model available for 2000, with no changes to its engine or running gear. A minor change was made to the floorboard mounting on the 2000 frame. There were no numbered frame plaques for standard production, but new color options were offered, including "Special Edison" (SE) metallic paints. Showa forks continued to be standard equipment for early 2000 (as did 5-gallon fuel tanks), but ILM forks were phased into later 2000 production. Total production for 2000 was reported to be 3,616.

2000 Chief Shown in Black

FREE SPIRIT. ONE OF A KIND. TRULY INDEPENDENT. THESE ARE THE, WORDS THAT DESCRIBE THE INDIAN OWNER. BECAUSE IT'S NOT ABOUT BELONGING TO ANY CLUBS. OR JOINING ANY GROUPS. IT'S ABOUT A TRULY UNIQUE MACHINE, BUILT BY HAND, WITH IT'S HISTORY INTACT. IT'S ABOUT WANTING TO GET OUT ON THE OPEN ROAD WHILE IT'S STILL OPEN.

2000 Chief Shown in Medium Metallic Blue & Gray
2000 Chief Shown in Black & Cream

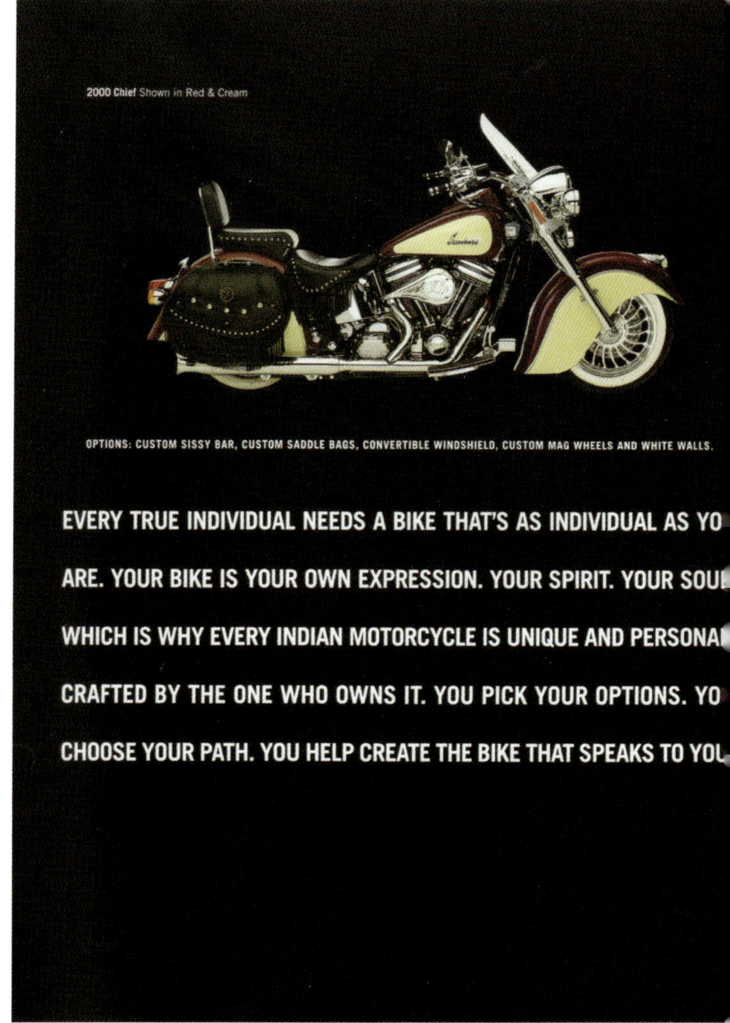
2000 Chief Shown in Red & Cream
OPTIONS: CUSTOM SISSY BAR, CUSTOM SADDLE BAGS, CONVERTIBLE WINDSHIELD, CUSTOM MAG WHEELS AND WHITE WALLS.
EVERY TRUE INDIVIDUAL NEEDS A BIKE THAT'S AS INDIVIDUAL AS YO
ARE. YOUR BIKE IS YOUR OWN EXPRESSION. YOUR SPIRIT. YOUR SOU
WHICH IS WHY EVERY INDIAN MOTORCYCLE IS UNIQUE AND PERSONA
CRAFTED BY THE ONE WHO OWNS IT. YOU PICK YOUR OPTIONS. YO
CHOOSE YOUR PATH. YOU HELP CREATE THE BIKE THAT SPEAKS TO YO

SHOW YOUR COLORS

2000 CHIEF SPECIFICATIONS

Engine

Type	S&S Super Stock 45 Degree V-Twin 4 Cycle
Displacement	88 Cubic inch (1442 cc)
Bore/Stroke	3.625" x 4.25"
Transmission	Constant Mesh, Foot Shift, 5-Speed
Fuel System	Gravity Feed Normally Aspirated
Exhaust System	2 Into 1
Primary Drive	Belt Drive — Dry Clutch
Final Drive	Belt Drive

Dimensions and Weights

Length	102" / 259 cm
Seat Height	24" / 60 cm
Ground Clearance	6" / 15 cm
Wheelbase	69" / 175 cm
Fuel Capacity	5 Gallon U.S. / 18.9 Liters
Oil Capacity	3.0 Quarts U.S. w/Filter / 2.8 Liters
Dryweight	650 lbs. / 294 kg

Wheels

Brakes	Front: 4 Piston Caliper, Billet Rear: 4 Piston Caliper, Billet
Tires	Front: 130 / 90-16 Rear: 130 / 90-16
Wheels	Front: 60 Spoke Chrome Rear: 60 Spoke Chrome

General

Instruments	LED Indicator Lights
Seat	Indian
Frame	Indian

Suspension

Front Suspension	41mm Hydraulic Dual-dampening conventional style
Rear Suspension	Nitrogen charged hydraulic absorber with adjustable pre-load

* SEE YOUR LOCAL DEALER FOR OPTIONS AVAILABLE FOR THE 2000 CHIEF

A later printing substituted this page for the previous image. The later printing includes "#IM5185-071500" on the back cover.

2000 CHIEF SPECIFICATIONS

Engine

Type	S&S Super Stock 45 Degree V-Twin 4 Cycle Assembled by Indian Motorcycle in Gilroy, CA
Displacement	88 Cubic inch (1442 cc)
Bore/Stroke	3.625" x 4.25"
Transmission	Constant Mesh, Foot Shift, 5-Speed
Fuel System	Gravity Feed Normally Aspirated
Exhaust System	2 Into 1
Primary Drive	Belt Drive — Dry Clutch
Final Drive	Belt Drive

Dimensions and Weights

Length	102" / 259 cm
Seat Height	24" / 60 cm
Ground Clearance	6" / 15 cm
Wheelbase	69" / 175 cm
Fuel Capacity	5 Gallon U.S. / 18.9 Liters
Oil Capacity	3.0 Quarts U.S. w/Filter / 2.8 Liters
Dryweight	650 lbs.

Wheels

Brakes	Front: 4 Piston Caliper, Billet Rear: 4 Piston Caliper, Billet
Tires	Front: 130 / 90-16 Rear: 130 / 90-16
Wheels	Front: 60 Spoke Chrome Rear: 60 Spoke Chrome

General

Instruments	LED Indicator Lights
Seat	Indian
Frame	Indian

Suspension

Front Suspension	41mm Hydraulic Dual-dampening conventional style
Rear Suspension	Nitrogen charged hydraulic absorber with adjustable pre-load

Indian Chief Colors

Solids	Red, Black
Two-tones	Red/Black, Red/Cream, Black/Gray, Maroon/Cream Black/Cream, Yellow/Cream
Two-tone Metallics	Medium Metallic Blue/Gray, Dark Metallic Blue/Cream Medium Metallic Red/Black, Dark Metallic Red/Gray

* ASK YOUR DEALER FOR OPTIONS AVAILABLE FOR THE 2000 CHIEF

Another page substitution from the later printing

The third and final page substitution from a later printing

2000 CHIEF & 2000 CHIEF SE SPECIFICATIONS

ENGINE

TYPE	S&S Super Stock 45 Degree V-Twin 4 Cycle
DISPLACEMENT	88 Cubic Inch (1442 cc)
BORE/STROKE	4.25" X 3.625"
TRANSMISSION	Constant Mesh, Foot Shift, 5-Speed
FUEL SYSTEM	Gravity Feed Normally Aspirated
EXHAUST SYSTEM	2 Into 1
PRIMARY DRIVE	Belt Drive-Dry Clutch
FINAL DRIVE	Belt Drive

DIMENSIONS AND WEIGHTS

LENGTH	102"/259cm
SEAT HEIGHT	24"/60cm
GROUND CLEARANCE	6"/15cm
WHEELBASE	69"/175cm
FUEL CAPACITY	5 Gallon U.S./18.9 Liters
OIL CAPACITY	3.0 Quarts U.S. w/Filter/2.8 Liters
DRYWEIGHT	650 lbs.

WHEELS

BRAKES	FRONT: 4 Piston Caliper, Billet
	REAR: 4 Piston Caliper, Billet
TIRE	FRONT: 130/90-16
	REAR: 130/90-16
WHEELS	FRONT: 60 Spoke Chrome
	REAR: 60 Spoke Chrome

GENERAL

INSTRUMENTS	LED Indicator Lights
SEAT	INDIAN
FRAME	INDIAN

INDIAN CHIEF COLORS

SOLIDS	Red, Black,
TWO-TONES	Red/Black, Red/Cream, Black/Gray,
	Maroon/Cream, Yellow/Cream, Black/Cream

INDIAN CHIEF SE COLORS,

TWO-TONES-METALLIC	Medium Metallic Blue/Gray,
	Dark Metallic Blue/Cream,
	Medium Metallic Red/Black,
	Dark Metallic Red/Gray

Note the special-edition colors available at the bottom of this card.

Special Editions

A special-edition uncataloged Chief called the "Millennium" was offered this year, featuring gray/white two-tone paint with dark-gray saddlebags and seat (252 were built). Another special edition for 2000 (also not cataloged) was the "Silver Cloud." This was painted silver and white with light-gray saddlebags and seat (227 were built). Oddly, there is no known promotional material for either the "Millennium" or the "Silver Cloud." The 2000 Silver Cloud reportedly began production quite late in the 2000 model year (August 28, 2000) and continued manufacture until January 19, 2001.

Ominous Developments

It was during 2000 that capital became a major problem for IMCOA. When asked in 2016 if the company was ever "within spitting distance of a profit," Rey Sotelo, former president and CEO of IMCOA, replied,

> No, never. Actually the first year we broke even. Second year [2000], they had major losses because they had money going in fifteen different directions.

The special-edition 2000 "Millennium" Chief. Original pipes were of two-into-one type. *Courtesy of James Bauer*

The special-edition 2000 "Silver Cloud" Chief. *Courtesy of Lee Maloney*

Concerned IMCOA investors brought in Frank O'Connell as a consultant (see chapter 4, "IMCOA Corporate History," for details). Despite the pinch, a brave face was maintained. Rosy predictions were given to the press, probably in anticipation of a public stock offering. The *Los Angeles Business Journal* reported in September 2000, "Indian Motorcycle expects to have about 300 dealerships by next year, when production is projected to increase to 25,000 units and the number of styles is to be expanded." The reality would be only a shadow of the dream.

Contributing to IMCOA's problems was the fact that the company was plagued by suppliers of poor-quality parts. Initially, a large number of parts had been purchased from Custom Chrome, and these provided good fit and finish. As the company's financial situation worsened, less expensive alternatives were sought. Some of the new overseas suppliers sent parts that didn't fit or were marred by substandard chrome (or both). One source in particular provided parts that failed Gilroy's quality inspections 50 percent of the time. Rather than refunding IMCOA, the supplier sent replacement parts—half of which again proved unacceptable. The situation became so bad that eventually, IMCOA acquired some parts "in the rough" and had them chromed and polished locally. All this bogged down quality control inspections, consuming so much time that deadlines for parts returns were occasionally missed. Management's failure to quickly remedy this situation resulted in routine parts shortages on the production line.

Indian had highly resourceful people running the assembly lines. They were driven to keep the lines running and turn out finished product. When they ran out of a component to keep the line moving, they would try to come up with a substitute—it was common to go to the local hardware store and buy small springs, for example. On some occasions they would buy Harley parts, since the early Indians had several similar components. It was a manufacturing professional's worst nightmare.

—Frank O'Connell, former president and CEO of IMCOA

2001 Model Year
The End of the Beginning

The year 2001 marked one hundred years of the Indian motorcycle brand. Appropriately, the company supplied a clutch cover with an engraved "100" on all 2001 models. This has often led owners to mistakenly believe their bikes to be special "Centennial" models. The Centennial Chief was painted black and gold, while the Centennial Scout was available in either black or tan (with a round headlight).

After over a half century, the Indian Scout was resurrected in 2001, just in time for the one hundredth anniversary of the brand. The first Scout off the line sported black paint with gold tank decals and was signed in gold pen by every IMCOA employee. Riding on a new Indian-designed frame, the Scout was powered by the trusty S&S Super Stock 88 V-twin, featuring staggered dual pipes. The Scout's engine was powder-coated all black for 2001. Early-production 2001 model year Scouts (other than the Centennial Scout) utilized a belt-driven dry primary, but this was soon replaced with the new proprietary Indian chain-driven wet primary. With its 32-degree rake and 67-inch wheelbase, and lighter by 65 pounds, the Scout was noticeably more agile than the Chief. A rigid-frame Sport Scout had been planned but was indefinitely postponed. The special "Centennial" Scout featured throwback paint jobs, a wet clutch, and a round headlight (215 built).

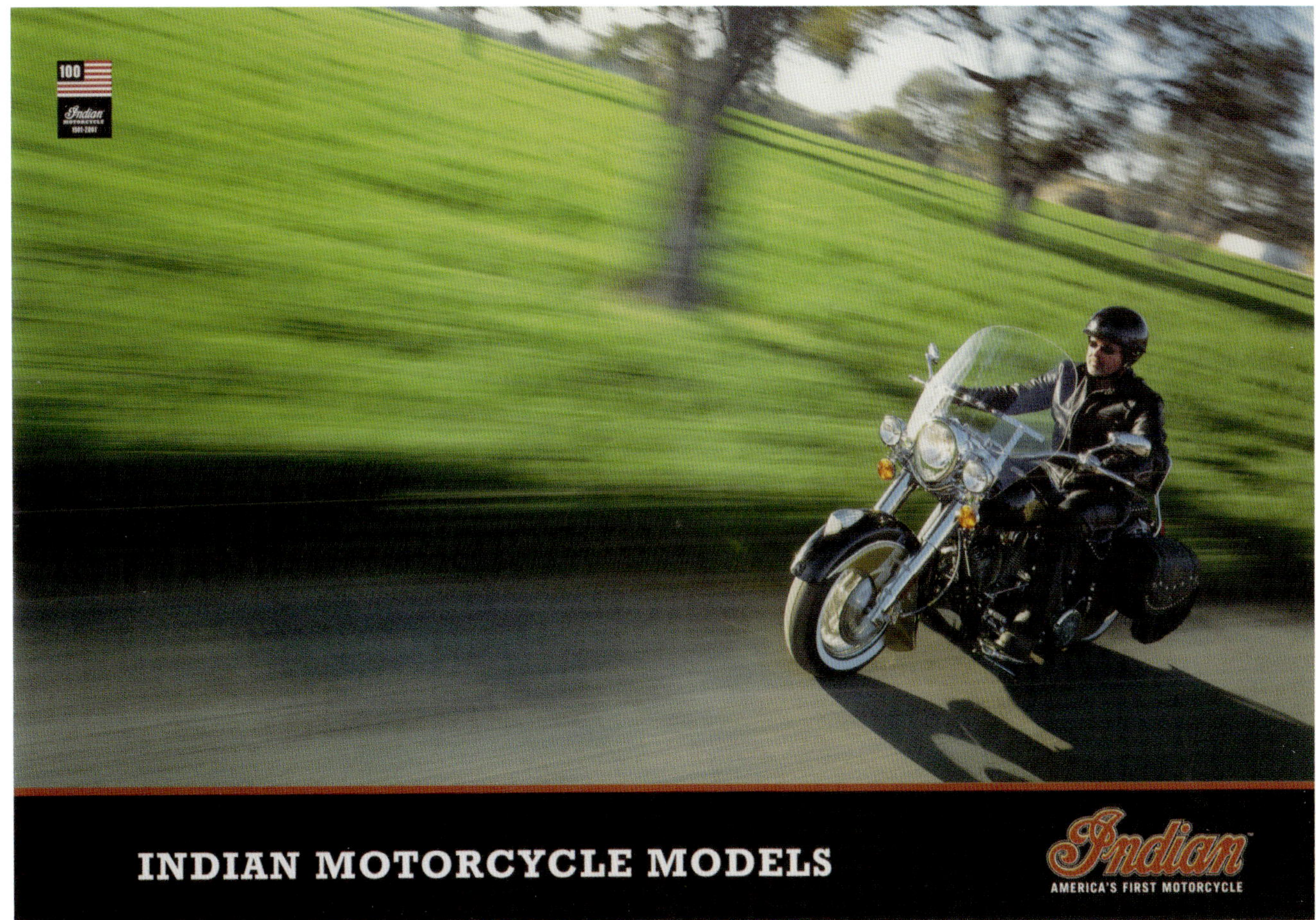

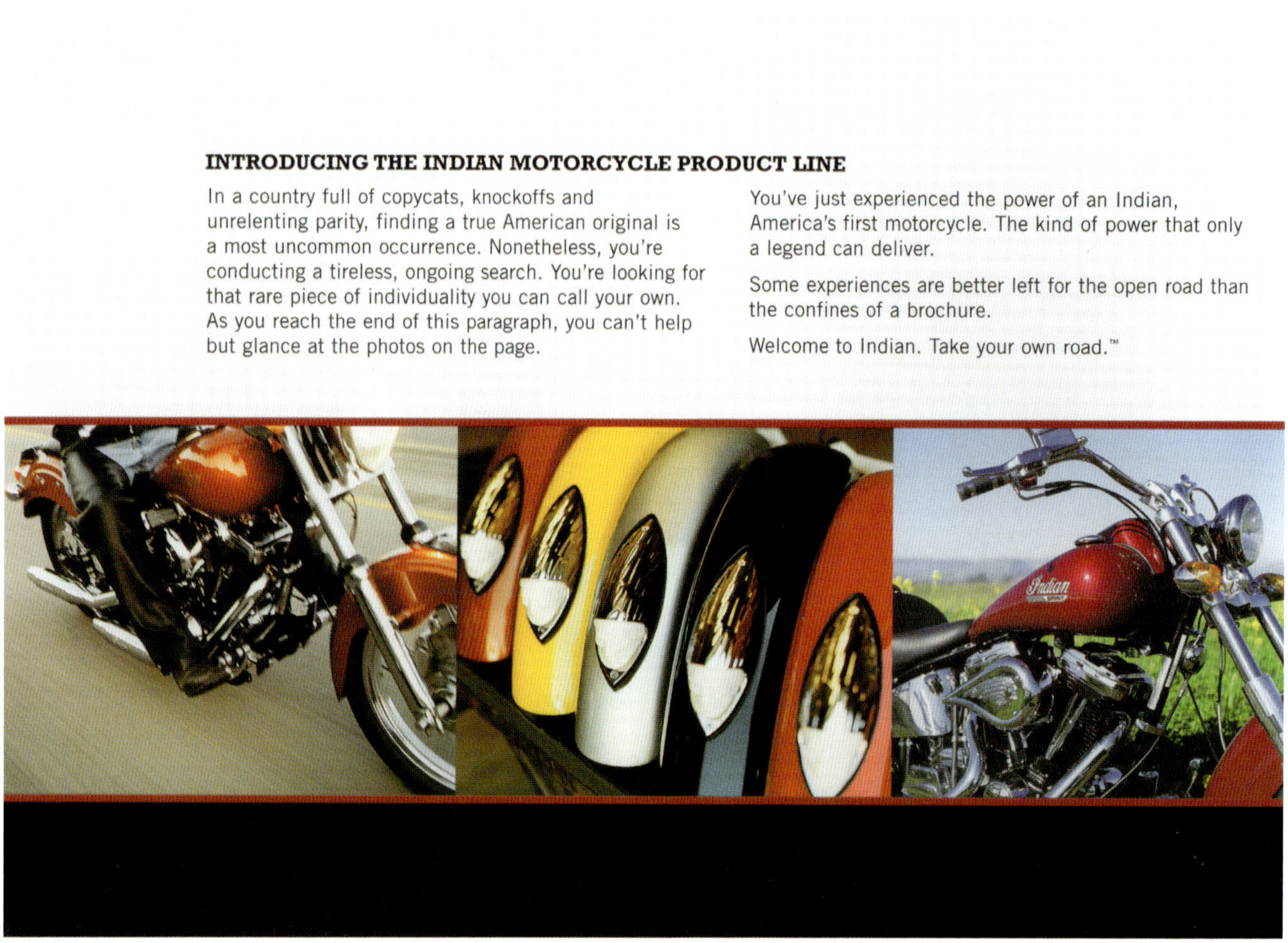

INTRODUCING THE INDIAN MOTORCYCLE PRODUCT LINE

In a country full of copycats, knockoffs and unrelenting parity, finding a true American original is a most uncommon occurrence. Nonetheless, you're conducting a tireless, ongoing search. You're looking for that rare piece of individuality you can call your own. As you reach the end of this paragraph, you can't help but glance at the photos on the page.

You've just experienced the power of an Indian, America's first motorcycle. The kind of power that only a legend can deliver.

Some experiences are better left for the open road than the confines of a brochure.

Welcome to Indian. Take your own road.™

Note the image at far right, which shows the round headlight supplied with the 2001 Spirits.

INDIAN MOTORCYCLE CO.
200 EAST TENTH STREET, GILROY, CA 95020
WWW.INDIANMOTORCYCLE.COM

THE INDIAN MOTORCYCLE LOGOS, INDIAN MOTORCYCLE, CHIEF, SCOUT, SPIRIT, THE SKIRTED FENDER DESIGN AND THE WAR BONNET LAMP DESIGN ARE REGISTERED TRADEMARKS OF IMCOA LICENSING AMERICA, INC. ©IMCOA LICENSING AMERICA, INC. 2001

PRICES AND SPECIFICATIONS SUBJECT TO CHANGE WITHOUT NOTICE. PAINT SWATCHES DEPICTED WITHIN ARE APPROXIMATIONS ONLY AND NOT REPRESENTATIONS OF ACTUAL PAINT COLOR.

MOTORCYCLES ARE TO BE USED ONLY ON THE ROAD BY A LICENSED RIDER. OBEY ALL LOCAL LAWS AND REGULATIONS. WE RECOMMEND THAT YOU ALWAYS WEAR A HELMET, PROTECTIVE CLOTHING AND EYEWEAR, AND THAT YOUR PASSENGERS DO THE SAME. NEVER RIDE UNDER THE INFLUENCE OF ALCOHOL OR DRUGS. RIDE WITH YOUR HEADLIGHT ON AT ALL TIMES AND RIDE SAFELY. READ YOUR OWNER'S MANUAL THOROUGHLY. WE RECOMMEND THAT ALL RIDERS COMPLETE A RECOGNIZED TRAINING PROGRAM PRIOR TO OPERATING A MOTORCYCLE.

Indian™
AMERICA'S FIRST MOTORCYCLE

98-044

2001 was the centennial year of the founding of the Indian brand. IMCOA celebrated with the Centennial Chief (always black and gold), and the Centennial Scout (a choice of cream or black).

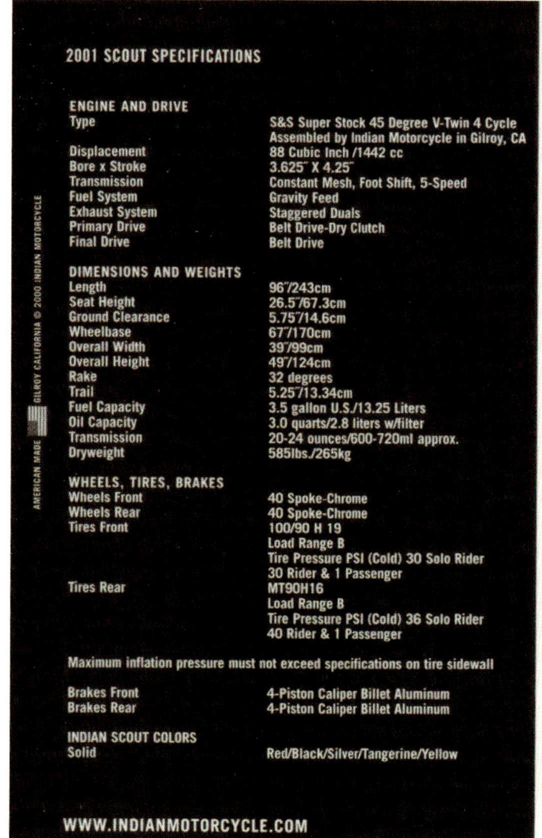

2001 SCOUT SPECIFICATIONS

ENGINE AND DRIVE	
Type	S&S Super Stock 45 Degree V-Twin 4 Cycle Assembled by Indian Motorcycle in Gilroy, CA
Displacement	88 Cubic Inch /1442 cc
Bore x Stroke	3.625" X 4.25"
Transmission	Constant Mesh, Foot Shift, 5-Speed
Fuel System	Gravity Feed
Exhaust System	Staggered Duals
Primary Drive	Belt Drive-Dry Clutch
Final Drive	Belt Drive

DIMENSIONS AND WEIGHTS	
Length	96"/243cm
Seat Height	26.5"/67.3cm
Ground Clearance	5.75"/14.6cm
Wheelbase	67"/170cm
Overall Width	39"/99cm
Overall Height	49"/124cm
Rake	32 degrees
Trail	5.25"/13.34cm
Fuel Capacity	3.5 gallon U.S./13.25 Liters
Oil Capacity	3.0 quarts/2.8 liters w/filter
Transmission	20-24 ounces/600-720ml approx.
Dryweight	585lbs./265kg

WHEELS, TIRES, BRAKES	
Wheels Front	40 Spoke-Chrome
Wheels Rear	40 Spoke-Chrome
Tires Front	100/90 H 19 Load Range B Tire Pressure PSI (Cold) 30 Solo Rider 30 Rider & 1 Passenger
Tires Rear	MT90H16 Load Range B Tire Pressure PSI (Cold) 36 Solo Rider 40 Rider & 1 Passenger

Maximum inflation pressure must not exceed specifications on tire sidewall

Brakes Front	4-Piston Caliper Billet Aluminum
Brakes Rear	4-Piston Caliper Billet Aluminum

INDIAN SCOUT COLORS	
Solid	Red/Black/Silver/Tangerine/Yellow

AMERICAN MADE GILROY CALIFORNIA © 2000 INDIAN MOTORCYCLE

WWW.INDIANMOTORCYCLE.COM

Postage

INDIAN PROUDLY INTRODUCES THE 2001 SCOUT.

In a country full of copycats, knockoffs and unrelenting parity, finding a true American original is a most uncommon occurrence. Nonetheless, you're conducting a tireless, ongoing search. You're looking for that rare piece of individuality you can call your own. As you reach the end of this paragraph, you can't help but glance at the photo on the facing page.

You've just experienced the power of an Indian, America's first motorcycle. While the Scout is Indian's performance cruiser, it has far more going for it than merely topnotch acceleration and handling. It also features incredible stopping power, even on the printed page. The kind of power that only a legend can deliver.

Indian

THERE'S NO QUICKER WAY TO EXPRESS YOUR INDIVIDUALITY.

When your gaze was inexplicably drawn to the classic design and styling of the Indian Scout, perhaps you noticed some of the unique facets of the machine such as the single down tube and higher controls. Or the specially modified S&S engine (1422cc) that is hand assembled by Indian.

Now we could tell you these features give you unsurpassed performance, but trust us, you'd much rather feel that for yourself. Some experiences are better left for the open road than the confines of a brochure. Welcome to Indian. Take your own road.™

THE BACKBONE OF AN INDIAN

The Indian single down-tube frame found on the Scout is nothing less than revolutionary. Virtually every other cruiser made has a double down-tube because most cruisers need the support of two tubes to hold the V-twin engines that power them. Our thinking was this: You don't design a frame to make the engine happy. You design a frame to make the rider happy. Our single down-tube frame is handwelded from seamless rolled steel and shaped with the utmost accuracy. Every single frame is qualified on our Coordinate Measuring Machine to ensure its exactness. All this means a flawless frame that gives you a smoother ride, more maneuverability and better handling.

Indian

AN INDIAN IS AN INDIAN IS AN INDIAN.

From it's braided stainless steel cabling to it's billet aluminum pegs to the almost spirit-like Indian chief head on the front fender, there are 450 parts on an Indian that are uniquely Indian. They are handcrafted at our factory in Gilroy by people whose dream is to build something perfect. There's lots of open space in Gilroy, but there's no room for compromise.

2001 COLORS & SPECIFICATIONS

BLACK HILLS

MOJAVE

RED ROCK

BONNEVILLE

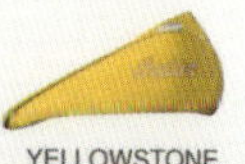
YELLOWSTONE

ENGINE AND DRIVE TRAIN	
TYPE	S&S SUPER STOCK 45 DEG. V-TWIN 4 CYCLE ASSEMBLED BY INDIAN MOTORCYCLE IN GILROY, CA
DISPLACEMENT	88 CUBIC INCH/1442CC
BORE X STROKE	3.625" X 4.25"
TRANSMISSION	CONSTANT MESH, FOOT SHIFT, 5-SPEED
CARBURETOR	S&S E TYPE 1 7/8" / 47.6MM BORE
EXHAUST SYSTEM	STAGGERED DUALS
PRIMARY DRIVE	BELT DRIVE-DRY CLUTCH
FINAL DRIVE	BELT DRIVE
DIMENSIONS AND WEIGHT	
SEAT HEIGHT	26.5" / 673 MM
GROUND CLEARANCE	5.75" / 146 MM
WHEELBASE	67" / 1702 MM
OVERALL LENGTH	96" / 2438 MM
OVERALL WIDTH	39" / 991 MM
OVERALL HEIGHT	49" / 1245 MM
RAKE	32DEG.
TRAIL	5.25" /133.4 MM
FUEL CAPACITY	3.5 GALLON U.S / 13.25 LITERS
OIL CAPACITY	3.0 QUARTS / 2.8 LITERS W/FILTER
DRY WEIGHT	585LBS. / 265KG.
WHEELS, TIRES & BRAKES	
FRONT WHEEL	40 SPOKE-CHROME, 2.25" X 19"
REAR WHEEL	40 SPOKE-CHROME, 3" X 16"
FRONT TIRE	100/90 H 19
REAR TIRE	130/90 H 16
FRONT BRAKE	4-PISTON CALIPER BILLET ALUM.
REAR BRAKE	4-PISTON CALIPER BILLET ALUM.

2001 SCOUT

There's no quicker way to express your individuality.

2001 SCOUT SPECIFICATIONS

DEngine: S&S Super Stock 45 Degree V-Twin 4 Cycle
Assembled by Indian Motorcycle in Gilroy, CA

Displacement: 88 Cubic Inch / 1442cc, Bore / Stroke: 3.625" / 4.25"

Transmission: Proprietary, Constant Mesh, Foot Shift, 5-Speed

Carburetor: S&S E TYPE, 1⅞" / 47.6mm Bore

Exhaust System: Staggered Duals

Primary Drive: Belt Drive, Dry Clutch

Final Drive: Belt Drive

Dimensions and Weight

Seat Height: 26.5" / 673mm **Ground Clearance:** 5.75" / 146mm

Overall Length: 96" / 2438mm **Overall Width:** 39" / 991mm
Overall Height: 49" / 1245mm

Wheelbase: 67" / 1702mm **Rake:** 32 Degrees

Trail: 5.25" /133.4mm

Dry Weight: 585lbs. / 265kg. GVWR 1085lbs. / 493 kg.

Oil Capacity: 3.0 quarts / 2.8 liters w/filter

Fuel Capacity: 3.5 US Gallons / 13.25 Liters;
Reserve .5 Gallons / 1.875 Liters

Front Wheel: 40-Spoke, Chrome, 2.15" x 19"
Rear Wheel: 40-Spoke, Chrome, 3" x 16"

Front Tire: 4.10" H-19
Rear Tire: MT-90 H-16

Front Brake: 4 Piston Caliper, Billet Aluminum
Rear Brake: 4 Piston Caliper, Billet Aluminum

General Instruments: LED indiacator lights

Seat: Indian **Frame:** Indian

Front Suspension: 41mm Hydraulic Dual-damping conventional style
Rear Suspension: Nitrogen charged hydraulic absorber with adjustable pre-load

Scout Colors

Solid: Black Hills Black • Mojave • Red Rock • Bonneville Silver
Yellowstone • Candy Apple Red • Cobalt Blue • Flint Black • Aspen White

Warranty: 2 years or 24,000 miles

MSRP: $18,995.00

The later 2001 full-line catalog showed more available colors for the Scout.

A quad-fold brochure showing the full 2001 line devoted one panel to custom paint for the Scout.

INDIAN MOTORCYCLE CO.
200 EAST TENTH STREET, GILROY, CA 95020
WWW.INDIANMOTORCYCLE.COM

Centennial Scout

2001 CENTENNIAL SCOUT

CENTENNIAL SCOUT SPECIFICATIONS

Engine: S&S Super Stock 45 Degree V-Twin 4 Cycle
Assembled by Indian Motorcycle in Gilroy, CA

Displacement: 88 Cubic Inch / 1442cc, Bore / Stroke: 3.625" / 4.25"

Transmission: Proprietary, Constant Mesh, Foot Shift, 5-Speed

Carburetor: S&S E TYPE, 1⅞" / 47.6mm Bore

Exhaust System: Staggered Duals

Primary Drive: Chain Drive-Proprietary Wet Clutch

Final Drive: Belt Drive

Dimensions and Weight

- **Seat Height:** 26.5" / 673mm **Ground Clearance:** 5.75" / 146mm
- **Overall Length:** 96" / 2438mm **Overall Width:** 41.5" / 1054mm
  Overall Height: 49.5" / 1257mm
- **Wheelbase:** 67" / 1702mm **Rake:** 32 Degrees
- **Trail:** 5.25" /133.4mm
- **Dry Weight:** 585lbs. / 265kg. GVWR 1085lbs. / 493 kg.

Fuel Capacity: 3.5 US Gallons/13.25 Liters; Reserve .5 Gallon/1.875 Liters

Oil Capacity: 3.0 Quarts / 2.8 Liters w/filter

Front Wheel: 40-Spoke, Black anodized, 2.15" x 19"
Rear Wheel: 40-Spoke, Black anodized, 3" x 16"

Front Tire: 4.10" H-19
Rear Tire: MT-90 H-16

Front Brake: 4 Piston Caliper, Billet Aluminum
Rear Brake: 4 Piston Caliper, Billet Aluminum

General Instruments: VDO analog speedometer with digital odometer & tripmeter. Proprietary bezel with V-shaped indicator lights layout.

Seat: Indian **Frame:** Indian

Front Suspension: 41mm Hydraulic Dual-damping conventional style
Rear Suspension: Nitrogen charged hydraulic absorber with adjustable pre-load

Centennial Scout Colors

- **Solid:** Cream with Red Rock Pin-Stripping • Black Hills Black

Warranty: 2 years or 24,000 miles

MSRP: $19,995.00

It's about a truly unique machine, with it's history intact.

Cream with
Red Rock Pinstriping

Black Hills Black

Note the round headlight on the first-year Spirits.

The new Spirit shared the new Indian frame of the Scout but featured the larger fuel tanks of the Chief, a different seat, 16-inch wheels front and rear, a two-into-one exhaust, the Indian wet primary, and fenders sized between those of the Scout and the Chief. Curiously, the 2001 Spirit featured a round headlight. Like the Scout, the 2001 Spirit's S&S 88 was powder-coated all black. Following the September 11, 2001, terrorist attacks, a "9/11" Spirit was offered in patriotic colors (seventy built).

All models of the 2001 Indians were equipped with new proprietary brake rotors featuring prominent teardrop-shaped vents around the axle (the 1999 and 2000 Chiefs had been supplied with Russell brake rotors).

The venerable Chief wasn't forgotten. Indian's heavy cruiser was given the proprietary Indian chain-driven wet clutch, retaining the belt final drive. ILM forks continued to be supplied for 2001, with an additional bolt on each lower fork tube to better secure the fender. A redesigned instrument panel featured LED indicators and a VDO speedometer with a digital odometer and trip meter. The 39-inch-wide "beach bars" of the 1999–2000 Chiefs were replaced by slightly narrower (37-inch) models.

A curious management decision dealt with a poor initial design for the Indian wet primaries. The first of these featured a channel between the inner and outer primary-drive housings that held an O-ring rather than a flat gasket. This design was prone to leakage, but rather than simply modifying the design, a new foundry was contracted to provide primary housings. The start-up tooling costs inherent with a new supplier might have been avoided by working with the original foundry on an improved design.

New paint options were available, including more special editions such as the black-and-gold "Centennial" Chief, which celebrated the one hundredth anniversary of the brand's founding (364 built), and the "Neiman Marcus" Chief (approximately forty built). The standard paint options for 2001 all featured solid-color fuel tanks; the "Neiman Marcus" tanks were the only exception. The black and gold "Centennial" Chief also sported a feature not seen on the fuel tanks of US Indian motorcycles since 1939: the image of an Indian in a full war bonnet. This classic depiction would reappear on the 2002 Chiefs and persist on Chiefs (except the "Vintage" and "Springfield") through the end of production.

2001 SPIRIT

Your bike is your own expression. your spirit. your soul.

2001 SPIRIT

Engine: S&S Super Stock 45 Degree V-Twin 4 Cycle
Assembled by Indian Motorcycle in Gilroy, CA

Displacement: 88 Cubic Inch / 1442cc, Bore / Stroke: 3.625" / 4.25"

Transmission: Proprietary, Constant Mesh, Foot Shift, 5-Speed

Carburetor: S&S E TYPE, 1⅞" / 47.6mm Bore

Exhaust System: 2 into 1

Primary Drive: Chain Drive-Proprietary Wet Clutch

Final Drive: Belt Drive

Dimensions and Weight

Seat Height: 28" / 711mm **Ground Clearance:** 5.75" / 146mm

Overall Length: 99.5" / 2527mm **Overall Width:** 43.5" / 1105mm
Overall Height: 49" / 1245mm

Wheelbase: 67" / 1702mm **Rake:** 32 Degrees

Trail: 5.25" /133.4mm

Dry Weight: 620lbs. / 282kgs.

Fuel Capacity: 4.75 US Gallons / 18 Liters; Reserve .44 Gallons / 1.65 Liters

Oil Capacity: 3.0 Quarts / 2.8 Liters w/filter

Front Wheel: 60-Spoke, Chrome, 3.5" x 16"
Rear Wheel: 60-Spoke, Chrome, 3.5" x 16"

Front Tire: 130/90-16 67H
Rear Tire: 130/90-16 73H

Front Brake: 4 Piston Caliper, Billet Aluminum
Rear Brake: 4 Piston Caliper, Billet Aluminum

General Instruments: VDO analog speedometer with digital odometer & tripmeter. Proprietary bezel with V-shaped indicator lights layout.

Seat: Indian **Frame:** Indian

Front Suspension: 41mm Hydraulic Dual-damping conventional style
Rear Suspension: Nitrogen charged hydraulic absorber with adjustable pre-load

Spirit Colors

Solids: Monterey Blue • Flint Black • Springfield Green • Sedona Red

Warranty: 2 years or 24,000 miles

MSRP: $20,995.00

Monterey Blue Flint Black Springfield Green Sedona Red

2001 CHIEF

Each is unique & personal, crafted by the one who owns it.

2001 CHIEF SPECIFICATIONS

Engine: S&S Super Stock 45 Degree V-Twin 4 Cycle
Assembled by Indian Motorcycle in Gilroy, CA

Displacement: 88 Cubic Inch / 1442cc, Bore / Stroke: 3.625˝ / 4.25˝

Transmission: Proprietary, Constant Mesh, Foot Shift, 5-Speed

Carburetor: S&S E TYPE, 1⅞˝ / 47.6mm Bore

Exhaust System: 2 Into 1

Primary Drive: Chain Drive-Proprietary Wet Clutch
Final Drive: Belt Drive

Dimensions and Weight

Seat Height: 25˝ / 635mm **Ground Clearance:** 6˝ / 152mm

Overall Length: 100˝ / 2540mm **Overall Width:** 44˝ / 1118mm
Overall Height: 46˝ / 1168mm

Wheelbase: 69˝ / 1752mm **Rake:** 36 Degrees

Dry Weight: 650 lbs. / 295kg. GVWR 1080 lbs. / 491 kg.

Fuel Capacity: 4.75 Gallons US / 18 Liters, Reserve 1.75 Quarts / 1.65 Liters

Oil Capacity: 3.0 Quarts US w/filter / 2.8 Liters

Front Wheel: 60-Spoke, Chrome, 3.5˝ x 16˝
Rear Wheel: 60-Spoke, Chrome, 3.5˝ x 16˝

Front Tire: 130/90-16
Rear Tire: 130/90-16

Front Brake: 4 Piston Caliper, Billet Aluminum
Rear Brake: 4 Piston Caliper, Billet Aluminum

General Instruments: VDO analog speedometer with digital odometer & tripmeter. Proprietary bezel with V-shaped indicator lights layout.

Seat: Indian **Frame:** Indian

Front Suspension: Proprietary 41mm Hydraulic Dual-damping conventional style

Rear Suspension: Nitrogen charged hydraulic absorber with adjustable pre-load

Chief Colors

Solid: Black Hills Black

Two-Tone: Yellowstone/Aspen White • Red Rock/Aspen White • Nashville Green/Bonneville Silver

Warranty: 2 years or 24,000 miles

MSRP: $23,995.00

Black Hills Black

Yellowstone & Aspen White

Red Rock & Aspen White

Nashville Green & Bonneville Silver

2001 CENTENNIAL CHIEF

CENTENNIAL CHIEF SPECIFICATIONS

Engine: S&S Super Stock 45 Degree V-Twin 4 Cycle
Assembled by Indian Motorcycle in Gilroy, CA

Displacement: 88 Cubic Inch / 1442cc, Bore / Stroke: 3.625" / 4.25"

Transmission: Proprietary, Constant Mesh, Foot Shift, 5-Speed

Carburetor: S&S E TYPE, 1⅞" / 47.6mm Bore

Exhaust System: 2 Into 1

Primary Drive: Chain Drive-Proprietary Wet Clutch
Final Drive: Belt Drive

Dimensions and Weight

Seat Height: 25" / 635mm **Ground Clearance:** 6" / 152mm
Overall Length: 100" / 2540mm **Overall Width:** 47" / 1194mm
Overall Height: 49" / 1245mm

Wheelbase: 69" / 1752mm **Rake:** 36 Degrees

Dry Weight: 670 lbs. / 304.5kg. GVWR 1080 lbs. / 491 kg.

Fuel Capacity: 4.75 Gallons US / 18 Liters; Reserve .44 Gallons / 1.65 Liters

Oil Capacity: 3.0 Quarts US w/filter 2.8 Liters

Front Wheel: 60-Spoke, Chrome, 3.5" x 16"
Rear Wheel: 60-Spoke, Chrome, 3.5" x 16"

Front Tire: MT90-16, Whitewall
Rear Tire: MT90-16, Whitewall

Front Brake: 4 Piston Caliper, Billet Aluminum
Rear Brake: 4 Piston Caliper, Billet Aluminum

General Instruments: VDO analog speedometer with digital odometer & tripmeter. Proprietary bezel with V-shaped indicator lights layout.

Seat: Indian **Frame:** Indian

Windshield: 19" Tall x 26" Wide / 482mm Tall x 660mm Wide

Saddle Bags: Capacity, Approximately 16" Long x 11" Tall x 4.5" Wide

Front Suspension: Proprietary 41mm Hydraulic Dual-damping conventional style

Rear Suspension: Nitrogen charged hydraulic absorber with adjustable pre-load

Centennial Chief Colors

Two-Tone: Black Hills Black / Gold

Warranty: 2 years or 24,000 miles

MSRP: $25,995.00

Every true individual needs a bike that's as individual as he is.

Black Hills Black & Gold

The Neiman Marcus Chief was the only 2001 model with two-tone tank paint. *From the Neiman Marcus 2001 Christmas catalog*

Despite the demand for the IMCOA Indian motorcycles, the numerous recalls and warranty repairs were becoming generally known in the motorcycling community. To counteract the bad press, the 2001 full-line catalog devoted two pages to stressing the company's commitment to quality.

> In many ways, it was amazing they could turn out good-looking bikes with Indian DNA that actually ran. The workforce was very dedicated and hardworking. Given the huge number of components, poor or erratic quality of parts, and unpredictable delivery schedules, it was magical that they could get the pieces to work at all. Even more amazing yet was that the brand was alive and well, even though the bikes were very expensive and the quality issues were all too well known. The bikes were in demand.
>
> *—Frank O'Connell, former president and CEO of IMCOA*

Despite everything, Indian was slowly, painfully moving in the right direction.

Reported production of the 2001 Scout, Spirit, and Chief totaled 3,856 in 2001.

MADE BY HEART AND HAND

Remaining faithful to a legend. That's the goal at Indian Motorcycle. Leading edge technology and state-of-the art facilities allow us to produce motorcycles that remain unerringly true to the heritage that is Indian Motorcycle.

From the braided stainless steel cabling, to the billet aluminum pegs and almost "spirit-like" Indian chief head on the front fender, there are more than 450 parts on an Indian Motorcycle that are uniquely Indian. They are handcrafted at our factory in Gilroy by people whose dream is to build the perfect motorcycle.

THE BACKBONE OF AN INDIAN

Frames are meticulously hand-welded to exacting specifications and individually inspected to maintain consistency and finish quality. To insure absolute build accuracy, all critical frame dimensions are measured by a Coordinate Measuring Machine (CMM) prior to powder coating.

STATE-OF-THE-ART POWDER COATING

Every part is visually inspected before and after the powder coating process to insure that it is free of defects and blemishes. Our state-of-the-art facility allows us to apply a coating that has greater chemical resistance, thermal durability and chip resistance than standard liquid paint.

AN INDIAN IS AN INDIAN IS AN INDIAN

Final assembly is performed by teams of people, not machines. A thorough inspection process is conducted to make certain each bike is assembled within strict tolerances and to a pristine finish. Every Indian Motorcycle must be mechanically sound and visually flawless.

Every motorcycle that leaves our factory is thoroughly test ridden by our team of experienced test riders. Our riders are so familiar with Indian motorcycles that they can scrutinize them at levels of detail few could ever discern. They make certain that each motorcycle will deliver the same incredible thrill of owning and riding an American Legend.

Find out for yourself why every Indian Motorcycle is unique and personal, crafted by the one who owns it. You pick your options. You choose your path. You help create the bike that speaks to you or the bike that answers back.

Take your own road™.

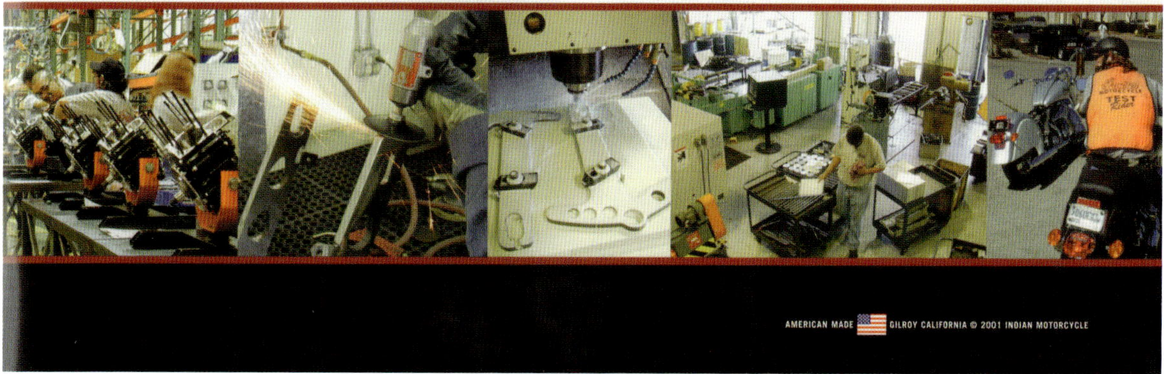

Note the image to the far right, showing a 2000 Silver Cloud with factory-supplied blackwall tires. In the absence of original promotional material for this model, such details can be helpful.

2002 Model Year
Beginning of the End

By 2002, IMCOA's fortunes seemed to be looking up. The company was slowly making progress toward all-Indian-designed motorcycles. The Scout (and new Scout Deluxe) and Spirit (and new Spirit Deluxe) were already riding on Indian-designed frames, and a new 92-cubic-inch Indian engine for these models was in the works. But the big news this year was the all-new Indian-designed 100-cubic-inch V-twin engine that was introduced for the Chief. It was called the "Powerplus," resurrecting the name first used in 1916 for a revolutionary new side-valve engine/motorcycle that was in production until 1924. IMCOA had high hopes for the Powerplus 100 and was not shy in its publicity for the new engine.

The handsome 2002–03 Indian "Powerplus" V-twin, commonly called the "bottlecap" due to its distinctive round-notched rocker boxes. At 100 cubic inches (1,638 cc)—this was the largest American OEM motorcycle power plant at the time. This engine—with improvements—would power Indian Chiefs through the Stellican era and the first years of Polaris ownership.

The Powerplus 100

We hadn't lived up to the brand. I wanted to have a motorcycle that said, "This is an Indian motorcycle. It's revived; it's back; it's reborn."

—Rey Sotelo, former president and CEO of IMCOA

In designing the first US Indian motorcycle engine to be manufactured since 1953, the company was faced with a dilemma. Should the power plant be an entirely new design, or should it be developed from a proven platform? A completely new engine design would consume more time and money—with a high risk of unforeseen design flaws and the added expense of proprietary parts. It was decided to build on a proven design, and Indian made a wise choice for its basic inspiration: Harley-Davidson's highly regarded Evolution V-twin. Although Indian's new Powerplus 100 would contain numerous unique parts, many of its internal components would be interchangeable with Milwaukee's proven mill. The exterior of the new Powerplus 100 would boast round, classic Indian-style cylinders, a Mikuni HSR

42 carburetor mounted on the left side in traditional Indian style, and rocker boxes suggestive of the vertical fins found on Indian's classic side-valve engines. These distinctive boxes would earn the engine its nickname: the "bottlecap."

In the spring of 2002, Fran O'Hagan reported,

> We did a lot of research to see what customers expected from an Indian engine. The three things that stood out were (1) it had to perform and have plentiful torque, (2) it had to have historic Indian design cues—as in carburetor on the left, round cylinders, vertical fins on top—and (3) [it had to] take the best of proven technology and create an engine that's both reliable and durable. —Fran O'Hagan, former senior vice president, product management and marketing, IMCOA

As for the new engine's development, O'Hagan remarked, "There were about fifteen Indian employees involved in designing, developing, and bringing the Powerplus 100 to production over . . . twenty-four months." Additionally, Indian brought in outside consultants, including Thunder Heart Performance Corp. (White House, Tennessee); VePro Ltd. (Leicestershire, England); the Ann Arbor and Southfield, Michigan, offices of England's Lotus Engineering; and Performance Assembly Solutions (Livonia, Michigan). PAS built the production engines in its facility and shipped the completed engines to Gilroy.

Thunder Heart assisted with engineering, supplied the dual-fire electronic ignition, and built the first prototype engine. VePro, which had earlier been involved in the design, engineering, and development of the short-lived (1999–2000) Excelsior-Henderson motorcycle, helped Indian finalize the design for the Powerplus 100, source the parts, and bring the engine into production. Lotus Engineering conducted much of the durability testing.

Performance Assembly Solutions (PAS), a subsidiary of Uniboring (Howell, Michigan) and Roush Industries (Livonia, Michigan), functioned as Indian's manufacturing partner for the Powerplus 100. It assumed production responsibility for the new engine, supplying complete operational units to Indian's Gilroy plant. According to Chris Zucker, vice president and general manager of PAS, his company employed seven people to assemble the engines (initially at 110 engines per week), with two additional support staff (on the basis of the number of 2002–03 Chiefs manufactured, this production schedule was not maintained for long).

The machined cylinders, cylinder heads, and cases were supplied by Uniboring, while Roush tested the finished engines. Torque-to-turn ratio, oil pressure, oil flow, and compression all were checked on each engine. One out of every thirty engines was pulled for a friction stabilization test and performance verification run. "If that engine meets specification," said Zucker, "and the other engines in that batch have passed their cold-test requirements, they are released for shipment to Indian."

The supply base for the PP 100 spanned half of the US and included Japan. Most or all 2002 crank cases were cast by Falco in Fresno, California (then machined by Uniboring), but these were eventually supplanted in 2003 by better-quality cases cast in Mansfield, Ohio. Toward the end of production in late 2003, a few Canadian Ramsden cases were utilized, but apparently in very small numbers.

However, the celebrated new Powerplus engine suffered from insufficient field testing, and failures began to occur. Imported flywheels often became unbalanced, pinion run-out became a serious problem, the oil pump was insufficient, and oil routing was faulty. Consultant Frank Aliano worked on solutions and eventually formed his own company (Blackhawk Motor Works) which specializes in Powerplus 100 rebuilds. As noted on the Blackhawk website,

The imported flywheels used by Indian Motorcycle Co. suffered from soft materials, machining problems, and unlike tapers. This has caused major problems with the flywheel assembly's ability to maintain its concentricity. Consequently, flywheels are shifting on the tapers and coming out of "true," leading to several problems like increased vibration, lower end knocks, broken pinion shafts, and the loosening of the cast-in case race insert in the right side case, rendering the cases bad.

A modified oil pump, rerouting for improved lubrication and cooling, and a relocated crankcase breather, along with new flywheels and connecting rods, would eventually prove to be the basic formula used by several reputable rebuilders of Powerplus 100 engines over the years. But until then, every failed engine had to be replaced at company expense.

The new Powerplus 100 engines—regarded by many as one of the most beautiful motorcycle engines ever built—were installed in an all-new Indian frame, making the 2002–03 Chiefs completely Indian-designed motorcycles.

The Indian Powerplus 100/105 engine is unique in being the only OEM engine offered by three different companies building Indian motorcycles: IMCOA/Gilroy (2002–03), Stellican/Kings Mountain (2009–11), and Polaris / Spirit Lake (2011–13).

The 2002–03 Indian Chiefs were awarded official OEM status by the National Highway Traffic Safety Administration. There was some public celebration of this development. Gibson even offered a commemorative Les Paul guitar with the time-honored Indian Chief war bonnet motif, a gesture from one classic American company to another.

The 2002 Chief received Brembo disc brakes and new, larger 5.5-gallon fuel tanks with a new instrument panel, along with its new Indian-designed frame (which reduced its rake to 34 degrees and wheelbase to 68.4 inches) and the new Powerplus engine.

Beginning in 2002, the Chief was offered in three models: the one-color Chief, the two-color Chief Deluxe (with whitewall tires), and the Chief Roadmaster (a Deluxe with saddlebags, two-up seating, passenger backrest, and a windshield). All three models of the Chief featured fuel tanks adorned with an Indian in full war bonnet, as seen on 1934-1939 Indian Motorcycles and resurrected on the 2001 Centennial. This depiction was based upon the real-life Passamaquoddy Chief Joseph Nicholas ("Leaping Deer"). Nicholas (1895-1948) was reportedly discovered by Indian officials demonstrating his basket making skills in Springfield, Massachusetts. He was duly photographed and compensated for the use of his handsome profile on Indian machines.

Indian was listening to its customers, as evident in the changes made to the 2002 Scout and Scout Deluxe. Narrower handlebars, relocated foot pegs, a reshaped rear fender, a larger speedometer, 5.8-gallon tanks, a beefier swing arm, and even a louder horn were improvements made after the first year's production. The S&S 88 V-twin was now being supplied to IMCOA ready to run, in what the Indian catalogs called "raw finish" (unpainted aluminum).

The Spirit was also improved with a teardrop headlight, 5.5-gallon Chief-style tanks, a larger speedometer, a louder horn, a stronger swing arm, a more comfortable seat, and floorboards. The Spirit was offered as a base model and a Spirit Deluxe (two-tone paint and whitewalls). Like the Scout, the base Spirit's S&S 88 V-twin was now being supplied to IMCOA ready to run, in what the Indian catalogs called "raw finish" (unpainted aluminum). The Spirit Deluxe featured an engine with "black finish."

Reported production of the Scout, Spirit, and Chief totaled 3,278 in 2002.

2002 Chief™
Chief™
Chief™ Deluxe
Chief™ Roadmaster
SPECIFICATIONS
Engine: Powerplus™ 100, 45-degree, V-twin
Displacement: 100 cubic inches (1638cc)
Bore x Stroke: 3.875" x 4.25"
Compression Ratio: 9.5:1
Valves: 1.94" intake, 1.615" exhaust, hydraulic lifters
Ignition: Electronic, computer-controlled
Carburetor: Mikuni HSR 42mm flat-slide
Exhaust System: 2-into-1
Transmission: Constant-mesh, five-speed
Final Drive: Aramid-reinforced belt
Frame: Hand-welded, high-tensile steel, powder-coated, black
Rake: 34 degrees Trail: 5.92 inches
Front Suspension: 41mm, hydraulic compression and rebound damping
Rear Suspension: Rising-rate, KW single shock with adjustable pre-load
Brakes: Stainless-steel 11.5" discs, 4-piston Brembo calipers
Front Wheel/Tire: 60-spoke, chrome, 16" x 3.5", MT90-16
Rear Wheel/Tire: 60-spoke, chrome, 16" x 3.5", MT90-16
Wheelbase: 68.4 inches
Seat Height: 28.5 inches
Dry Weight: Chief: 687 lbs., Chief Deluxe: 690 lbs., Roadmaster: 716 lbs.
Fuel Capacity: 5.8 U.S. gallons including 1.2 gallon reserve
Instruments: Analog speedometer with digital odometer & tripmeter
Colors: CHIEF: Black, Red Metallic, Silver
CHIEF DELUXE / CHIEF ROADMASTER: Black/Red Metallic, Black/Cream, Crimson/Cream, Copper/Black, Blue Metallic/Silver, Black/Silver
Warranty: 12 months/unlimited mileage
MSRP: CHIEF: $20,495 U.S. dollars
CHIEF DELUXE: $21,795 U.S. dollars
CHIEF ROADMASTER: $22,995 U.S. dollars
BLACK
RED METALLIC
SILVER
BLACK/ RED METALLIC
BLACK/CREAM
CRIMSON/ CREAM
COPPER/ BLACK
BLUE METALLIC/ SILVER
BLACK/SILVER
Indian™
AMERICA'S FIRST MOTORCYCLE
For more information visit our website at www.newchief.com.
INDIAN MOTORCYCLE CORPORATION • 200 EAST TENTH STREET • GILROY, CA 95020
INDIAN, script INDIAN, INDIAN MOTORCYCLE, CHIEF, the Indian Motorcycle logos, the skirted fender design, and the war bonnet lamp design are trademarks of IMCOA Licensing America, Inc. in the U.S. and foreign countries. © 2002 IMCOA Licensing America, Inc.
Prices and specifications subject to change without notice.
Motorcycles are to be used only on the road by a licensed rider. Obey all local laws and regulations. We recommend that you always wear a helmet, protective clothing and eyewear, and that your passengers do the same. Never ride under the influence of alcohol or drugs. Ride with your headlight on at all times and ride safely. Read your owner's manual thoroughly. We recommend that all riders complete a recognized training program prior to operating a motorcycle.

The 2002 Chief catalog was the company's most elaborate to date. At 8.5 × 11 in., plus additional 6 in. gatefolds, Indian's flagship motorcycle was shown to best advantage.

IT'S ABSOLUTELY NEW.
BUT IT'S INSPIRED BY 101 YEARS OF HISTORY.
It began over a century ago. Oscar Hedstrom, a talented inventor, and George Hendee, a champion bicyclist, gave America a new kind of freedom. They built America's first motorcycle—and started a movement that changed the world.
That movement led, among other places, to England's Isle of Man. Where, in 1911, Indian® motorcycles placed 1, 2, and 3—and showed the rest of the world just how a motorcycle should be built. In 1914, it propelled Cannonball Baker, riding an original Powerplus™ V-twin, across the American continent in record time. And in 1937, it took Ed Kretz to victory in the first-ever Daytona 200.
Now, 101 years after that movement began, we're doing it all over again. Indian Motorcycle Corporation is bringing back the legendary motorcycles that captivated the world. And doing it with the same commitment to exhilarating performance, handcrafted quality and technological excellence that made Indian a revered marque from the racetracks of Europe to the dirt-track fairgrounds of America.
This new 2002 Chief™, with its all-new, all-Indian® Powerplus 100 engine, is the result of three years of long, hard hours and inspired moments. Three years of CAD-CAM design and seemingly endless dyno runs. Three years of fine-tuning, and countless miles of on-the-road testing. Three years of intensive labor. And every minute, a labor of love.
Every member of the Indian Motorcycle team is justifiably proud of what we have accomplished. And we are inspired, every day, by knowing that the founders of Indian would be just as proud as we are.
USA
THE Indian
THE INDIAN NEWS—Voice of 100,000 Riders!
INDIAN MOTOCYCLE CO., Springfield, Mass., U.S.A.
"DAWN OF NEW RECORDS"
AMERICA'S FIRST
SINCE
Indian
1901
MOTORCYCLE

CHIEF

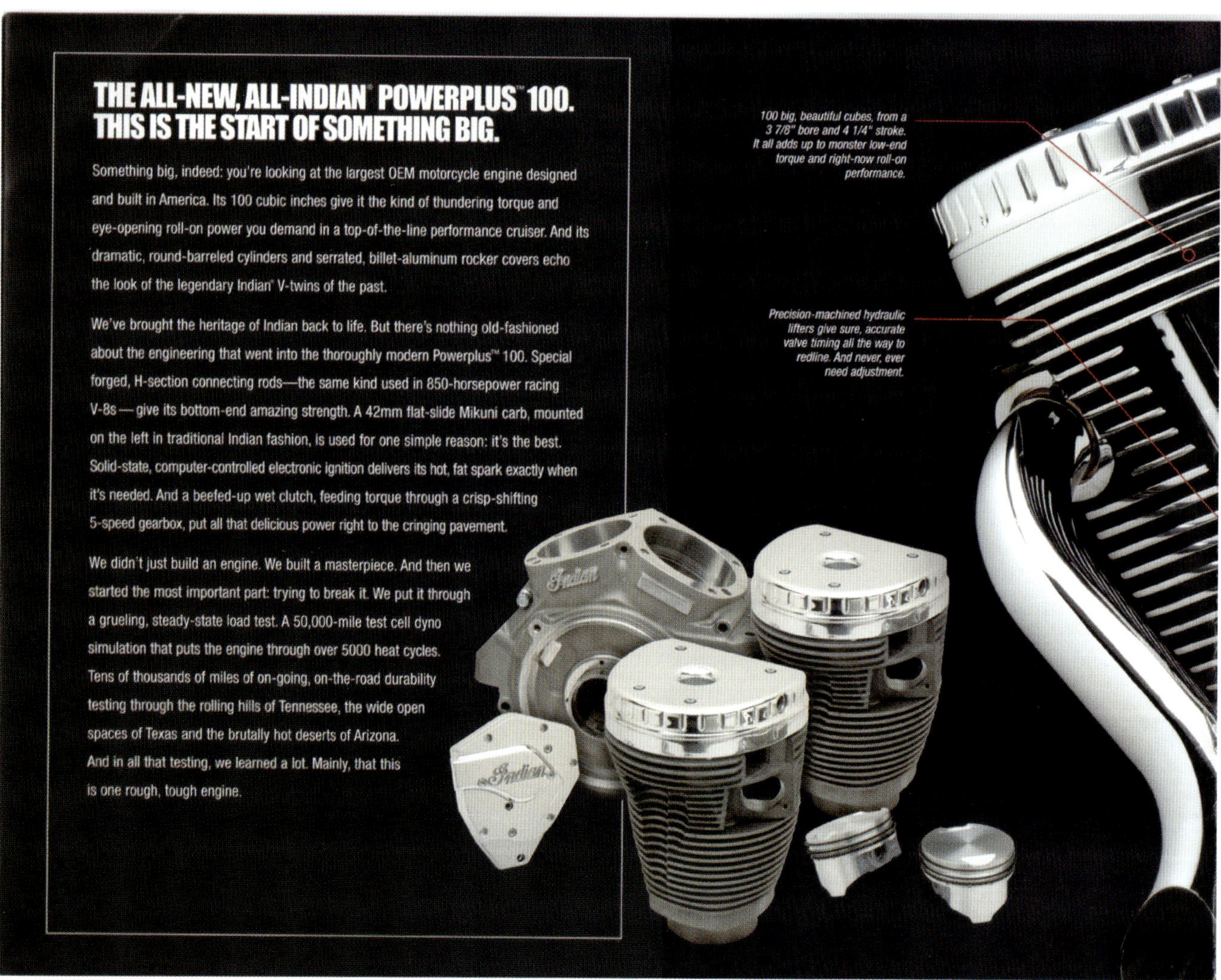

Despite the hype of extensive testing for this "rough, tough engine," its rushed development would manifest itself in widespread bottom-end failures.

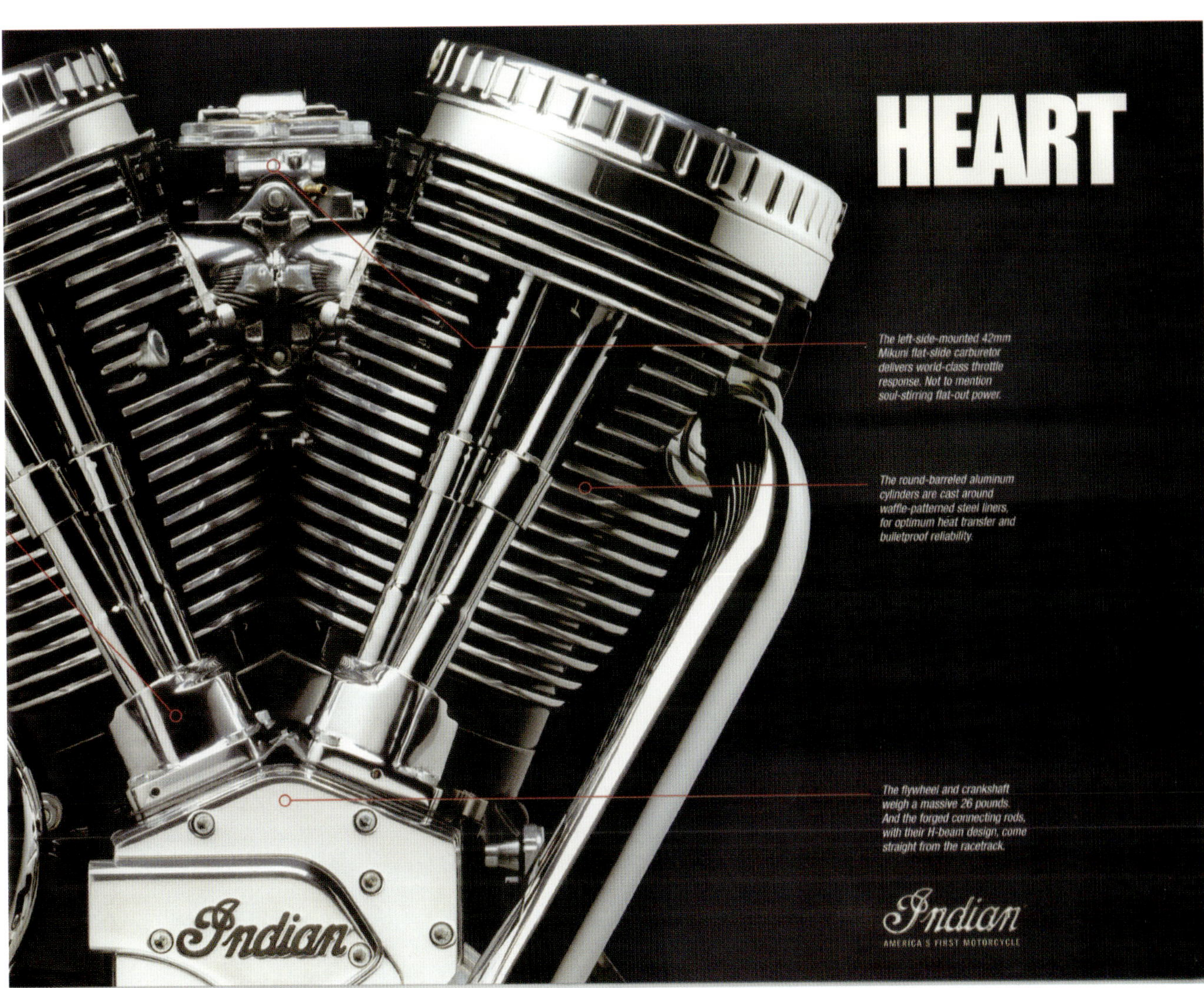

Preproduction photos of the PP 100 show chromed lifter blocks, but these didn't make it to production bikes.

The attractive painted fender darts are found only on the 2002 Chief Deluxe and Chief Roadmaster.

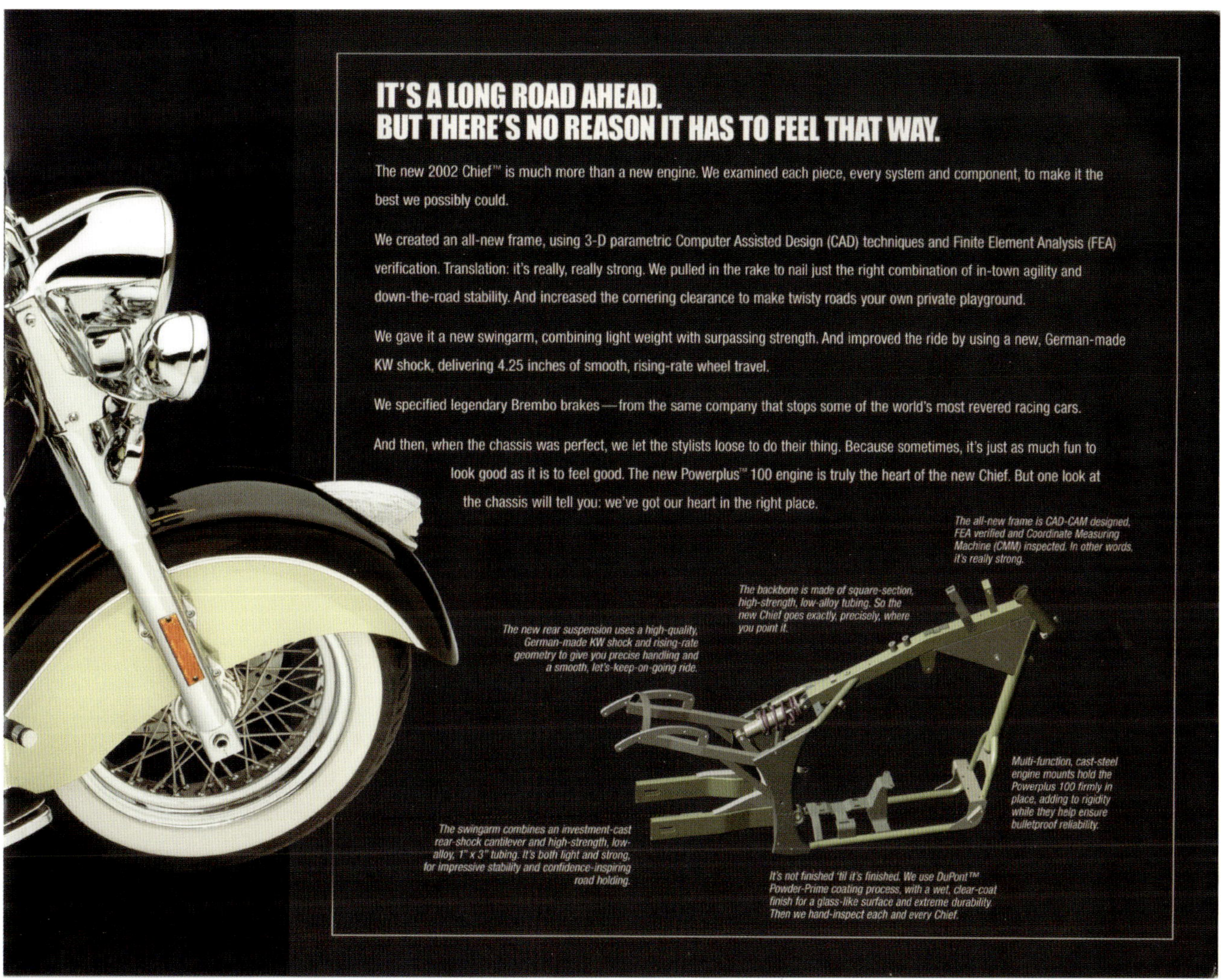

The new Chief frame modified the bike's rake to a more traditional (and more maneuverable) 34 degrees. To prevent the problem of "wet sumping" so common to motorcycles whose oil tanks were mounted higher than the crankcase, Indian's design placed a long, shallow oil tank at the bottom of the frame, below crankcase level. Oil could no longer pool in the crankcase during periods of nonuse. This frame would serve Indian's future corporate owners for years to come.

CHIEF™
Indian
Indian

IT WON'T FIT IN THE BEDROOM.
BUT YOU CAN ALWAYS SLEEP IN THE GARAGE.
You lie awake. You can think of nothing else. That's OK—our engineers know just how you feel. They've spent the last three years building this new Chief™ motorcycle from the pavement up. From the tip of its deep-valanced front fender to the ergonomic curve of its all-new seat, they sweated each and every detail. They gave it 60-spoke chrome wheels, Brembo brakes, and a precision-calibrated, German-made KW shock. They bolted in the all-new, all-Indian® Powerplus™ 100 engine—the biggest American OEM engine you—or anyone else—can get. And when they were done, they knew that they had done it right—striking the perfect balance between the legendary heritage of Indian and the comfort, style and bulletproof performance you demand in an American original.

The left-side views of the Chief, Chief Deluxe, and Chief Roadmaster on this and the following pages are rarely seen in IMCOA advertising. This is probably due to the black-plastic air box, which is conceded by most Gilroy fans to be . . . well, ugly. These days, it's rare to find one of these original air boxes still in place.

CHIEF™ deluxe

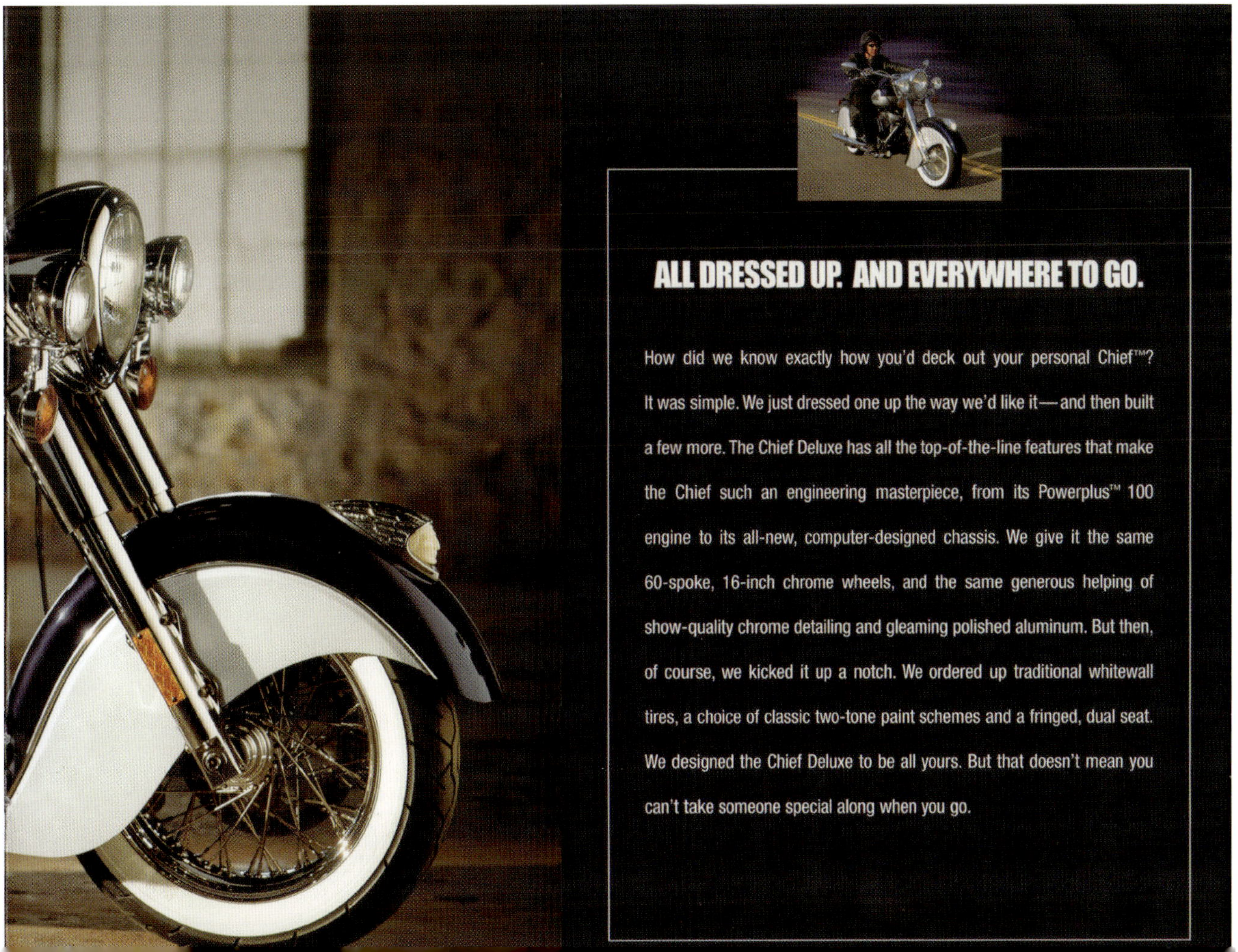

ALL DRESSED UP. AND EVERYWHERE TO GO.

How did we know exactly how you'd deck out your personal Chief™? It was simple. We just dressed one up the way we'd like it—and then built a few more. The Chief Deluxe has all the top-of-the-line features that make the Chief such an engineering masterpiece, from its Powerplus™ 100 engine to its all-new, computer-designed chassis. We give it the same 60-spoke, 16-inch chrome wheels, and the same generous helping of show-quality chrome detailing and gleaming polished aluminum. But then, of course, we kicked it up a notch. We ordered up traditional whitewall tires, a choice of classic two-tone paint schemes and a fringed, dual seat. We designed the Chief Deluxe to be all yours. But that doesn't mean you can't take someone special along when you go.

CHIEF™
deluxe
SPECIFICATIONS
Engine: Powerplus™ 45-degree V-twin
Displacement: 100 cubic inches (1638cc)
Bore x Stroke: 3.875" x 4.25"
Compression Ratio: 9.5:1
Valves: 1.94" intake, 1.615" exhaust, hydraulic lifters
Ignition: Electronic, computer-controlled
Carburetor: Mikuni HSR 42mm flat-slide
Exhaust System: 2-into-1
Transmission: Constant-mesh, five-speed
Final Drive: Aramid-reinforced belt
Frame: High-tensile steel, powder-coated, black
Rake/Trail: 34 degrees / 5.92"
Front Suspension: 41mm, hydraulic compression and rebound damping
Rear Suspension: Rising-rate, KW single shock with adjustable preload
Brakes: Stainless-steel 11.5" discs, 4-piston Brembo calipers
Front Wheel/Tire: 60-spoke, chrome, 16" x 3.5", MT90-16
Rear Wheel/Tire: 60-spoke, chrome, 16" x 3.5", MT90-16
Wheelbase: 68.4"
Seat Height: 28.5"
Dry Weight: 690 lbs.
Fuel Capacity: 5.5 U.S. gallons including 1.2 gallon reserve
Instruments: Analog speedometer with digital odometer & tripmeter
Warranty: 12 months/unlimited mileage
MSRP: $21,795 U.S. dollars
2002 Color Selection
BLACK/ RED METALLIC
BLACK/CREAM
CRIMSON/CREAM
COPPER/BLACK
BLUE METALLIC/ SILVER
BLACK/SILVER
CHIEF DELUXE FEATURES
• Fringed dual seat. Yes, you can take her with you.
• Classic whitewall tires. Authentic 1950's style.
• Exclusive two-tone paint schemes. The legendary look of the Indian® Chief.™
Indian
AMERICA'S FIRST MOTORCYCLE

CHIEF roadmaster

SOME PEOPLE JUST DON'T KNOW WHEN TO STOP.

Some things, you just can't get enough of. Things like an endless road, a wide-open sky and an insatiable hunger for adventure. We know how it is. And we know how to build the perfect Chief™ for your long-range ambitions. Start with the class and comfort of the Chief Deluxe, with its big, beautiful Powerplus™ 100 engine, state-of-the-art chassis and sunrise-to-sunset comfort. Factor in its whitewall tires, fringed dual seat and two-tone paint schemes. Then add an elegantly sculpted windshield, to help persuade the atmosphere to step aside. Mount up innovative, exclusively Indian saddlebags, to help you look as good at dinner as you do on the road. And bolt on a custom-engineered, chrome passenger backrest, to keep your best friend as comfortable as you are. You may not know exactly where you're going. But you do know you're going in classic style.

CHIEF™ roadmaster

SPECIFICATIONS

Engine:	Powerplus™ 45-degree V-twin
Displacement:	100 cubic inches (1638cc)
Bore x Stroke:	3.875" x 4.25"
Compression Ratio:	9.5:1
Valves:	1.94" intake, 1.615" exhaust, hydraulic lifters
Ignition:	Electronic, computer-controlled
Carburetor:	Mikuni HSR 42mm flat-slide
Exhaust System:	2-into-1
Transmission:	Constant-mesh, five-speed
Final Drive:	Aramid-reinforced belt
Frame:	High-tensile steel, powder-coated, black
Rake/Trail:	34 degrees/5.92"
Front Suspension:	41mm, hydraulic compression and rebound damping
Rear Suspension:	Rising-rate, KW single shock with adjustable preload
Brakes:	Stainless-steel 11.5" discs, 4-piston Brembo calipers
Front Wheel/Tire:	60-spoke, chrome, 16" x 3.5", MT90-16
Rear Wheel/Tire:	60-spoke, chrome, 16" x 3.5", MT90-16
Wheelbase:	68.4"
Seat Height:	28.5"
Dry Weight:	716 lbs.
Fuel Capacity:	5.5 U.S. gallons including 1.2 gallon reserve
Instruments:	Analog speedometer with digital odometer & tripmeter
Warranty:	12 months/unlimited mileage
MSRP:	$22,995 U.S. dollars

2002 Color Selection

BLACK/ RED METALLIC

BLACK/CREAM

CRIMSON/CREAM

COPPER/BLACK

BLUE METALLIC/ SILVER

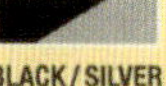
BLACK/SILVER

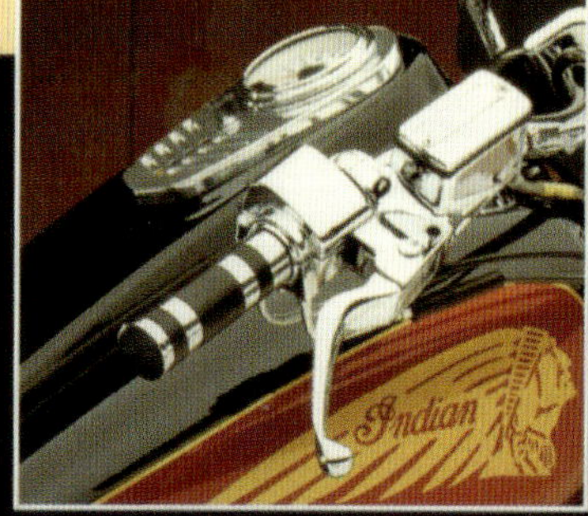

CHIEF ROADMASTER FEATURES

- **Heavy-duty Lucite® L acrylic windshield.** Long-haul weather protection.
- **Custom fringed saddlebags.** Yes, you can take it with you.
- **Fringed dual seat.** Yes, you can take her with you.
- **Chrome passenger backrest.** Added passenger comfort and confidence.
- **Classic whitewall tires.** Authentic 1950's style.
- **Exclusive two-tone paint schemes.** The legendary look of the Indian® Chief.™

Indian

Despite a reputation for recalls and warranty problems, IMCOA's quality was slowly improving.

GENUINE INDIAN RIDER WEAR
Show your allegiance with our full line of leather jackets, pants and gloves, as well as casual wear for both men and women. You'll also enjoy our selection of collectibles and unique gift items. Visit indianmotorcycle.com or stop in at your local Indian Motorcycle dealer.
INDIAN RIDERS GROUP
Share the love. Of riding your Indian Motorcycle, that is. The Indian Riders Group was founded to help you meet and socialize with other Indian riders and enthusiasts. If there's already an Indian Riders Group chapter in your area, you'll certainly want to join. And if there isn't, why not start one? Each chapter is dedicated to promoting rides, get-togethers and charity events and to spreading the word about how good life can be from the seat of an Indian Motorcycle. Ask your local dealer about joining or forming a chapter near you.
Indian
AMERICA'S FIRST MOTORCYCLE
Indian
MOTORCYCLE
POWERPLUS™ 100

This is the 2002 police bike #2 used in the Arnold Schwarzenegger movie *Terminator 3*. Unlike another example that was destroyed during filming, this one survives in pristine condition, with only 350 miles on the odometer.
Courtesy of Mark Peterson

Indian™
AMERICA'S FIRST MOTORCYCLE
2002
SCOUT
SCOUT DELUXE
SPIRIT
SPIRIT DELUXE

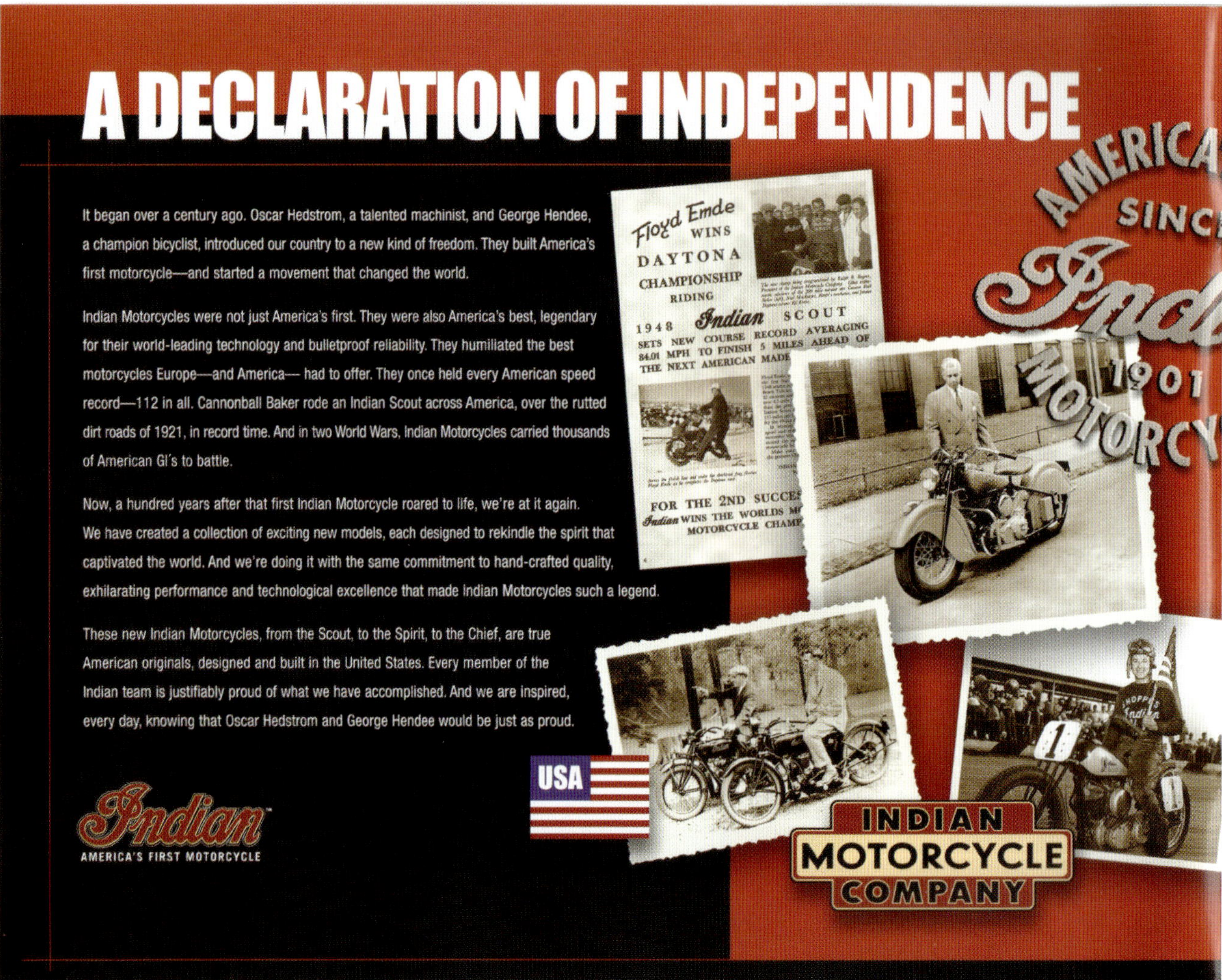
A DECLARATION OF INDEPENDENCE
It began over a century ago. Oscar Hedstrom, a talented machinist, and George Hendee, a champion bicyclist, introduced our country to a new kind of freedom. They built America's first motorcycle—and started a movement that changed the world.
Indian Motorcycles were not just America's first. They were also America's best, legendary for their world-leading technology and bulletproof reliability. They humiliated the best motorcycles Europe—and America— had to offer. They once held every American speed record—112 in all. Cannonball Baker rode an Indian Scout across America, over the rutted dirt roads of 1921, in record time. And in two World Wars, Indian Motorcycles carried thousands of American GI's to battle.
Now, a hundred years after that first Indian Motorcycle roared to life, we're at it again. We have created a collection of exciting new models, each designed to rekindle the spirit that captivated the world. And we're doing it with the same commitment to hand-crafted quality, exhilarating performance and technological excellence that made Indian Motorcycles such a legend.
These new Indian Motorcycles, from the Scout, to the Spirit, to the Chief, are true American originals, designed and built in the United States. Every member of the Indian team is justifiably proud of what we have accomplished. And we are inspired, every day, knowing that Oscar Hedstrom and George Hendee would be just as proud.
Floyd Emde WINS DAYTONA CHAMPIONSHIP RIDING
1948 Indian SCOUT
SETS NEW COURSE RECORD AVERAGING 84.01 MPH TO FINISH 5 MILES AHEAD OF THE NEXT AMERICAN MADE
FOR THE 2ND SUCCES
Indian WINS THE WORLDS M
MOTORCYCLE CHAMP
USA
Indian
AMERICA'S FIRST MOTORCYCLE
INDIAN MOTORCYCLE COMPANY
1901

2002
INDIAN MOTORCYCLES
www.indianmotorcycle.com

SCOUT

2002 SPECIFICATIONS

Engine:	45-degree S&S Super Stock V-twin, raw finish
Displacement:	88 cubic inches
Bore x Stroke:	3.625" x 4.25"
Compression Ratio:	9.4:1
Ignition:	Electronic, computer-controlled
Carburetor:	S&S Super E, 1 7/8" venturi
Exhaust System:	Chrome, shorty duals
Transmission:	Constant-mesh, five-speed
Final Drive:	Aramid-reinforced belt
Frame:	Hand-welded, high-tensile steel, powder-coated, black
Rake:	32 degrees Trail: 5.25 inches
Front Suspension:	41mm, hydraulic compression and rebound damping
Rear Suspension:	Nitrogen-charged hydraulic dampers, coil springs with adjustable pre-load
Brakes:	Stainless-steel disc, 4-piston billet-aluminum caliper
Front Wheel/Tire:	40-spoke, chrome, 19" x 2.15", 4.10-19
Rear Wheel/Tire:	40-spoke, chrome, 16"x 3.0", MT90-16
Wheelbase:	67 inches
Seat Height:	26.5 inches
Dry Weight:	606 lbs.
Fuel Capacity:	5.8 U.S. gallons including 1.2 gallon reserve
Instruments:	VDO speedometer with digital odometer & tripmeter
Colors:	Black • Cobalt Blue
Warranty:	12 months/unlimited mileage
MSRP:	$16,995 U.S. dollars

THE ENGINE IS BIG. THE TANK IS BIG. BUT WITH SCOUT'S NEW ERGONOMICS, YOU DON'T HAVE TO I

The Scout has been improved and reconfigured for 2002, with an emphasis on making it ev for a wider range of riders. We've also added narrower handlebars and relocated footpegs. T reshaped for a more classic look, the speedometer is bigger, for easier viewing, the swingar and the horn is louder. Well, what else would you expect from a bike that's been making itse heard for over 80 years?

BLACK
COBALT BLUE
2002 COLOR OPTIONS
Indian SCOUT
comfortable,
fender is
onger,
Indian
AMERICA'S FIRST MOTORCYCLE

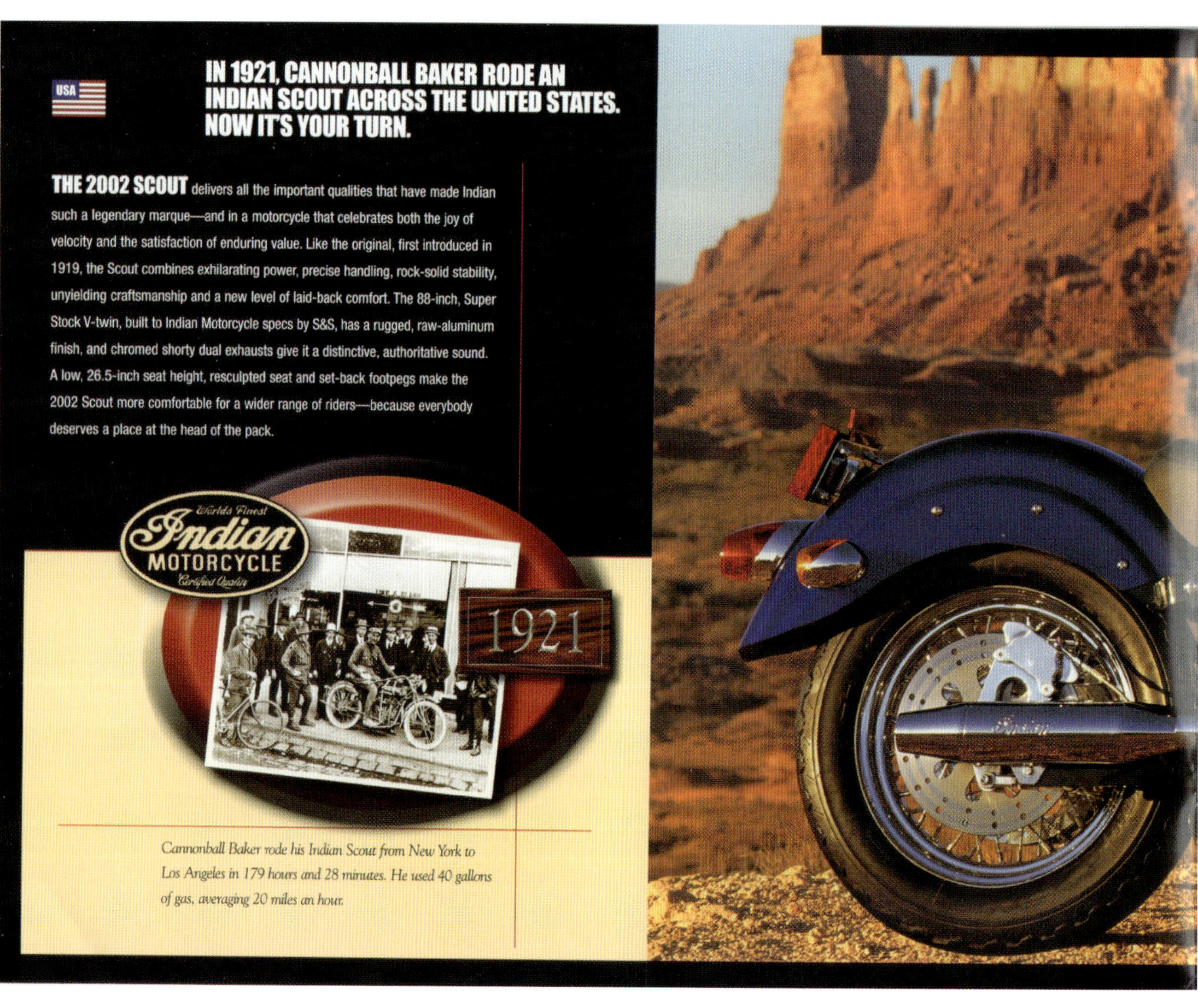
USA
IN 1921, CANNONBALL BAKER RODE AN INDIAN SCOUT ACROSS THE UNITED STATES. NOW IT'S YOUR TURN.
THE 2002 SCOUT delivers all the important qualities that have made Indian such a legendary marque—and in a motorcycle that celebrates both the joy of velocity and the satisfaction of enduring value. Like the original, first introduced in 1919, the Scout combines exhilarating power, precise handling, rock-solid stability, unyielding craftsmanship and a new level of laid-back comfort. The 88-inch, Super Stock V-twin, built to Indian Motorcycle specs by S&S, has a rugged, raw-aluminum finish, and chromed shorty dual exhausts give it a distinctive, authoritative sound. A low, 26.5-inch seat height, resculpted seat and set-back footpegs make the 2002 Scout more comfortable for a wider range of riders—because everybody deserves a place at the head of the pack.
World's Finest
Indian
MOTORCYCLE
Certified Quality
1921
Cannonball Baker rode his Indian Scout from New York to Los Angeles in 179 hours and 28 minutes. He used 40 gallons of gas, averaging 20 miles an hour.

SCOUT
Indian
SCOUT

SCOUT deluxe

2002 SPECIFICATIONS

Engine:	45-degree S&S Super Stock V-twin, raw finish
Displacement:	88 cubic inches
Bore x Stroke:	3.625" x 4.25"
Compression Ratio:	9.4:1
Ignition:	Electronic, computer-controlled
Carburetor:	S&S Super E, 1 7/8" venturi
Exhaust System:	Chrome, shorty duals
Transmission:	Constant-mesh, five-speed
Final Drive:	Aramid-reinforced belt
Frame:	Hand-welded, high-tensile steel, powder-coated, color-matched
Rake:	32 degrees Trail: 5.25 inches
Front Suspension:	41mm, hydraulic compression and rebound damping
Rear Suspension:	Nitrogen-charged hydraulic dampers, coil springs with adjustable pre-load
Brakes:	Stainless-steel disc, 4-piston billet-aluminum caliper
Front Wheel/Tire:	40-spoke, chrome, 19" x 2.15", 4.10-19
Rear Wheel/Tire:	40-spoke, chrome, 16"x 3.0", MT90-16
Wheelbase:	67 inches
Seat Height:	26.5 inches
Dry Weight:	606 lbs.
Fuel Capacity:	5.8 U.S. gallons including 1.2 gallon reserve
Instruments:	VDO speedometer with digital odometer & tripmeter
Colors:	Red • Silver • White
Warranty:	12 months/unlimited mileage
MSRP:	$17,495 U.S. dollars

A NEW 5.8-GALLON TANK, TO TAKE YOU FARTHER. AND NEW ACCOMMODATIONS, TO KEEP YOU SMILING EVERY

The 2002 Scout Deluxe has a long list of improvements—because like you, we at Indian ar staying still. The handlebar has a new bend, with a narrower width, and the pegs are moved to fit more riders. The powder-coated frame is color matched to the body parts, and the rea reshaped for a more dramatic look. The speedometer is bigger, the swingarm is even strong the horn is louder. As if you'd need any help attracting attention.

RED
SILVER
WHITE
2002 COLOR OPTIONS
Indian
SCOUT
OF THE WAY.
omfortable
es back,
Indian
AMERICA'S FIRST MOTORCYCLE

USA
WE INTRODUCED THE SCOUT IN 1919. AS YOU MIGHT EXPECT, WE'VE MADE A FEW IMPROVEMENTS SINCE THEN.
THE INDIAN SCOUT DELUXE is the latest incarnation of a proud line of motorcycles—motorcycles that helped make America a leader in the sport, the world over. The Scout Deluxe starts with all the attributes of the Scout, and adds a distinctive, color-matched frame—just the way we did it back in 1919. Like the original, the Scout Deluxe represents all the legendary qualities that have made Indian such a respected name, combining uncompromising craftsmanship, inspiring power, agile handling and relaxed comfort. The 88-inch, Super Stock V-twin, built to Indian Motorcycle specs by S&S, has a rugged, raw-aluminum finish, and chromed shorty dual exhausts give it a throaty, authoritative sound all its own. And a low, 26.5-inch seat height, recontoured seat and moved-back footpegs make the Scout Deluxe more accommodating for a wider range of riders.
Indian
MOTORCYCLE
1927
The original Scout was so revered, it even inspired a poem:
"You'll never wear out The Indian Scout, or its brother,
The Indian Chief. They're built like rocks. To take hard knocks.
It's the others that cause the grief."

SCOUT
deluxe
Indian
SCOUT

SPIRIT
Indian
SPIRIT

SOME PEOPLE EXPRESS THEMSELVES WITH A PAINT BRUSH. WE PREFER TO USE A THROTTLE.
USA
THE 2002 SPIRIT gives you all the torquey power, stable handling and laid-back comfort you demand, styled to achieve a clean, elegant look. It's powered by the rumbling, 88-inch Super Stock V-twin, built to Indian Motorcycle specs by legendary performance tuner S&S, and presented with a distinctive, full-metal, raw-aluminum finish. The Spirit is fitted out with a powder-coated frame, responsive steering geometry, polished disc brakes and 60-spoke, 16-inch chrome wheels. The new long-haul, 5.8-gallon fuel tank and valanced fenders complete the picture, finished in classic black or gleaming silver. Others will sit up and take notice, but you get to sit back and relax with a new, ergonomically designed seat and roomy, Indian-logo floorboards. Deep inside, you always knew you were going places—isn't it time you hit the road?
Indian
MOTORCYCLE
SINCE 1901
1937
Indian won the first-ever Daytona 200, run in 1937 on the beach and the paved coast road. Ed Kretz was the winning rider—he was famous for his bravery, conditioning and determination.

SPIRIT

2002 SPECIFICATIONS

Engine:	45-degree S&S Super Stock V-twin, raw finish
Displacement:	88 cubic inches
Bore x Stroke:	3.625" x 4.25"
Compression Ratio:	9.4:1
Ignition:	Electronic, computer-controlled
Carburetor:	S&S Super E, 1 7/8" venturi
Exhaust System:	Chrome, 2-into-1
Transmission:	Constant-mesh, five-speed
Final Drive:	Aramid-reinforced belt
Frame:	Hand-welded, high-tensile steel, powder-coated black
Rake:	32 degrees Trail: 5.25 inches
Front Suspension:	41mm, hydraulic compression and rebound damping
Rear Suspension:	Nitrogen-charged hydraulic dampers, coil springs with adjustable pre-load
Brakes:	Stainless-steel disc, 4-piston billet-aluminum caliper
Front Wheel/Tire:	60-spoke, chrome, 16" x 3.5", 130/90-16
Rear Wheel/Tire:	60-spoke, chrome, 16" x 3.5", 130/90-16
Wheelbase:	67 inches
Seat Height:	28 inches
Dry Weight:	626 lbs.
Fuel Capacity:	5.8 U.S. gallons including 1.2 gallon reserve
Instruments:	VDO speedometer with digital odometer & tripmeter
Colors:	Black • Medium Silver
Warranty:	12 Months/unlimited mileage
MSRP:	$17,995 U.S. dollars

INDIAN HAS ALWAYS BEEN KNOWN FOR INNOVATION—AND WE'RE NOT ABOUT TO SLOW DOWN NOW.

New Spirit features for 2002 include a new teardrop-style headlight, a huge, 5.8-gallon fue dual aviation-style, lockable gas caps. The speedometer is bigger, the horn is louder, and th is 33% stronger. The seat is recontoured, to keep your body just as gratified as your soul. And new Indian-logo, vibration-absorbing floorboards keep your feet just as comfortable as the rest of you.

BLACK
MEDIUM SILVER
2002 COLOR OPTIONS
Indian
SPIRIT
d
arm
Indian
MERICA'S FIRST MOTORCYCLE

SPIRIT
deluxe
Indian

EVERY MOVEMENT NEEDS A LEADER.
USA
THE INDIAN SPIRIT DELUXE is what American cruising is all about. Its 88-inch Super Stock V-twin, built to Indian Motorcycle specs by legendary performance tuner S&S, delivers the kind of roll-on power and low-end torque you demand. Its roomy new floorboards give you an extra measure of laid-back comfort. And its low, low chassis, with 16-inch, 60-spoke wheels, front and rear, make the Spirit Deluxe just as comfortable in town as it is on the way to the next horizon. Dress it all up with the flawless finish, unmatched quality and elegant lines inherent in any Indian. Finish it off with a classic selection of two-tone color schemes. And get ready to turn heads, just as easily as you crank out miles.
INDIAN
MOTORCYCLE
COMPANY
1911
1911 was a big year for Indian. We placed 1, 2, 3 at the Isle of Man, sending European motorcycle designers back to their drawing boards. By the end of the year, Indian possessed every single American speed and distance record-112 in all.

SPIRIT deluxe

2002 SPECIFICATIONS

Engine:	45-degree S&S Super Stock V-twin, black finish
Displacement:	88 cubic inches
Bore x Stroke:	3.625" x 4.25"
Compression Ratio:	9.4:1
Ignition:	Electronic, computer-controlled
Carburetor:	S&S Super E, 1 7/8" venturi
Exhaust System:	Chrome, 2-into-1
Transmission:	Constant-mesh, five-speed
Final Drive:	Aramid-reinforced belt
Frame:	Hand-welded, high-tensile steel, powder-coated black
Rake:	32 degrees Trail: 5.25 inches
Front Suspension:	41mm, hydraulic compression and rebound damping
Rear Suspension:	Nitrogen-charged hydraulic dampers, coil springs with adjustable pre-load
Brakes:	Stainless-steel disc, 4-piston billet-aluminum caliper
Front Wheel/Tire:	60-spoke, chrome, 16" x 3.5", 130/90-16
Rear Wheel/Tire:	60-spoke, chrome, 16" x 3.5", 130/90-16
Wheelbase:	67 inches
Seat Height:	28 inches
Dry Weight:	626 lbs.
Fuel Capacity:	5.8 U.S. gallons including 1.2 gallon reserve
Instruments:	VDO speedometer with digital odometer & tripmeter
Colors:	Black/Red • Black/Silver • Black/Cream • Red/Cream
Warranty:	12 Months/unlimited mileage
MSRP:	$18,995 U.S. dollars

FOR 2002, WE MADE THE FUEL TANK BIGGER-BECAUSE SPIR JUST DON'T WANT TO STOP.

The Indian Spirit was a massive hit in 2001. So, naturally, we went all out to make it even teardrop-style headlight, a huge, 5.8-gallon fuel tank and dual aviation-style, lockable gas new, more ergonomic, fringed seat, and comfortable, Indian-logo floorboards. We made the the horn louder, and the swingarm even beefier. Then we hopped on, flicked the starter, an rumbled off into the sunset. And haven't been heard from since.

BLACK/
RED
BLACK/
SILVER
BLACK/
CREAM
RED/
CREAM
2002 COLOR OPTIONS
ERS
e gave it a new
bolted on a
neter bigger,
Indian
MERICA'S FIRST MOTORCYCLE

A PROUD TRADITION OF QUALITY
From the beginning, Indian Motorcycles have been known for leading-edge technology and meticulous craftsmanship. We are committed to remaining true to that heritage–and to building some of the highest-quality, handcrafted motorcycles money can buy.
Our state-of-the-art factory is equipped with the latest computer-aided technology. But it's the hands and eyes of our people that give each Indian Motorcycle its distinctive personality.
From the Indian head sculpture on the front fender to the billet-aluminum controls and flawless finish, each Indian Motorcycle is built to be a bold statement of craftsmanship, an icon of excellence in a mass-produced world.
Indian
AMERICA'S FIRST MOTORCYCLE

The 2002 Scout/Spirit catalog touts the quality of the engine built "to Indian specs by legendary performance leader S&S Cycle." Note the raw-aluminum finish. The Scout and Spirit models were the only models still equipped with the S&S 88-cubic-inch engine.

2003 Model Year
Downfall

By mid-2003, improvements to the Powerplus were slowly being implemented at the factory, and a 92-cubic-inch S&S-built Indian engine was coming online for 2004 model year Scouts and Spirits. Gilroy was on the brink of achieving its goal of 100 percent Indian-designed motorcycles. The "Vintage" Chief (655 built) was introduced this year at the January 12, 2003, National Dealer Convention, along with the "Springfield" Scouts, Spirits, and Chiefs. The Chief / Chief Deluxe / Chief Roadmaster options continued, as well as a Spirit Deluxe / Spirit Roadmaster with a wide choice of color combinations. Paioli forks were introduced during 2003 Chief production. A special uncataloged-edition "T3" Chief was offered (fifty-two built) as a tribute bike for the Arnold Schwarzenegger film *Terminator 3*. The depiction of Chief Joseph Nicholas ("Leaping Deer") continued to be a feature on 2003 Chief fuel tanks except the "Vintage" and the "Springfield."

The Scout and Spirit underwent some interesting changes for 2003. The base Scout was no longer available in black, the 2003 choices being cobalt blue and blackberry metallic (a far cry from the nine available colors for the base Scout in 2001). For the Scout Deluxe, silver was dropped in favor of yellow. For the base Spirit, 2003 was even more interesting . . . because there wasn't one. Only the Spirit Deluxe (two-tone paint plus whitewalls) and Spirit Roadmaster (two-tone paint, whitewalls, saddlebags, and a passenger backrest) were offered in IMCOA's final year. In addition, the two Spirit models featured polished fins on their S&S 88 V-twins.

May 2003 was the IMCOA's highest sales month yet. But as Indian's momentum was gaining steam, the cost of numerous recalls and warranty repairs/replacements on the Powerplus engines was choking the lifeblood from the company. By mid-2003, an additional infusion of capital was desperately needed. Indian's primary investor, Audax, having burned through approximately $100 million over twenty-seven months and still writing weekly checks to keep Indian afloat, finally withdrew its financial support (see chapter 4, "IMCOA Corporate History," for details on Audax's involvement with IMCOA). With no other investors stepping forward, operating funds were quickly exhausted. Abruptly on September 19, 2003, the Indian motorcycle factory in Gilroy, California, closed its doors and laid off its workers (see chapter 4, "IMCOA Corporate History," for details on the shutdown). Reported production of the Scout, Spirit, and Chief totaled 3,900–4,000 for 2003, a few of which were 2004 models that had finally achieved an all-Indian line of motorcycles. The first resurrection of the Indian motorcycle had ended.

Like the previous year's large catalog for the Chief, 2003's version was 8.5 × 11 in. plus 6 in. gatefolds. Note the inclusion of the new Chief Vintage, which was introduced in January. Prospective customers (and potential investors) could never have guessed by this catalog that IMCOA was slowly circling the drain.

WE'VE STARTED SOMETHING BIG.
NOW IT'S YOUR TURN.
IT BEGAN 103 YEARS AGO. OSCAR HEDSTROM, AN INGENIOUS INVENTOR, AND GEORGE HENDEE, A CHAMPION BICYCLE RACER, GAVE TO AMERICA A NEW KIND OF FREEDOM. THEY CREATED AMERICA'S FIRST MOTORCYCLE. AND ON THE WAY, STARTED A MOVEMENT THAT CHANGED THE WORLD.
NOW, MORE THAN A CENTURY AFTER THAT FIRST INDIAN MOTORCYCLE HIT THE ROAD, WE'RE CHANGING THE WORLD AGAIN. WE'RE BRINGING THOSE LEGENDARY MOTORCYCLES BACK TO LIFE—THE MOTORCYCLES THAT CAPTURED THE WORLD'S IMAGINATION. AND WE'RE DOING IT WITH THE SAME COMMITMENT TO SOUL-STIRRING PERFORMANCE, HANDCRAFTED QUALITY AND ADVANCED TECHNOLOGY THAT HAVE MADE THE INDIAN BRAND WORLD-RENOWNED SINCE 1901.
AS THE TOP OF THE INDIAN MOTORCYCLE'S LINEUP, THE INDIAN CHIEF IS A ROLLING DECLARATION OF EVERYTHING WE STAND FOR. WE CONCEIVED AND BUILT ITS ALL-AMERICAN, ALL-INDIAN POWERPLUS™ 100 ENGINE TO DELIVER THE MASSIVE TORQUE AND HEART-POUNDING POWER A MACHINE LIKE THIS DESERVES. WE BUILT ITS COMPUTER-DESIGNED CHASSIS TO MAKE IT AS EASY TO HANDLE AS IT IS TO LOOK AT. WE MADE IT A SHOWPIECE OF MODERN TECHNOLOGY—AND A TRIBUTE TO THE LEGENDARY CHIEFS OF THE PAST.
FROM THE EXCITING NEW CHIEF VINTAGE, WITH ITS AUTHENTIC '40S APPEAL TO THE STUNNING CHIEF DELUXE AND THE FULL LINE UP OF OTHER CHIEF MODELS, EACH IS DESIGNED TO REFLECT THE SOUL OF INDIAN MOTORCYCLES—AND TO KICKSTART THE HEART OF ITS FORTUNATE OWNER.
Indian®
ESTABLISHED
1901
2
2003 CHIEF®

The new Chief Vintage

Indian was responding to customers wanting a Chief with even more 1940s characteristics.

Note the standard forks and lack of a headlight nacelle.

A STREETBIKE NAMED DESIRE.
WE SWEATED EVERY DETAIL OF THE CHIEF® MODEL, FROM ITS DEEP-VALANCED FRONT FENDER TO THE COMFORTABLE CURVE OF ITS NEW SWEPT-BACK HANDLEBAR. ITS HEART IS THE POWERPLUS™ 100 ENGINE—AN AMERICAN POWERHOUSE DESIGNED TO DELIVER PLENTY OF TORQUE AND OUTSTANDING ROLL-ON PERFORMANCE. IT RIDES ON BEEFY 60-SPOKE CHROME WHEELS AND SLOWS WITH WORLD-FAMOUS BREMBO BRAKES. ITS HIGH-STRENGTH, HIGH-TECH CHASSIS USES A PRECISE, GERMAN-MADE KW MONOSHOCK FOR SURE CORNERING AND GREAT STRAIGHT-LINE STABILITY. ITS LOOK IS SIMPLY TIMELESS—JUST WHAT YOU'D EXPECT FROM AMERICA'S ORIGINAL MOTORCYCLE.
CHIEF FEATURES
Powerplus™ 100 engine. Big-inch power, big-time torque.
Computerized ignition. No guesswork, no maintenance.
High-strength CAD-CAM designed steel frame. In-town agility, long-haul stability.
Brembo brakes. From Formula 1 to Highway 1.
Show quality chrome and polished trim. The custom look comes standard.
German KW shock. Precision built, precision ride.
6
CHIEF®

Jet Black
Volcano Red Metallic
Cobalt Blue Metallic
7

WE READ YOUR MIND.
NOT TO MENTION YOUR HEART.
DESIGNING THE CHIEF® DELUXE WAS EASY. WE DRESSED UP THE CHIEF THE WAY WE'D LIKE IT OURSELVES—AND THEN BUILT JUST A FEW MORE. IT HAS ALL THE IMPRESSIVE TECHNOLOGY THAT MAKES THE CHIEF MODEL SUCH AN ENGINEERING STANDOUT, FROM ITS POWERPLUS™ 100 ENGINE TO ITS COMPUTER-DESIGNED CHASSIS. WE KEPT THE CHIEF'S ERGONOMIC NEW PULLBACK HANDLEBAR, THE 60-SPOKE, 16-INCH CHROME WHEELS, THE GLEAMING CHROME AND THE POLISHED ALUMINUM. WE ADDED TRADITIONAL WHITEWALL TIRES AND CLASSIC NEW TWO-TONE PAINT SCHEMES. NOT TO MENTION A FRINGED DUAL SEAT—BECAUSE A MACHINE THIS SPECIAL IS TOO GOOD NOT TO SHARE.
CHIEF DELUXE FEATURES
• Fringed dual seat. You can take her with you.
• Classic whitewall tires. Authentic 1950s style.
• Classic two-tone paint schemes. Some things are too good to change.
• Powerplus™ 100 engine. Big-inch power, big-time torque.
• Brembo brakes. From Formula 1 to Highway 1.
8
CHIEF® DELUXE

Jet Black/
Volcano Red Metallic
Deep Red/
Vanilla Cream
Copper Metallic/
Jet Black
Blackberry Metallic/
Jet Black
Jet Black/
Pearl White
Cobalt Blue Metallic/
Pearl White
9

CELEBRATING THE HERITAGE OF AMERICA'S ORIGINAL MOTORCYCLE.
IT ALL STARTED IN SPRINGFIELD, MASSACHUSETTS, 103 YEARS AGO. AND THIS SPECIAL CHIEF® MODEL COMMEMORATES THE LOOK AND WORLD-ROCKING PERFORMANCE OF THOSE BEAUTIFUL FIRST INDIAN® MODELS. LIKE MANY EARLY INDIAN MOTORCYCLES, THE CHIEF SPRINGFIELD COMES IN A MONOCHROME PAINT SCHEME, WITH THE CLASSIC GOLD SCRIPT TANK LOGO FIRST SEEN IN 1910, SURROUNDED BY RICH GOLD PINSTRIPES—A DESIGN UNVEILED ON THE 1917 INDIAN POWERPLUS. A SLEEK SOLO SEAT, 16-INCH, 60-SPOKE WIRE WHEELS AND TRADITIONAL BLACKWALL TIRES COMPLETE THE NOSTALGIC PRE-WAR—WORLD WAR ONE, THAT IS—MOTIF.
CHIEF SPRINGFIELD FEATURES
• Gold script logo and pinstripes. Legendary Springfield look.
• Traditional blackwall tires. Same as it ever was.
• Powerplus™ 100 engine. Big-inch power, big-time torque.
• High-strength CAD-CAM designed steel frame. In-town agility, long-haul stability.
• Brembo brakes. From Formula 1 to Highway 1.
• German KW shock. Precision built, precision ride.
Indian
10
CHIEF® SPRINGFIELD

Indian
Jet Black
Deep Red
11

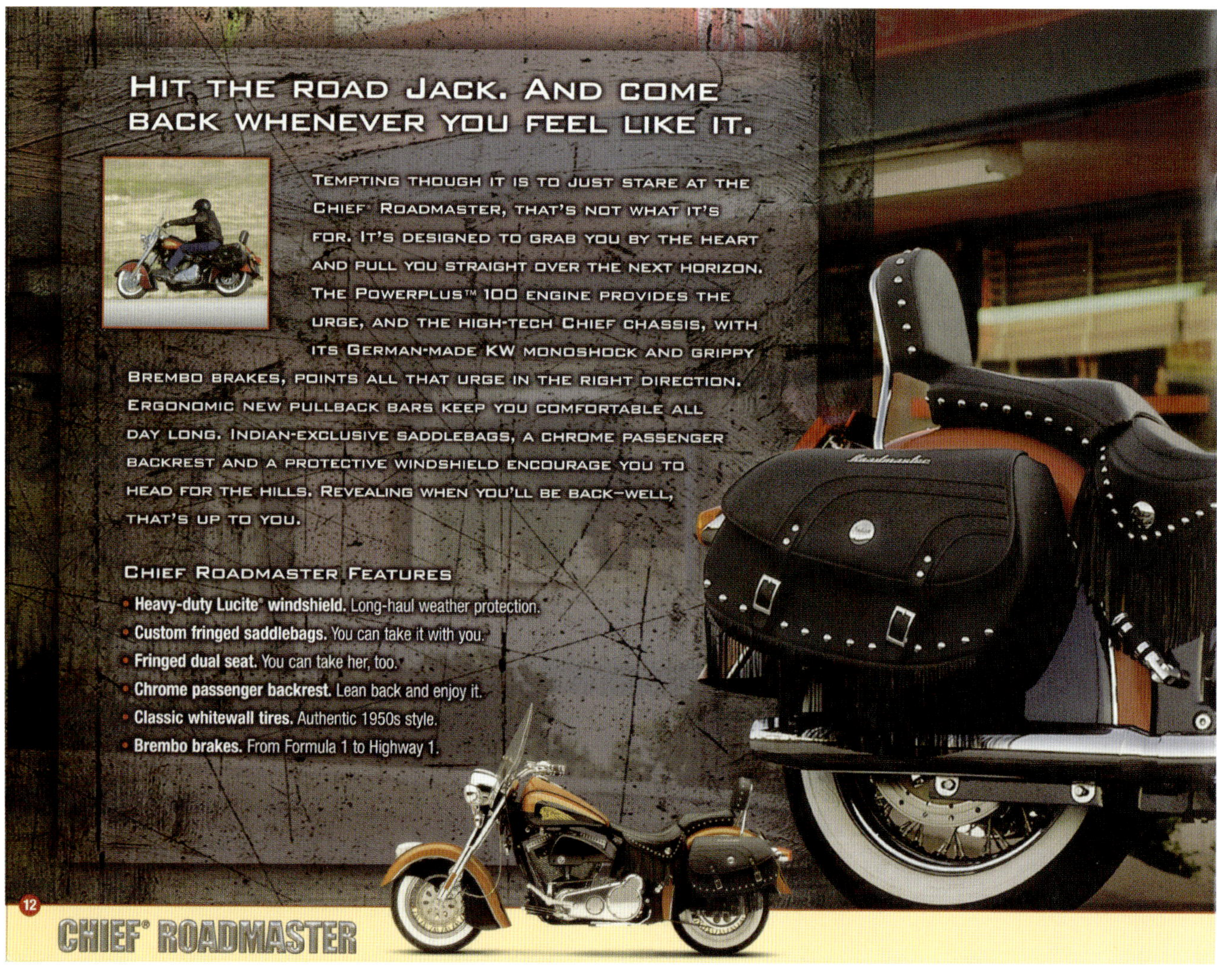
HIT THE ROAD JACK. AND COME BACK WHENEVER YOU FEEL LIKE IT.
TEMPTING THOUGH IT IS TO JUST STARE AT THE CHIEF® ROADMASTER, THAT'S NOT WHAT IT'S FOR. IT'S DESIGNED TO GRAB YOU BY THE HEART AND PULL YOU STRAIGHT OVER THE NEXT HORIZON. THE POWERPLUS™ 100 ENGINE PROVIDES THE URGE, AND THE HIGH-TECH CHIEF CHASSIS, WITH ITS GERMAN-MADE KW MONOSHOCK AND GRIPPY BREMBO BRAKES, POINTS ALL THAT URGE IN THE RIGHT DIRECTION. ERGONOMIC NEW PULLBACK BARS KEEP YOU COMFORTABLE ALL DAY LONG. INDIAN-EXCLUSIVE SADDLEBAGS, A CHROME PASSENGER BACKREST AND A PROTECTIVE WINDSHIELD ENCOURAGE YOU TO HEAD FOR THE HILLS. REVEALING WHEN YOU'LL BE BACK—WELL, THAT'S UP TO YOU.
CHIEF ROADMASTER FEATURES
• Heavy-duty Lucite® windshield. Long-haul weather protection.
• Custom fringed saddlebags. You can take it with you.
• Fringed dual seat. You can take her, too.
• Chrome passenger backrest. Lean back and enjoy it.
• Classic whitewall tires. Authentic 1950s style.
• Brembo brakes. From Formula 1 to Highway 1.
12
CHIEF® ROADMASTER

Jet Black
Volcano Red Metallic
Cobalt Blue Metallic
Jet Black / Volcano Red Metallic
Deep Red / Vanilla Cream
Copper Metallic / Jet Black
Blackberry Metallic / Jet Black
Jet Black / Pearl White
Cobalt Blue Metallic / Pearl White
Indian
Indian
13

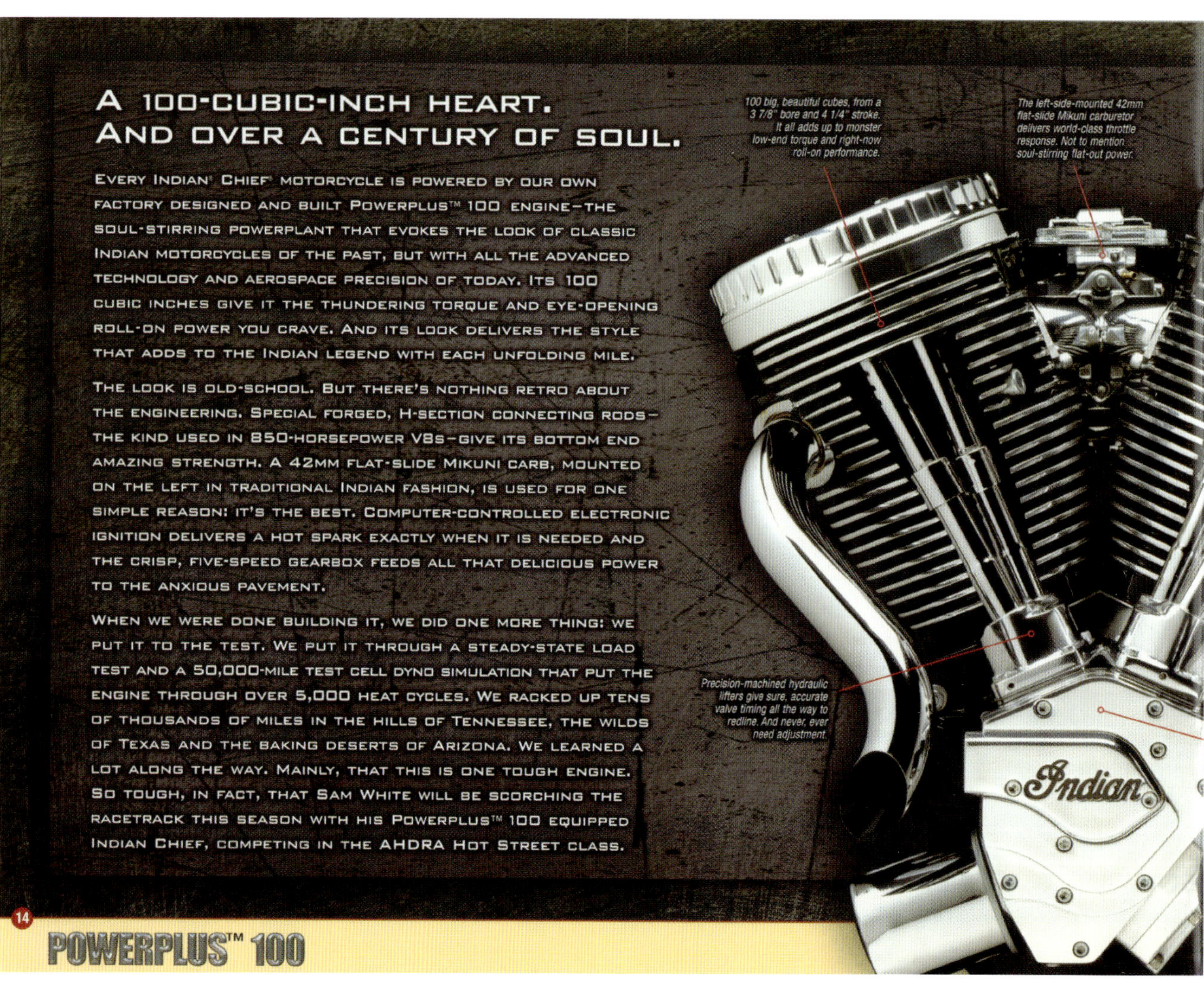
A 100-CUBIC-INCH HEART.
AND OVER A CENTURY OF SOUL.
Every Indian® Chief® motorcycle is powered by our own factory designed and built PowerPlus™ 100 engine—the soul-stirring powerplant that evokes the look of classic Indian motorcycles of the past, but with all the advanced technology and aerospace precision of today. Its 100 cubic inches give it the thundering torque and eye-opening roll-on power you crave. And its look delivers the style that adds to the Indian legend with each unfolding mile.
The look is old-school. But there's nothing retro about the engineering. Special forged, H-section connecting rods—the kind used in 850-horsepower V8s—give its bottom end amazing strength. A 42mm flat-slide Mikuni carb, mounted on the left in traditional Indian fashion, is used for one simple reason: it's the best. Computer-controlled electronic ignition delivers a hot spark exactly when it is needed and the crisp, five-speed gearbox feeds all that delicious power to the anxious pavement.
When we were done building it, we did one more thing: we put it to the test. We put it through a steady-state load test and a 50,000-mile test cell dyno simulation that put the engine through over 5,000 heat cycles. We racked up tens of thousands of miles in the hills of Tennessee, the wilds of Texas and the baking deserts of Arizona. We learned a lot along the way. Mainly, that this is one tough engine. So tough, in fact, that Sam White will be scorching the racetrack this season with his PowerPlus™ 100 equipped Indian Chief, competing in the AHDRA Hot Street class.
100 big, beautiful cubes, from a 3 7/8" bore and 4 1/4" stroke. It all adds up to monster low-end torque and right-now roll-on performance.
The left-side-mounted 42mm flat-slide Mikuni carburetor delivers world-class throttle response. Not to mention soul-stirring flat-out power.
Precision-machined hydraulic lifters give sure, accurate valve timing all the way to redline. And never, ever need adjustment.
Indian
14
POWERPLUS™ 100

The round-barreled aluminum cylinders are cast around waffle-patterned steel liners, for optimum heat transfer and bulletproof reliability.
IT'S A LONG ROAD AHEAD. BUT THERE'S NO REASON IT HAS TO FEEL THAT WAY.
THE CHIEF MOTORCYCLE HAS A HUGE HEART AND A RIGHTEOUS SOUL. ITS HANDLING MANNERS ARE JUST AS STUNNING AS ITS STYLING, WITH THE PERFECT COMBINATION OF DOWNTOWN AGILITY AND DOWN-THE-ROAD STABILITY. WITH THIS KIND OF CHASSIS PERFORMANCE, YOU CAN TURN TWISTY ROADS INTO YOUR OWN PRIVATE PLAYGROUND. IT STARTS WITH A HELL-FOR-STRONG CAD-CAM DESIGNED, COORDINATE MEASURING MACHINE-INSPECTED BACKBONE. THE CHIEF CHASSIS WAS CREATED USING 3-D PARAMETRIC COMPUTER ASSISTED DESIGN TECHNIQUES AND FINITE ELEMENT ANALYSIS VERIFICATION. TRANSLATION: IT'S INCREDIBLY PRECISE AND EVERY BIT AS STRONG AS IT LOOKS. A 41MM PAIOLI FORK KEEPS THE FRONT WHEEL FIRMLY IN LINE AND A GERMAN-MADE KW SHOCK STRIKES THE PERFECT BALANCE BETWEEN COMFORT AND CONTROL. THE POWERPLUS™ 100 IS THE HEART OF THE CHIEF AND ONE LOOK AT ITS CHASSIS WILL TELL YOU WE'VE GOT OUR HEART IN THE RIGHT PLACE.
The frame is CAD-CAM designed, FEA verified and Coordinate Measuring Machine (CMM) inspected. In other words, it's really strong.
The backbone is made of square-section, high-strength, low-alloy tubing. So the new Chief goes exactly, precisely, where you point it.
The rear suspension uses a high-quality, German-made KW shock and rising-rate geometry to give you precise handling and a smooth, let's-keep-on-going ride.
Multi-function, cast-steel engine mounts hold the Powerplus 100 firmly in place, adding to rigidity while they help ensure bulletproof reliability.
The swingarm combines an investment-cast rear-shock cantilever and high-strength, low-alloy, 1" x 3" tubing. It's both light and strong, for impressive stability and confidence-inspiring road holding.
The flywheel and crankshaft weigh a massive 26 pounds. And the forged connecting rods, with their H-beam design, come straight from the racetrack.
It's not finished 'til it's finished. We use DuPont™ Powder-Prime coating process, with a wet, clear-coat finish for a glass-like surface and extreme durability. Then we hand-inspect each and every Chief.
15
CHASSIS

IMCOA's "Exotic Color Shop" was capable of outstanding custom paint for those who wanted something extraordinary and were willing to pay for it. Multiple coats of metallic paint plus multiple applications of clearcoat resulted in a three-dimensional effect. The price of this artistry and labor varied, but added approximately $3000-$3500 to the price of a new Chief.
Courtesy of Mark Peterson

Courtesy of Mark Peterson

This catalog showing the entire 2003 Indian line measures 4 × 9 in. Note that the Chief Vintage (introduced in January) was not yet included in the lineup.

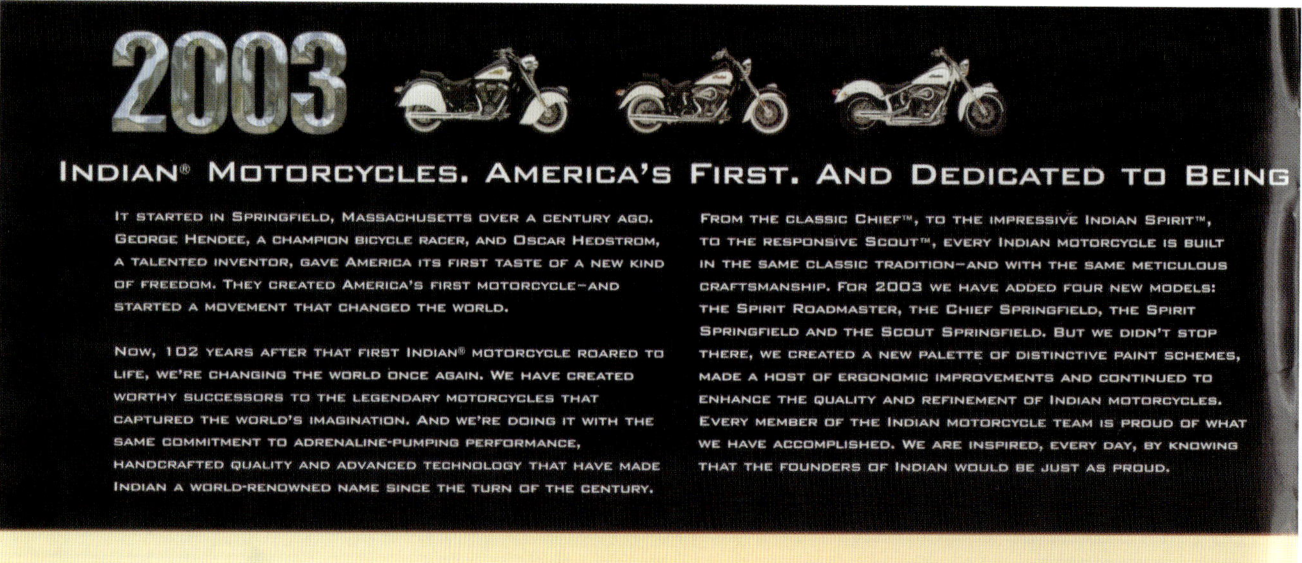

STREETBIKE NAMED DESIRE.

: SWEATED EVERY DETAIL OF THE CHIEF™, FROM ITS
EP-VALANCED FRONT FENDER TO THE COMFORTABLE
RVE OF ITS NEW SWEPT-BACK HANDLEBAR. ITS HEART
THE POWERPLUS™ 100–AN AMERICAN POWERHOUSE
SIGNED TO DELIVER PLENTY OF TORQUE AND
TSTANDING ROLL-ON PERFORMANCE. IT RIDES ON BEEFY
-SPOKE CHROME WHEELS AND SLOWS WITH
RLD-FAMOUS BREMBO BRAKES. ITS
H-STRENGTH, HIGH-TECH CHASSIS
ES A PRECISE, GERMAN-MADE KW
NOSHOCK FOR SURE CORNERING
D GREAT STRAIGHT-LINE STABILITY.
LOOK IS SIMPLY TIMELESS–JUST
AT YOU'D EXPECT FROM
ERICA'S ORIGINAL MOTORCYCLE.

IEF™

Jet Black
Volcano Red Metallic
Cobalt Blue Metallic

/E READ YOUR MIND.
IOT TO MENTION YOUR HEART.

ESIGNING THE CHIEF™ DELUXE WAS EASY. WE DRESSED
P THE CHIEF THE WAY WE'D LIKE IT OURSELVES–AND
HEN BUILT JUST A FEW MORE. IT HAS ALL THE IMPRESSIVE
ECHNOLOGY THAT MAKES THE CHIEF SUCH AN ENGINEERING
TANDOUT, FROM ITS POWERPLUS™ 100 ENGINE
O ITS COMPUTER-DESIGNED CHASSIS.
/E KEPT THE CHIEF'S ERGONOMIC
IEW PULLBACK HANDLEBAR, THE
O-SPOKE, 16-INCH CHROME
/HEELS, THE GLEAMING CHROME
ND THE POLISHED ALUMINUM.
/E ADDED TRADITIONAL
/HITEWALL TIRES AND CLASSIC
IEW TWO-TONE PAINT SCHEMES.
IOT TO MENTION A FRINGED DUAL
EAT–BECAUSE A MACHINE THIS
PECIAL IS TOO GOOD NOT TO SHARE.

CHIEF™ DELUXE

Jet Black /
Deep Red /
Copper Metallic /
Blackberry Metallic /
Jet Black /
Cobalt Blue Metallic /

HIT THE ROAD, JACK. AND COME BACK WHENEVER YOU FEEL LIKE IT.
TEMPTING THOUGH IT IS TO JUST STARE AT THE CHIEF™ ROADMASTER, THAT'S NOT WHAT IT'S FOR. IT'S DESIGNED TO GRAB YOU BY THE HEART AND PULL YOU STRAIGHT OVER THE NEXT HORIZON. THE POWERPLUS™ 100 ENGINE PROVIDES THE URGE, AND THE HIGH-TECH CHIEF CHASSIS, WITH ITS GERMAN-MADE KW MONOSHOCK AND GRIPPY BREMBO BRAKES, POINTS ALL THAT URGE IN THE RIGHT DIRECTION. ERGONOMIC NEW PULLBACK BARS KEEP YOU COMFORTABLE ALL DAY LONG. INDIAN-EXCLUSIVE SADDLEBAGS, A CHROME PASSENGER BACKREST AND A PROTECTIVE WINDSHIELD ENCOURAGE YOU TO HEAD FOR THE HILLS. REVEALING WHEN YOU'LL BE BACK—WELL, THAT'S UP TO YOU.
CHIEF™ ROADMASTER
Jet Black
Volcano Red Metallic
Cobalt Blue Metallic
Jet Black / Volcano Red Metallic
Deep Red / Vanilla Cream
Copper Metallic / Jet Black
Blackberry Metallic / Jet Black
Jet Black / Pearl White
Cobalt Blue Metalli Pearl White
THE 2003 SPRINGFIELD EDITIONS: CELEBRATING THE HERITAGE OF AMERICA'S ORIGINAL MOTORCYCLE.
THE CLASSIC LOOK AND FEEL OF THE EARLY INDIAN® MOTORCYCLES IS AN ESSENTIAL PART OF THEIR ENDURING APPEAL AND A MAJOR ELEMENT OF THE INDIAN MYSTIQUE. TO CELEBRATE THE MACHINES THAT FIRST PUT AMERICA ON TWO WHEELS WE CREATED THREE DISTINCTIVE SPRINGFIELD EDITION INDIAN MOTORCYCLES.
THE SPRINGFIELD EDITIONS WEAR THE CLASSIC LARGE INDIAN SCRIPT LOGO IN RICH GOLD, SURROUNDED BY DOUBLE GOLD PINSTRIPING ON A GLEAMING BACKGROUND FINISH OF SOLID RED OR BLACK. THIS FLOWING SCRIPT LOGO WAS INTRODUCED IN 1910. THE COMPLETE LOOK, WITH THE SURROUNDING GOLD PINSTRIPING, WAS FIRST SEEN ON THE 1917 INDIAN POWERPLUS™ STREET TWIN.
SPRINGFIELD EDITIONS

'HE 2003 POWERPLUS™ 100 ENGINE:
START SOMETHING BIG.
AST YEAR, WE ROCKED THE MOTORCYCLING WORLD WITH
HE ALL-INDIAN® POWERPLUS™ 100—THE LARGEST OEM
IOTORCYCLE ENGINE DESIGNED AND BUILT IN AMERICA.
HIS YEAR, OF COURSE, IT'S BACK—AND WITH A
ENGEANCE. IT STILL HAS EVERY BIT OF THE EARTH-
HAKING TORQUE THAT MADE IT SUCH A SENSATION.
VERY PULSE OF ITS EYE-OPENING ROLL-ON
OWER. AND EVERY BIT OF THE LOOK
HAT HAS MADE INDIAN MOTORCYCLES
UCH ICONS OF CLASSIC DESIGN.
S WE SAID, LAST YEAR WE ROCKED
HE MOTORCYCLING WORLD. NOW
'S TIME TO ROCK YOURS.
'OWERPLUS™ 100 ENGINE
Indian

Indian
Indian
Deep Red
Jet Black

SPIRIT DELUXE

BURGERS
SHAKES
SOD AS
'S A BIG COUNTRY.
ET THE NEW SPIRIT ROADMASTER SHRINK
DOWN TO SIZE.
E 2003 SPIRIT ROADMASTER IS DESIGNED TO QUENCH UR THIRST FOR ADVENTURE. IT'S EQUIPPED WITH A SSENGER BACKREST AND SADDLEBAGS DESIGNED FOR E LONG HAUL—NO MATTER HOW MANY MILES IT TAKES SATISFY YOUR RESTLESS SOUL. THE LONG, LOW CHASSIS D 60-SPOKE, 16-INCH CHROME WHEELS GIVE THE IRIT THE PERFECT COMBINATION OF IN-TOWN ILITY AND HORIZON-SEEKING STABILITY. AND STINCTIVE NEW TWO-TONE PAINT SCHEMES ND POLISHED COOLING FINS ADD THE NISHING TOUCH. TURN HEADS IN TOWN—OR JRN THE ODOMETER OVER ALL DAY LONG. THER WAY, THE SPIRIT ROADMASTER IS E ALL-AMERICAN CRUISER YOU'VE BEEN AITING FOR.
Indian
PIRIT ROADMASTER
Jet Black
Jet Black/
Red Rock/
Jet Black/
Jet Black/
Chrome Yellow/

'S A FREE COUNTRY.
EEL FREE TO SEE IT ALL.
E SCOUT™ DELUXE IS WHAT HAPPENS WHEN YOU TAKE N IRRESISTIBLE V-TWIN CRUISER AND GIVE IT AN EXTRA HOT OF CLASSIC STYLE. THE POWDER-COATED FRAME IS OLOR-MATCHED TO AN EXCLUSIVE CHOICE OF WHITE, RED R NEW YELLOW BODYWORK—RECREATING THE LEGENDARY NDIAN LOOK. UNDER THE SKIN, THE SCOUT DELUXE IS L MUSCLE, FROM ITS 88-INCH SUPER TOCK™ HEART TO ITS PRECISE, AGILE- ANDLING CHASSIS. ERGONOMIC NEW ULLBACK BARS INCREASE YOUR OMFORT AND A REDESIGNED DING POSITION AND LOW SEAT EIGHT MAKE THE SCOUT DELUXE VEN MORE FRIENDLY TO SMALLER IDERS. HEAD ACROSS TOWN OR CROSS THE COUNTRY. AND FEEL FREE O GRIN EVERY INCH OF THE WAY.
Indian
SCOUT™ DELUXE
Aspen White
Citrus Yellow
Red Rock

SCOUT SPECIFICATIONS

Engine:	45-degree S&S Super Stock™ V-twin, raw finish
Displacement:	88 cubic inches (1442cc)
Bore x Stroke:	3.625" x 4.25"
Compression Ratio:	9.4:1
Ignition:	Electronic, computer-controlled
Valves:	2" intake, 1.605" exhaust, hydraulic lifters
Carburetor:	S&S Super E, 1 7/8" venturi
Exhaust System:	Chrome, shorty duals
Transmission:	Constant-mesh, five-speed
Final Drive:	Aramid-reinforced belt
Frame:	High-tensile steel, powder-coated
Rake / Trail:	32 degrees / 5.25"
Front Suspension:	41mm, hydraulic compression and rebound damping
Rear Suspension:	Nitrogen-charged hydraulic dampers, coil springs with adjustable preload
Brakes:	Stainless-steel discs, 4-piston billet-aluminum calipers
Front Wheel/Tire:	40-spoke, chrome, 19" x 2.15", 100/90-19
Rear Wheel/Tire:	40-spoke, chrome, 16"x 3.0", 130/90-16
Wheelbase:	67"
Seat Height:	26.5"
Dry Weight:	Scout/Deluxe/Springfield: 606 lbs.
Fuel Capacity:	5.5 U.S. gallons including 1.2 gallon reserve
Instruments:	Speedometer with digital odometer & tripmeter
Warranty:	12 months/unlimited mileage
MSRP:	**SCOUT:** $16,995 U.S. dollars **SCOUT SPRINGFIELD:** $17,495 U.S. dollars **SCOUT DELUXE:** $17,795 U.S. dollars

SPIRIT SPECIFICATIONS

Engine:	45-degree S&S Super Stock™ V-twin, raw finish, polished fins
Displacement:	88 cubic inches (1442cc)
Bore x Stroke:	3.625" x 4.25"
Compression Ratio:	9.4:1
Ignition:	Electronic, computer-controlled
Valves:	2" intake, 1.605" exhaust, hydraulic lifters
Carburetor:	S&S Super E, 1 7/8" venturi
Exhaust System:	Chrome, 2-into-1
Transmission:	Constant-mesh, five-speed
Final Drive:	Aramid-reinforced belt
Frame:	High-tensile steel, powder-coated, black
Rake / Trail:	32 degrees / 5.42"
Front Suspension:	41mm, hydraulic compression and rebound damping
Rear Suspension:	Nitrogen-charged hydraulic dampers, coil springs with adjustable preload
Brakes:	Stainless-steel discs, 4-piston billet-aluminum calipers
Front Wheel/Tire:	60-spoke, chrome, 16" x 3.5", 130/90-16
Rear Wheel/Tire:	60-spoke, chrome, 16" x 3.5", 130/90-16
Wheelbase:	67"
Seat Height:	28"
Dry Weight:	Deluxe: 626 lbs., Roadmaster: 644 lbs., Springfield: 624 lbs.
Fuel Capacity:	5.5 U.S. gallons including 1.2 gallon reserve
Instruments:	Speedometer with digital odometer & tripmeter
Warranty:	12 months/unlimited mileage
MSRP:	**SPIRIT SPRINGFIELD:** $18,495 U.S. dollars **SPIRIT DELUXE:** $18,995 U.S. dollars **SPIRIT ROADMASTER:** $19,995 U.S. dollars

CHIEF SPECIFICATIONS

Engine:	Powerplus™ 45-degree V-twin, black finish, polishe
Displacement:	100 cubic inches (1638cc)
Bore x Stroke:	3.875" x 4.25"
Compression Ratio:	9.5:1
Ignition:	Electronic, computer-controlled
Valves:	1.94" intake, 1.615" exhaust, hydraulic lifters
Carburetor:	Mikuni HSR 42mm flat-slide
Exhaust System:	Chrome, 2-into-1
Transmission:	Constant-mesh, five-speed
Final Drive:	Aramid-reinforced belt
Frame:	High-tensile steel, powder-coated, black
Rake / Trail:	34 degrees / 5.92"
Front Suspension:	41mm, hydraulic compression and rebound dampin
Rear Suspension:	Rising-rate, KW single shock with adjustable preloac
Brakes:	Stainless-steel 11.5" discs, 4-piston Brembo caliper
Front Wheel/Tire:	60-spoke, chrome, 16" x 3.5", 130/90-16
Rear Wheel/Tire:	60-spoke, chrome, 16" x 3.5", 130/90-16
Wheelbase:	68.4"
Seat Height:	28.5"
Dry Weight:	Chief: 687 lbs., Deluxe: 690 lbs. Roadmaster: 716 lbs., Springfield: 687 lbs.
Fuel Capacity:	5.5 U.S. gallons including 1.2 gallon reserve
Instruments:	Speedometer with digital odometer & tripmeter
Warranty:	12 months/unlimited mileage
MSRP:	**CHIEF:** $20,995 U.S. dollars **CHIEF SPRINGFIELD:** $21,495 U.S. dollars **CHIEF DELUXE:** $21,995 U.S. dollars **CHIEF ROADMASTER:** $23,495 U.S. dollars

SPECIFICATIONS

Swan Song

Indian launched its online newsletter, *The Legend*, on September 18, 2003—the day before the factory closure (a full newsletter page is shown in chapter 4). One item is of particular interest:

While the first 2004 Indian motorcycles were being assembled that fateful September, the last of the 2003 Chiefs were given distinctive silver and white paint and outfitted as Chief Roadmasters. It is unknown how many of these "Run-Out Specials" were built, but at the time of this writing, only ten of these motorcycles have been documented worldwide. Former IMCOA dealer Joe Malfa recalled that fifty of these specials were to have been produced, but it's likely that time ran out before that number was reached. There were a number of silver/white sets of tanks and fenders in the factory at the time of closure. These were subsequently used in custom-built bikes.

2003 Model Year Run-Out Specials

While there is still plenty of riding season left, grab a special deal on a new 2003 Indian motorcycle! Indian Motorcycle has introduced new Factory to Dealer Incentives to help you get that bike you've always wanted. **Visit your local dealer** to get the best deals on a new Indian Chief, Spirit or Scout motorcycle. As an added incentive, we are proud to introduce very special 2003 model year run-out edition Chief Roadmaster. Reminiscent of the popular 2000 Chief Silver Cloud Special Editions, these motorcycles are uniquely painted in Noble Silver and Pearl White. A striking color combination not offered on any previous Indian motorcycle and not part of the 2003 line up. Production is limited! Need we say more?

Courtesy of Norm Zabala, founder, the Gilroy Era of Indian Motorcycles

A 2003 "Run-Out Special" Chief Roadmaster, factory-built just before the closure

It took three years before IMCOA's vision of all-Indian motorcycles had been partially achieved; it was fully attained only with the stillborn 2004 line. The Gilroy Indians had suffered a number of teething pains that needed to be sorted out, and the Powerplus engine debacle (much like the Indian Torque models of 1949–50) only exacerbated the difficulties faced by IMCOA. This and other congenital challenges with production, management, and financing had slowly killed the company. Even so, some beautiful new American Indian motorcycles had been manufactured. The Gilroy Indians, many of which have had their initial flaws set right, now proudly prowl the streets of the world as survivors of the first resurrection of the legendary Indian Motorcycle brand. Only approximately 13,000 of these historic machines were manufactured from 1999 to 2003.

CHAPTER 3

IMCOA Accessories

From the earliest years of the twentieth century, some motorcycle manufacturers understood that their profits need not end after the sale of a motorcycle. Lighting, saddlebags, speedometers, cold-weather gear (windshields, handshields, etc.), and cycling apparel (jackets, goggles, boots, gloves, etc.) could keep riders coming back into the store and spending their money. As the years passed, the sale of accessories and apparel became a major source of revenue for some motorcycle companies. Currently, some wags maintain that one well-known brand is simply a clothing company, selling motorcycles as a sideline. Even if true, there's no denying success.

The manufacturing and assembly operations of the Indian Motorcycle Company of America (IMCOA) were a direct outgrowth of the California Motorcycle Company, so the mass sale of branded merchandise was a new experience for the workforce. Unfortunately, as sometimes occurred in production, there were few experienced people to take the reins of the accessory/apparel side of the business. After all, the new company had its hands full developing and manufacturing motorcycles and expanding its dealer network. As a result, the 1999 Indian Motorcycle catalog showed no accessories or apparel. This omission would slowly be made good over the next four years.

This chapter makes no claim to illustrate all accessories offered by IMCOA (especially apparel), but nearly all optional bike hardware will be found here.

Missing Link

In 1999, when director of logistics Guy Auyeung began working at IMCOA, the company employed fewer than one hundred people. He soon discovered to his surprise that there was no service warehouse to support Indian dealers with parts and accessories. This only made worse the chronic shortage of parts (as discussed in chapter 2)—the result of poor quality that didn't pass Indian QC standards. IMCOA often lacked a sufficient number of parts for the production line, resulting in little if any surplus for dealers, and had no efficient service warehouse to handle dealer orders if/when the parts became available. This meant that in order to service customers, dealers often had to rob parts from new bikes sitting in showrooms.

During 2000, this situation began to improve. Once the service warehouse was established to supply parts, accessories, and apparel, it became the only component of IMCOA that was turning a profit. Even so, Frank O'Connell was troubled by what he found:

> I had walked through the apparel warehouse across the street from the factory, looking at the stacks of apparel and clothing accessories. I was blown away by the number of SKUs and the amount of inventory, much of which I could tell by the box dates hadn't moved in weeks. This was a totally separate and complex business with no one running it, at least no one who had the necessary experience. It immediately hit me that this was a separate business, one that Indian should license out and not produce itself.
>
> *—Frank J. O'Connell, former president and CEO of IMCOA*

Over IMCOA's five years of life, its offerings of accessories and apparel grew significantly. Beginning with a handful of accessories shown in the 2000 motorcycle catalog, more and more items appeared in 2001 (including a Centennial Apparel Collection catalog), 2002, and 2003. In that final year of IMCOA, an extensive accessories/apparel catalog was published, offering a range of performance enhancement and eye candy designed to compel Indian riders to reach for their wallets. Guy Auyeung witnessed the orders flowing through the service warehouse:

> It was the only part of Indian that was making money—it wasn't the bikes! *—Guy Auyeung, former director of logistics, IMCOA*

In the end, however, it wasn't nearly enough.

Limited accessories in the early 2000 motorcycle catalog: wheels, leather, and windshield

A later 2000 motorcycle catalog substituted this page, showing a few more accessories.

A 2001 flyer showing a pricey replacement for the standard Chief passenger backrest

A 2001 flyer for new Scout accessories

The only customizing options shown in the 2001 motorcycle catalog

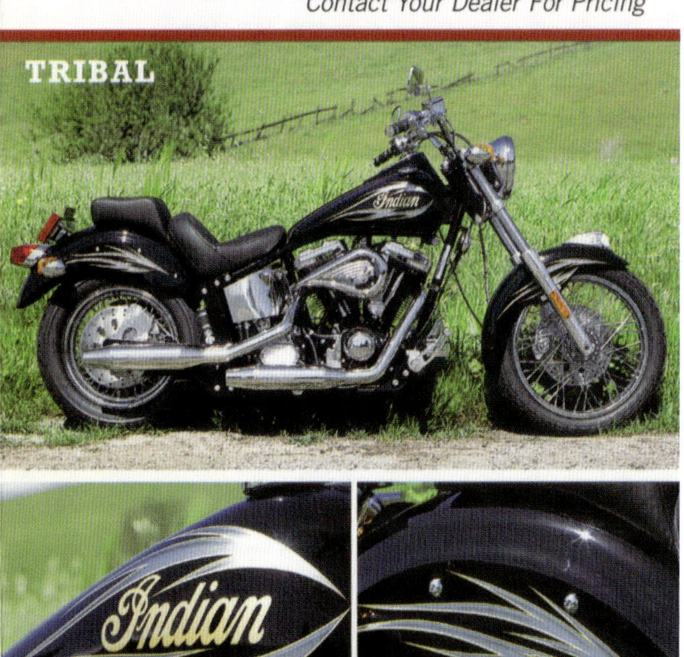

In the 2002 Chief catalog, IMCOA encouraged customers either to go online or visit their dealer for apparel. No bike accessories were shown.

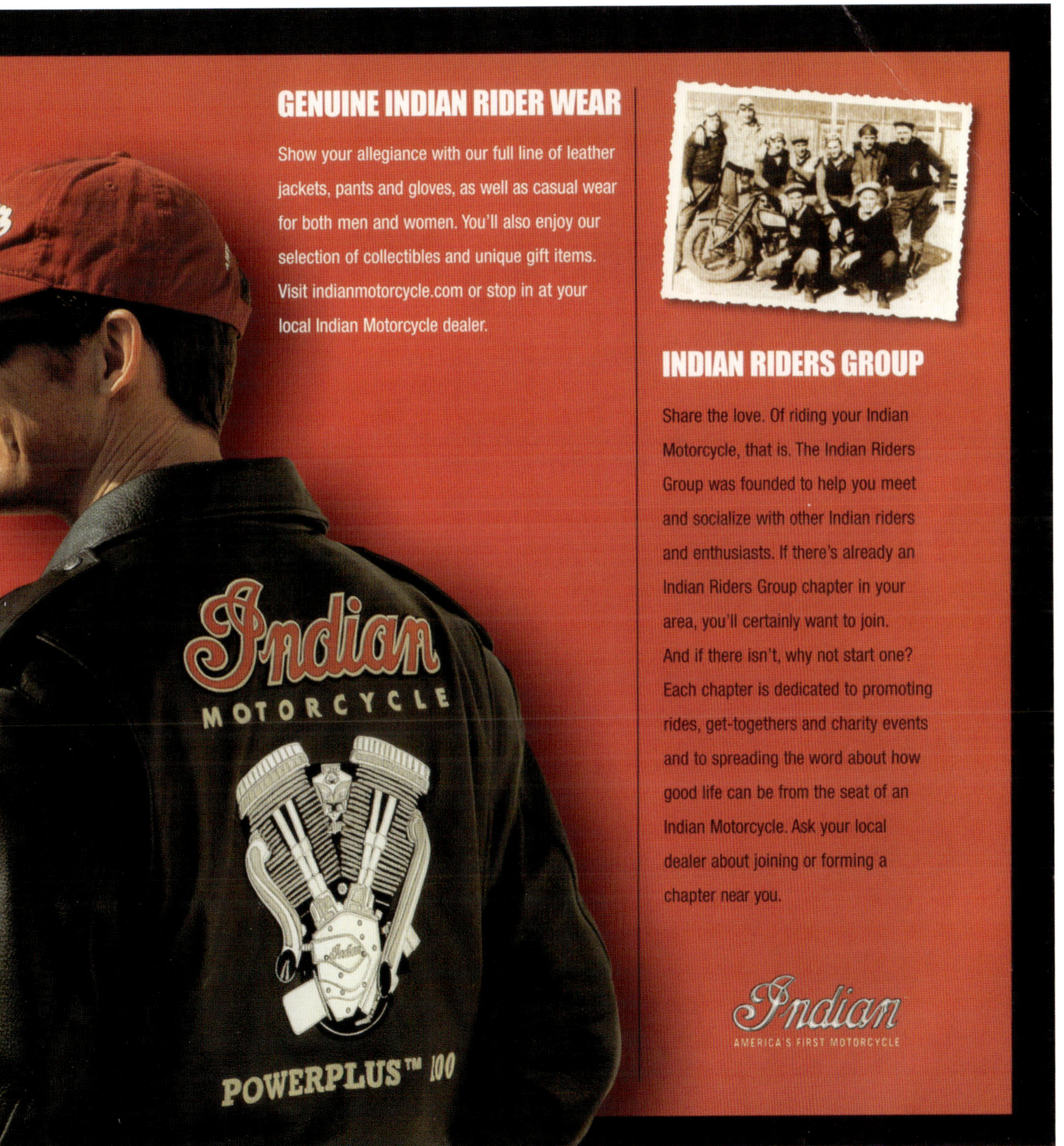

The 2002 Scout/Spirit catalog still directed riders to the website or dealer, but a smattering of accessories was shown.

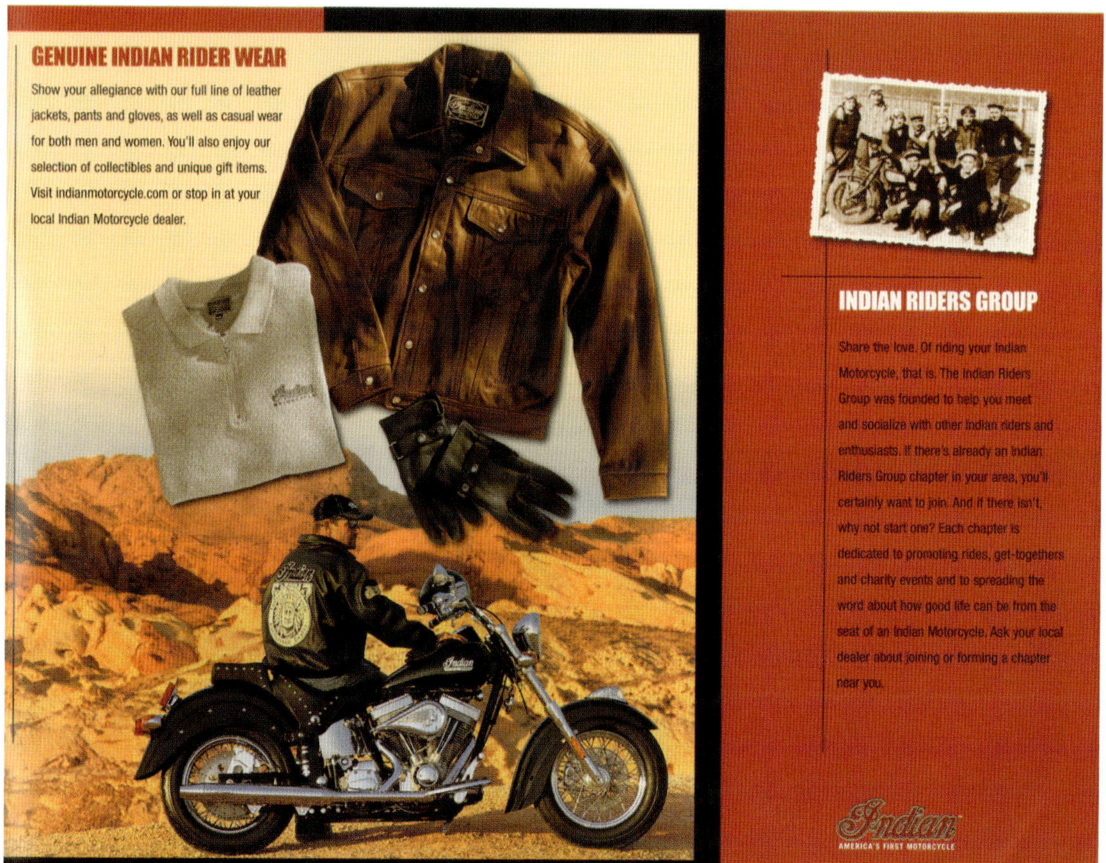

For apparel in 2002, IMCOA's website or a dealer was still the recommended portal.

The following seven pages from the 2003 Chief catalog offered accessories specific to IMCOA's flagship model.

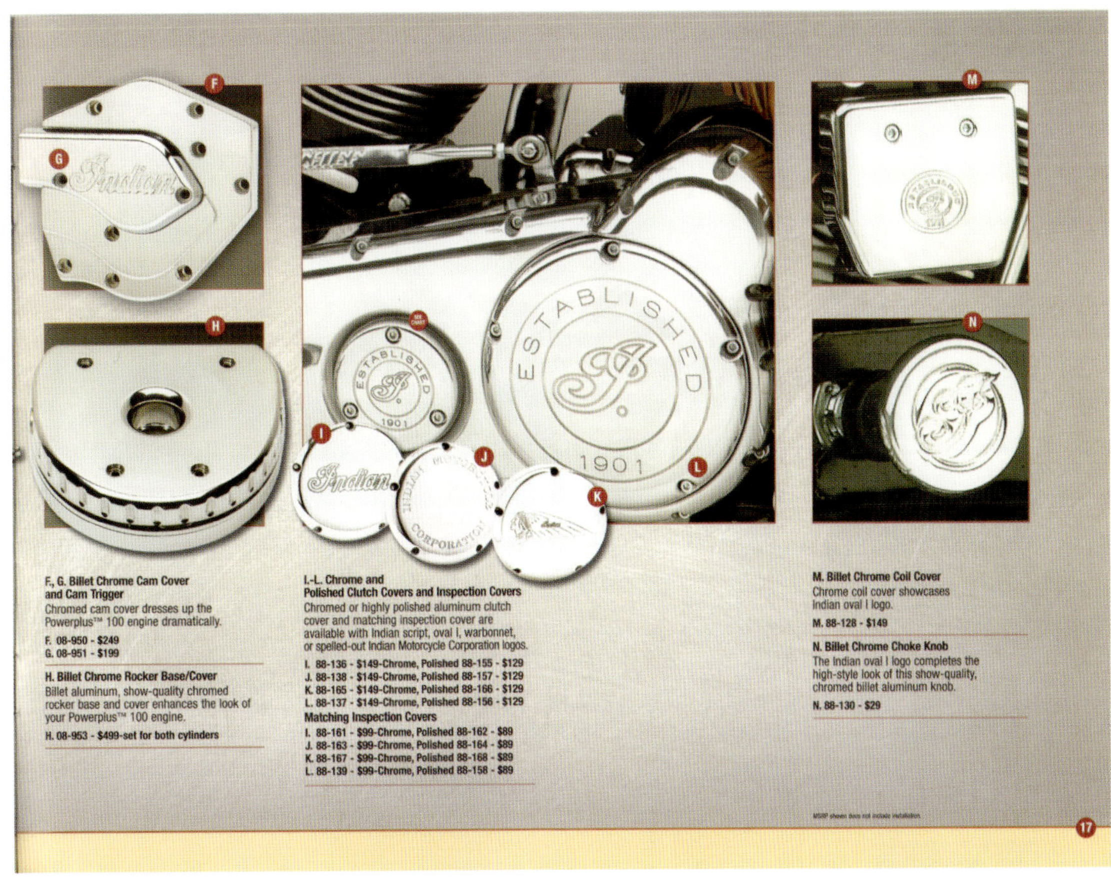

A. Billet Chrome Rear Passenger Floorboards
Rear passenger floorboards fold up when not in use, includes rubber inserts for added comfort.
A. 49-955 - $249
B., C. Billet Chrome Forward Controls
Billet chrome forward controls with stylized levers give the Chief an extra dose of custom panache. Designed to work with standard Chief floorboards. Shown with optional billet chrome shifter/brake pedal tips.
B. 49-950 - $789 - Billet Chrome Forward Controls
C. 49-953 - $179 - Billet Chrome Shifter/Brake Pedal Tips
D. Billet Chrome Handlebar Mount Tachometer
Mount replaces handlebar riser cover, provides precise engine speed data for maximum performance.
D. 56-056 - $399
E. Gold Plated Indian Head Fender Ornament
Your Chief will be as good as gold with this beautiful fender ornament.
E. 66-124 - $79
F. LED License Plate Frame
Chromed, billet aluminum frame is backlit with red LED's for a distinctive, dramatic styling statement.
F. 67-002 - $179
18
ACCESSORIES

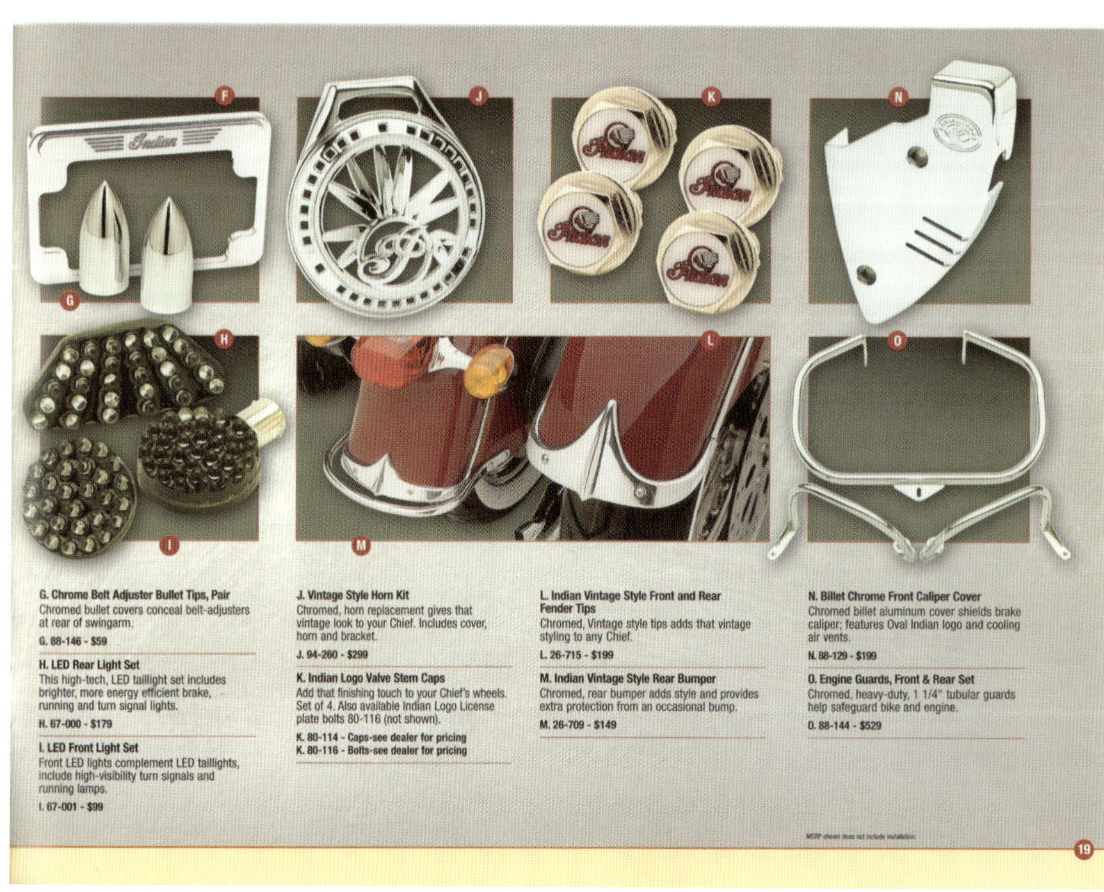
G. Chrome Belt Adjuster Bullet Tips, Pair
Chromed bullet covers conceal belt-adjusters at rear of swingarm.
G. 88-146 - $59
H. LED Rear Light Set
This high-tech, LED taillight set includes brighter, more energy efficient brake, running and turn signal lights.
H. 67-000 - $179
I. LED Front Light Set
Front LED lights complement LED taillights, include high-visibility turn signals and running lamps.
I. 67-001 - $99
J. Vintage Style Horn Kit
Chromed, horn replacement gives that vintage look to your Chief. Includes cover, horn and bracket.
J. 94-260 - $299
K. Indian Logo Valve Stem Caps
Add that finishing touch to your Chief's wheels. Set of 4. Also available Indian Logo License plate bolts 80-116 (not shown).
K. 80-114 - Caps-see dealer for pricing
K. 80-116 - Bolts-see dealer for pricing
L. Indian Vintage Style Front and Rear Fender Tips
Chromed, Vintage style tips adds that vintage styling to any Chief.
L. 26-715 - $199
M. Indian Vintage Style Rear Bumper
Chromed, rear bumper adds style and provides extra protection from an occasional bump.
M. 26-709 - $149
N. Billet Chrome Front Caliper Cover
Chromed billet aluminum cover shields brake caliper; features Oval Indian logo and cooling air vents.
N. 88-129 - $199
O. Engine Guards, Front & Rear Set
Chromed, heavy-duty, 1 1/4" tubular guards help safeguard bike and engine.
O. 88-144 - $529
19

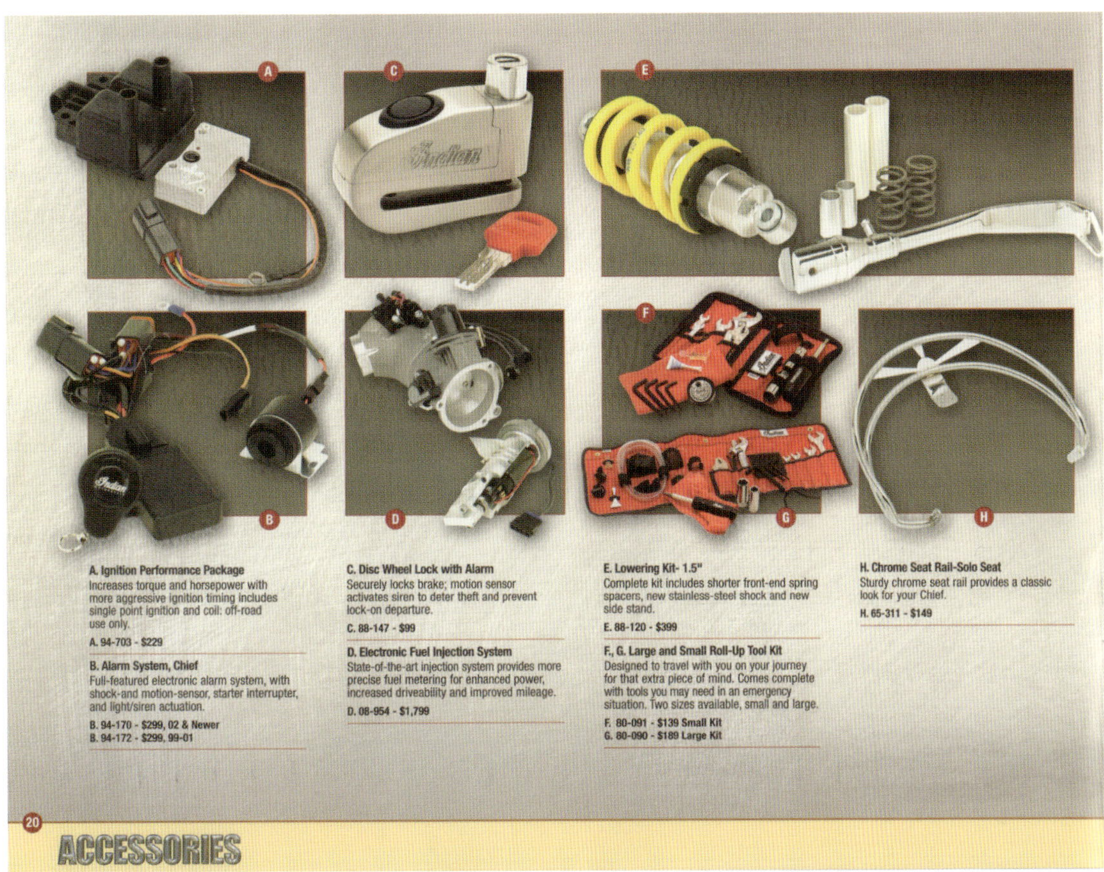

A. Ignition Performance Package
Increases torque and horsepower with more aggressive ignition timing includes single point ignition and coil: off-road use only.
A. 94-703 - $229

B. Alarm System, Chief
Full-featured electronic alarm system, with shock-and motion-sensor, starter interrupter, and light/siren actuation.
B. 94-170 - $299, 02 & Newer
B. 94-172 - $299, 99-01

C. Disc Wheel Lock with Alarm
Securely locks brake; motion sensor activates siren to deter theft and prevent lock-on departure.
C. 88-147 - $99

D. Electronic Fuel Injection System
State-of-the-art injection system provides more precise fuel metering for enhanced power, increased driveability and improved mileage.
D. 08-954 - $1,799

E. Lowering Kit- 1.5"
Complete kit includes shorter front-end spring spacers, new stainless-steel shock and new side stand.
E. 88-120 - $399

F., G. Large and Small Roll-Up Tool Kit
Designed to travel with you on your journey for that extra piece of mind. Comes complete with tools you may need in an emergency situation. Two sizes available, small and large.
F. 80-091 - $139 Small Kit
G. 80-090 - $189 Large Kit

H. Chrome Seat Rail-Solo Seat
Sturdy chrome seat rail provides a classic look for your Chief.
H. 65-311 - $149

20
ACCESSORIES

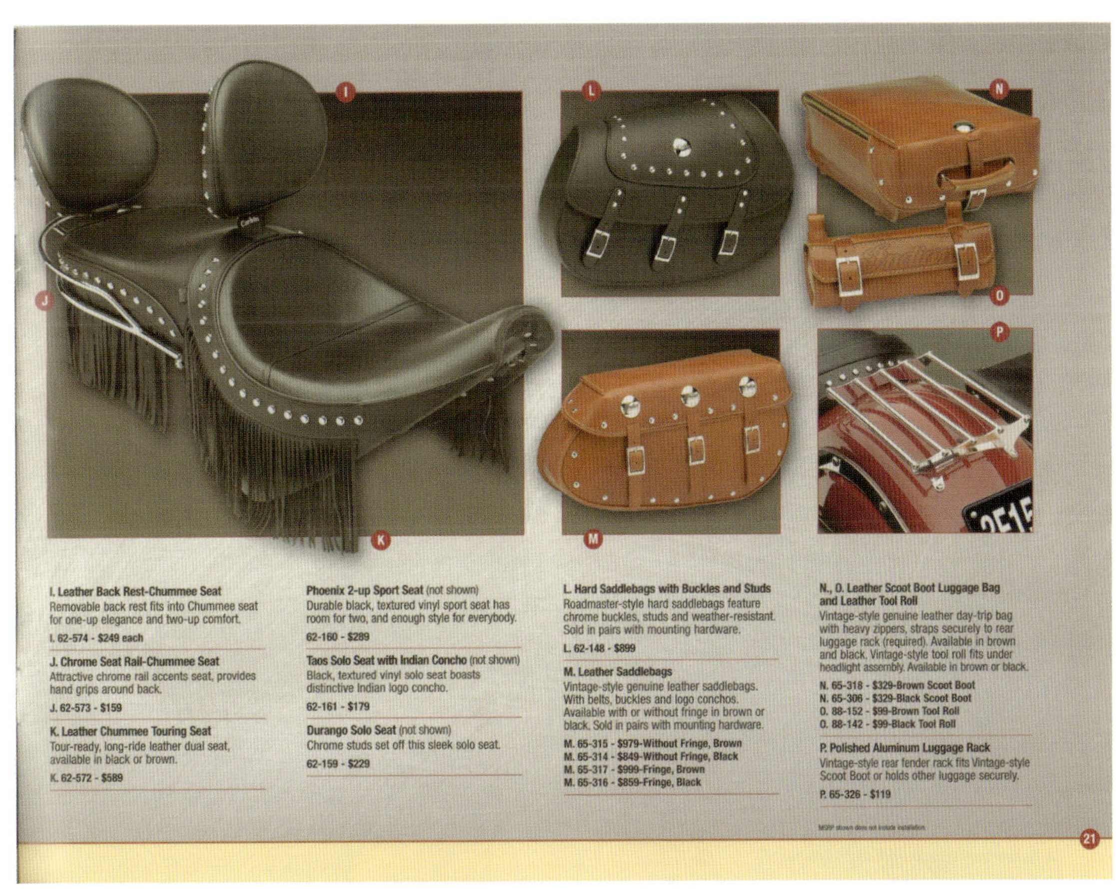

I. Leather Back Rest-Chummee Seat
Removable back rest fits into Chummee seat for one-up elegance and two-up comfort.
I. 62-574 - $249 each

J. Chrome Seat Rail-Chummee Seat
Attractive chrome rail accents seat, provides hand grips around back.
J. 62-573 - $159

K. Leather Chummee Touring Seat
Tour-ready, long-ride leather dual seat, available in black or brown.
K. 62-572 - $589

Phoenix 2-up Sport Seat (not shown)
Durable black, textured vinyl sport seat has room for two, and enough style for everybody.
62-160 - $289

Taos Solo Seat with Indian Concho (not shown)
Black, textured vinyl solo seat boasts distinctive Indian logo concho.
62-161 - $179

Durango Solo Seat (not shown)
Chrome studs set off this sleek solo seat.
62-159 - $229

L. Hard Saddlebags with Buckles and Studs
Roadmaster-style hard saddlebags feature chrome buckles, studs and weather-resistant. Sold in pairs with mounting hardware.
L. 62-148 - $899

M. Leather Saddlebags
Vintage-style genuine leather saddlebags. With belts, buckles and logo conchos. Available with or without fringe in brown or black. Sold in pairs with mounting hardware.
M. 65-315 - $979-Without Fringe, Brown
M. 65-314 - $849-Without Fringe, Black
M. 65-317 - $999-Fringe, Brown
M. 65-316 - $859-Fringe, Black

N., O. Leather Scoot Boot Luggage Bag and Leather Tool Roll
Vintage-style genuine leather day-trip bag with heavy zippers, straps securely to rear luggage rack (required). Available in brown and black. Vintage-style tool roll fits under headlight assembly. Available in brown or black.
N. 65-318 - $329-Brown Scoot Boot
N. 65-306 - $329-Black Scoot Boot
O. 88-152 - $99-Brown Tool Roll
O. 88-142 - $99-Black Tool Roll

P. Polished Aluminum Luggage Rack
Vintage-style rear fender rack fits Vintage-style Scoot Boot or holds other luggage securely.
P. 65-326 - $119

MSRP shown does not include installation.

21

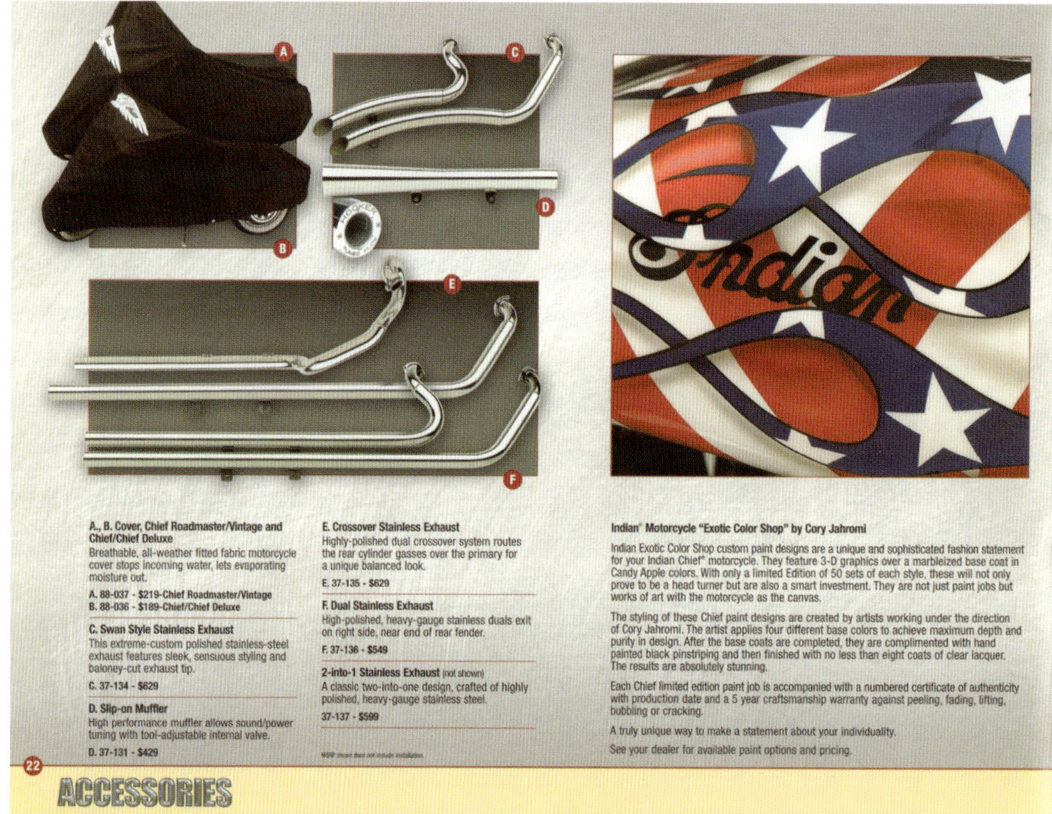

A., B. Cover, Chief Roadmaster/Vintage and Chief/Chief Deluxe
Breathable, all-weather fitted fabric motorcycle cover stops incoming water, lets evaporating moisture out.

A. 88-037 - $219-Chief Roadmaster/Vintage
B. 88-036 - $189-Chief/Chief Deluxe

C. Swan Style Stainless Exhaust
This extreme-custom polished stainless-steel exhaust features sleek, sensuous styling and baloney-cut exhaust tip.

C. 37-134 - $629

D. Slip-on Muffler
High performance muffler allows sound/power tuning with tool-adjustable internal valve.

D. 37-131 - $429

E. Crossover Stainless Exhaust
Highly-polished dual crossover system routes the rear cylinder gasses over the primary for a unique balanced look.

E. 37-135 - $629

F. Dual Stainless Exhaust
High-polished, heavy-gauge stainless duals exit on right side, near end of rear fender.

F. 37-136 - $549

2-into-1 Stainless Exhaust (not shown)
A classic two-into-one design, crafted of highly polished, heavy-gauge stainless steel.

37-137 - $599

Indian® Motorcycle "Exotic Color Shop" by Cory Jahromi

Indian Exotic Color Shop custom paint designs are a unique and sophisticated fashion statement for your Indian Chief® motorcycle. They feature 3-D graphics over a marbleized base coat in Candy Apple colors. With only a limited Edition of 50 sets of each style, these will not only prove to be a head turner but are also a smart investment. They are not just paint jobs but works of art with the motorcycle as the canvas.

The styling of these Chief paint designs are created by artists working under the direction of Cory Jahromi. The artist applies four different base colors to achieve maximum depth and purity in design. After the base coats are completed, they are complimented with hand painted black pinstriping and then finished with no less than eight coats of clear lacquer. The results are absolutely stunning.

Each Chief limited edition paint job is accompanied with a numbered certificate of authenticity with production date and a 5 year craftsmanship warranty against peeling, fading, lifting, bubbling or cracking.

A truly unique way to make a statement about your individuality.

See your dealer for available paint options and pricing.

22 ACCESSORIES

This 2003 IMCOA catalog was devoted entirely to accessories and apparel. In addition to a line of clothing and collectibles, accessories for the Scout and Spirit were featured.

Indian® Scout™ 240 Fat Tire Kit.
Fat: It's where it's at.

The Indian Scout™ Fat-Tire Conversion Kit is all-new for 2003. It gives your Scout the wild styling and performance of a one-off custom, but with the heritage and factory proven technology you've come to expect from Indian. The kit provides everything you need to give your Scout a complete wide-tire makeover, including a specially engineered swingarm, 8 1/2-inch-wide rear wheel and a beautiful strutless rear fender. The kit offers various options including forged aluminum chrome-plated 5-spoke wheels, matching pulley and rotors, stainless steel exhaust system and bullet marker light set.

When installed by your Indian Motorcycle dealer, the kit carries the full Indian Motorcycle warranty. So if the outrageous look of the Scout Fat-Tire Conversion Kit moves you, get moving to your Indian Motorcycle dealer and get started remaking your Indian Scout today.

See your dealer for application, availability and pricing for your motorcycle.

4

ACCESSORIES

Indian® Motorcycle
"Exotic Color Shop"

Indian Exotic Color Shop custom paint designs are a unique and sophisticated fashion statement for your Indian Spirit™ or Scout™ motorcycle. They feature 3-D graphics over a marbleized base coat in Candy Apple colors. Since these are limited editions, each style will not only prove to be a head turner but are also a smart investment. They are not just paint jobs but works of art with the motorcycle as the canvas.

The styling of these paint designs are created to be unique and as individual as you are. The artist applies four different base colors to achieve maximum depth and purity in design. After the base coats are completed, they are complimented with hand painted black pinstriping and then finished with no less than eight coats of clear. The results are absolutely stunning.

Each Scout or Spirit limited edition paint job is accompanied with a numbered certificate of authenticity and a 5-year craftsmanship warranty against peeling, fading, lifting, bubbling or cracking.

A truly unique way to make a statement about your individuality.
See your dealer for available paint options and pricing.

5

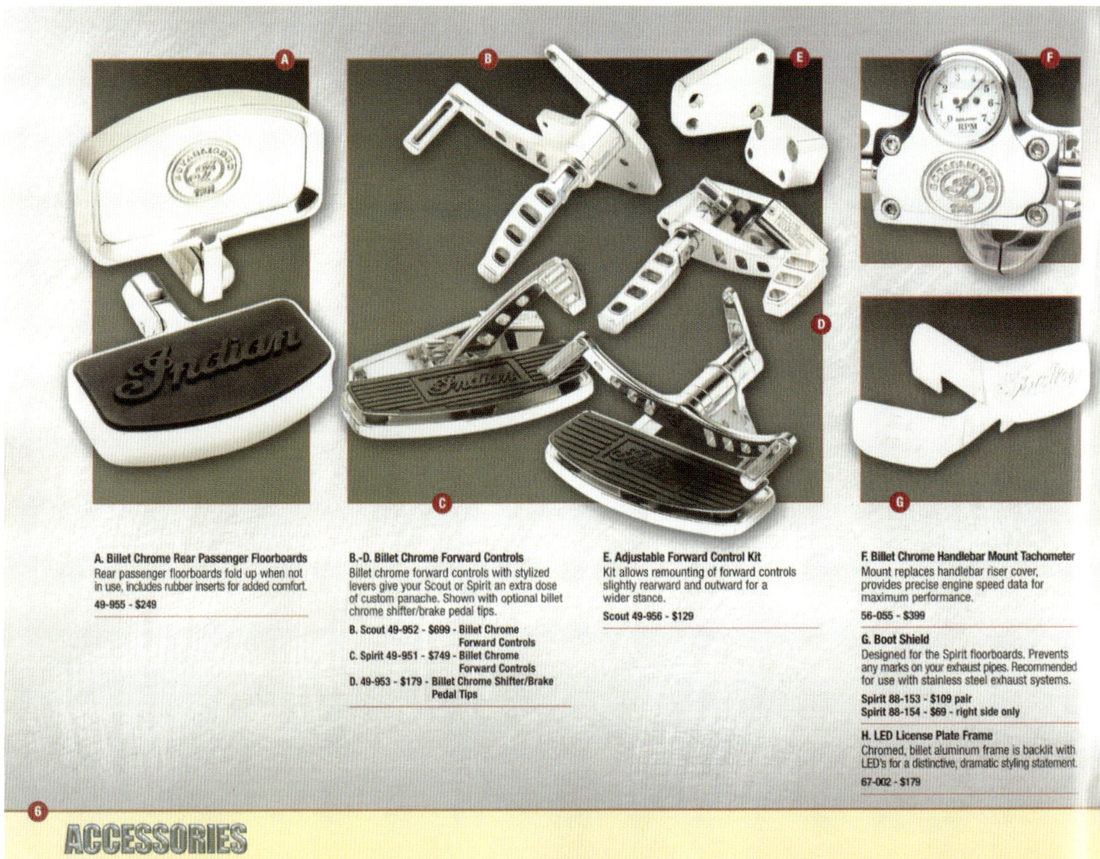

A. Billet Chrome Rear Passenger Floorboards
Rear passenger floorboards fold up when not in use, includes rubber inserts for added comfort.
49-955 - $249

B.-D. Billet Chrome Forward Controls
Billet chrome forward controls with stylized levers give your Scout or Spirit an extra dose of custom panache. Shown with optional billet chrome shifter/brake pedal tips.
B. Scout 49-952 - $699 - Billet Chrome Forward Controls
C. Spirit 49-951 - $749 - Billet Chrome Forward Controls
D. 49-953 - $179 - Billet Chrome Shifter/Brake Pedal Tips

E. Adjustable Forward Control Kit
Kit allows remounting of forward controls slightly rearward and outward for a wider stance.
Scout 49-956 - $129

F. Billet Chrome Handlebar Mount Tachometer
Mount replaces handlebar riser cover, provides precise engine speed data for maximum performance.
56-055 - $399

G. Boot Shield
Designed for the Spirit floorboards. Prevents any marks on your exhaust pipes. Recommended for use with stainless steel exhaust systems.
Spirit 88-153 - $109 pair
Spirit 88-154 - $69 - right side only

H. LED License Plate Frame
Chromed, billet aluminum frame is backlit with LED's for a distinctive, dramatic styling statement.
67-002 - $179

6 ACCESSORIES

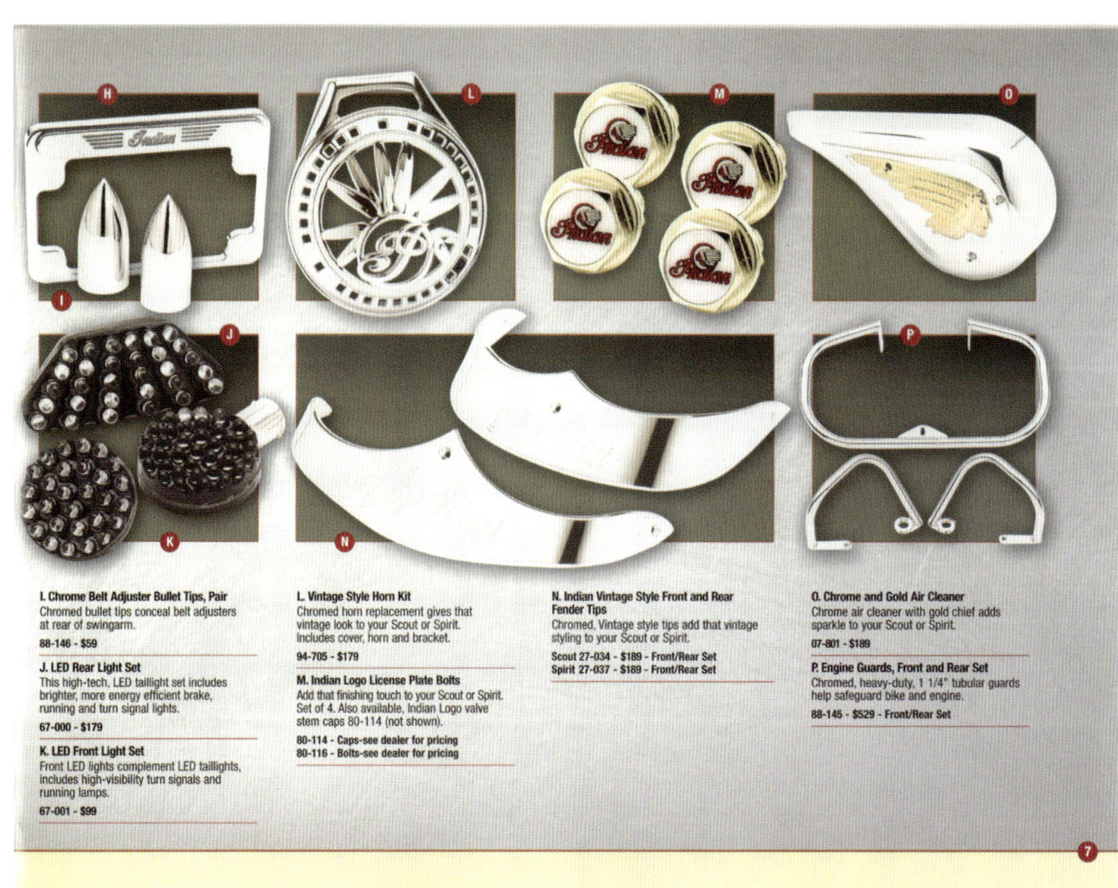

I. Chrome Belt Adjuster Bullet Tips, Pair
Chromed bullet tips conceal belt adjusters at rear of swingarm.
88-146 - $59

J. LED Rear Light Set
This high-tech, LED taillight set includes brighter, more energy efficient brake, running and turn signal lights.
67-000 - $179

K. LED Front Light Set
Front LED lights complement LED taillights, includes high-visibility turn signals and running lamps.
67-001 - $99

L. Vintage Style Horn Kit
Chromed horn replacement gives that vintage look to your Scout or Spirit. Includes cover, horn and bracket.
94-705 - $179

M. Indian Logo License Plate Bolts
Add that finishing touch to your Scout or Spirit. Set of 4. Also available, Indian Logo valve stem caps 80-114 (not shown).
80-114 - Caps-see dealer for pricing
80-116 - Bolts-see dealer for pricing

N. Indian Vintage Style Front and Rear Fender Tips
Chromed, Vintage style tips add that vintage styling to your Scout or Spirit.
Scout 27-034 - $189 - Front/Rear Set
Spirit 27-037 - $189 - Front/Rear Set

O. Chrome and Gold Air Cleaner
Chrome air cleaner with gold chief adds sparkle to your Scout or Spirit.
07-801 - $189

P. Engine Guards, Front and Rear Set
Chromed, heavy-duty, 1 1/4" tubular guards help safeguard bike and engine.
88-145 - $529 - Front/Rear Set

7

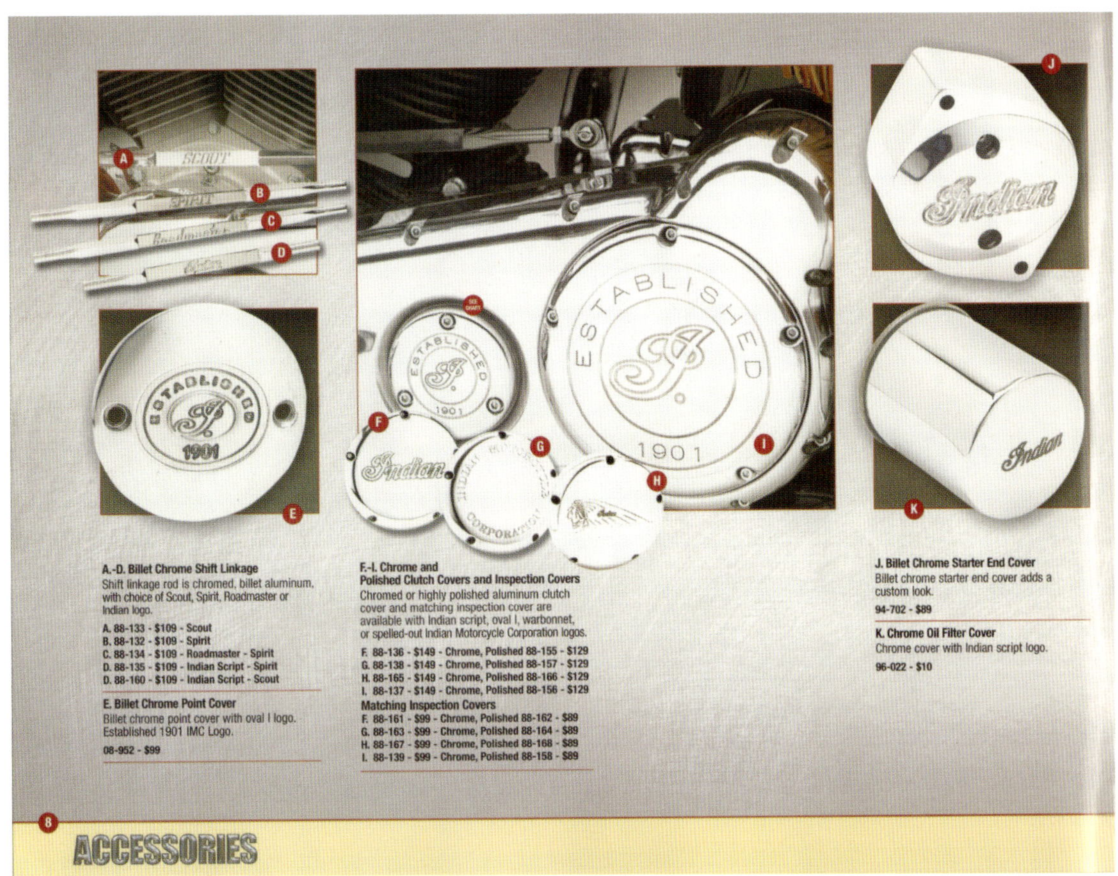

A.-D. Billet Chrome Shift Linkage
Shift linkage rod is chromed, billet aluminum, with choice of Scout, Spirit, Roadmaster or Indian logo.

A. 88-133 - $109 - Scout
B. 88-132 - $109 - Spirit
C. 88-134 - $109 - Roadmaster - Spirit
D. 88-135 - $109 - Indian Script - Spirit
D. 88-160 - $109 - Indian Script - Scout

E. Billet Chrome Point Cover
Billet chrome point cover with oval I logo. Established 1901 IMC Logo.

08-952 - $99

F.-I. Chrome and Polished Clutch Covers and Inspection Covers
Chromed or highly polished aluminum clutch cover and matching inspection cover are available with Indian script, oval I, warbonnet, or spelled-out Indian Motorcycle Corporation logos.

F. 88-136 - $149 - Chrome, Polished 88-155 - $129
G. 88-138 - $149 - Chrome, Polished 88-157 - $129
H. 88-165 - $149 - Chrome, Polished 88-166 - $129
I. 88-137 - $149 - Chrome, Polished 88-156 - $129

Matching Inspection Covers
F. 88-161 - $99 - Chrome, Polished 88-162 - $89
G. 88-163 - $99 - Chrome, Polished 88-164 - $89
H. 88-167 - $99 - Chrome, Polished 88-168 - $89
I. 88-139 - $99 - Chrome, Polished 88-158 - $89

J. Billet Chrome Starter End Cover
Billet chrome starter end cover adds a custom look.

94-702 - $89

K. Chrome Oil Filter Cover
Chrome cover with Indian script logo.

96-022 - $10

8 ACCESSORIES

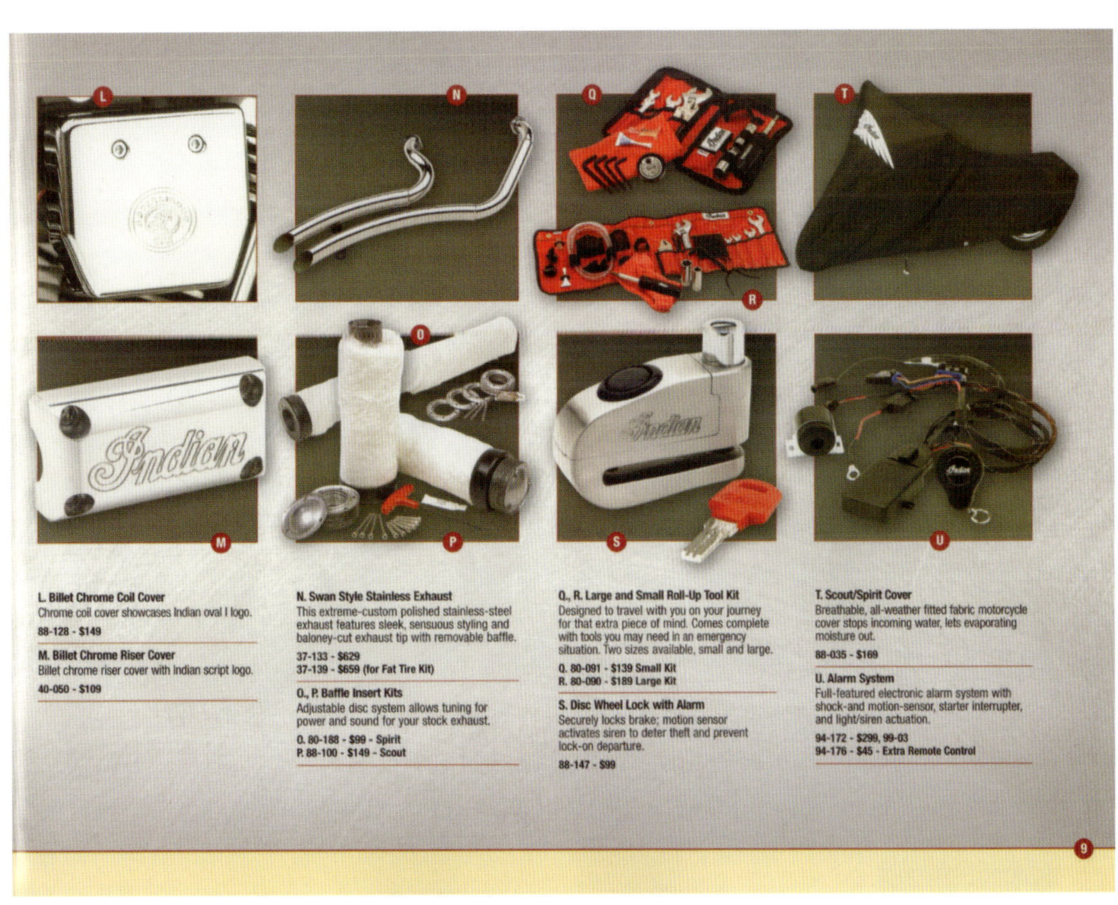

L. Billet Chrome Coil Cover
Chrome coil cover showcases Indian oval I logo.

88-128 - $149

M. Billet Chrome Riser Cover
Billet chrome riser cover with Indian script logo.

40-050 - $109

N. Swan Style Stainless Exhaust
This extreme-custom polished stainless-steel exhaust features sleek, sensuous styling and baloney-cut exhaust tip with removable baffle.

37-133 - $629
37-139 - $659 (for Fat Tire Kit)

O., P. Baffle Insert Kits
Adjustable disc system allows tuning for power and sound for your stock exhaust.

O. 80-188 - $99 - Spirit
P. 88-100 - $149 - Scout

Q., R. Large and Small Roll-Up Tool Kit
Designed to travel with you on your journey for that extra piece of mind. Comes complete with tools you may need in an emergency situation. Two sizes available, small and large.

Q. 80-091 - $139 Small Kit
R. 80-090 - $189 Large Kit

S. Disc Wheel Lock with Alarm
Securely locks brake; motion sensor activates siren to deter theft and prevent lock-on departure.

88-147 - $99

T. Scout/Spirit Cover
Breathable, all-weather fitted fabric motorcycle cover stops incoming water, lets evaporating moisture out.

88-035 - $169

U. Alarm System
Full-featured electronic alarm system with shock-and motion-sensor, starter interrupter, and light/siren actuation.

94-172 - $299, 99-03
94-176 - $45 - Extra Remote Control

9

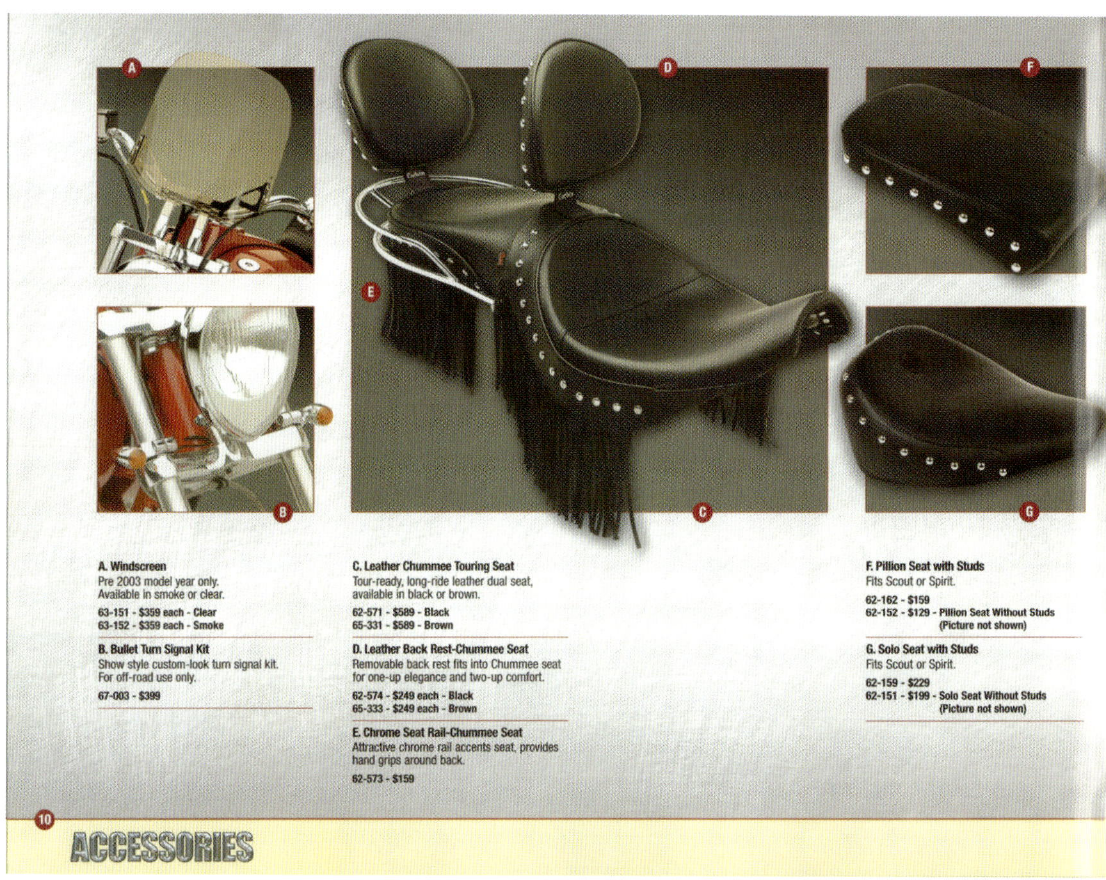

A. Windscreen
Pre 2003 model year only.
Available in smoke or clear.
63-151 - $359 each - Clear
63-152 - $359 each - Smoke

B. Bullet Turn Signal Kit
Show style custom-look turn signal kit.
For off-road use only.
67-003 - $399

C. Leather Chummee Touring Seat
Tour-ready, long-ride leather dual seat, available in black or brown.
62-571 - $589 - Black
65-331 - $589 - Brown

D. Leather Back Rest-Chummee Seat
Removable back rest fits into Chummee seat for one-up elegance and two-up comfort.
62-574 - $249 each - Black
65-333 - $249 each - Brown

E. Chrome Seat Rail-Chummee Seat
Attractive chrome rail accents seat, provides hand grips around back.
62-573 - $159

F. Pillion Seat with Studs
Fits Scout or Spirit.
62-162 - $159
62-152 - $129 - Pillion Seat Without Studs (Picture not shown)

G. Solo Seat with Studs
Fits Scout or Spirit.
62-159 - $229
62-151 - $199 - Solo Seat Without Studs (Picture not shown)

10 ACCESSORIES

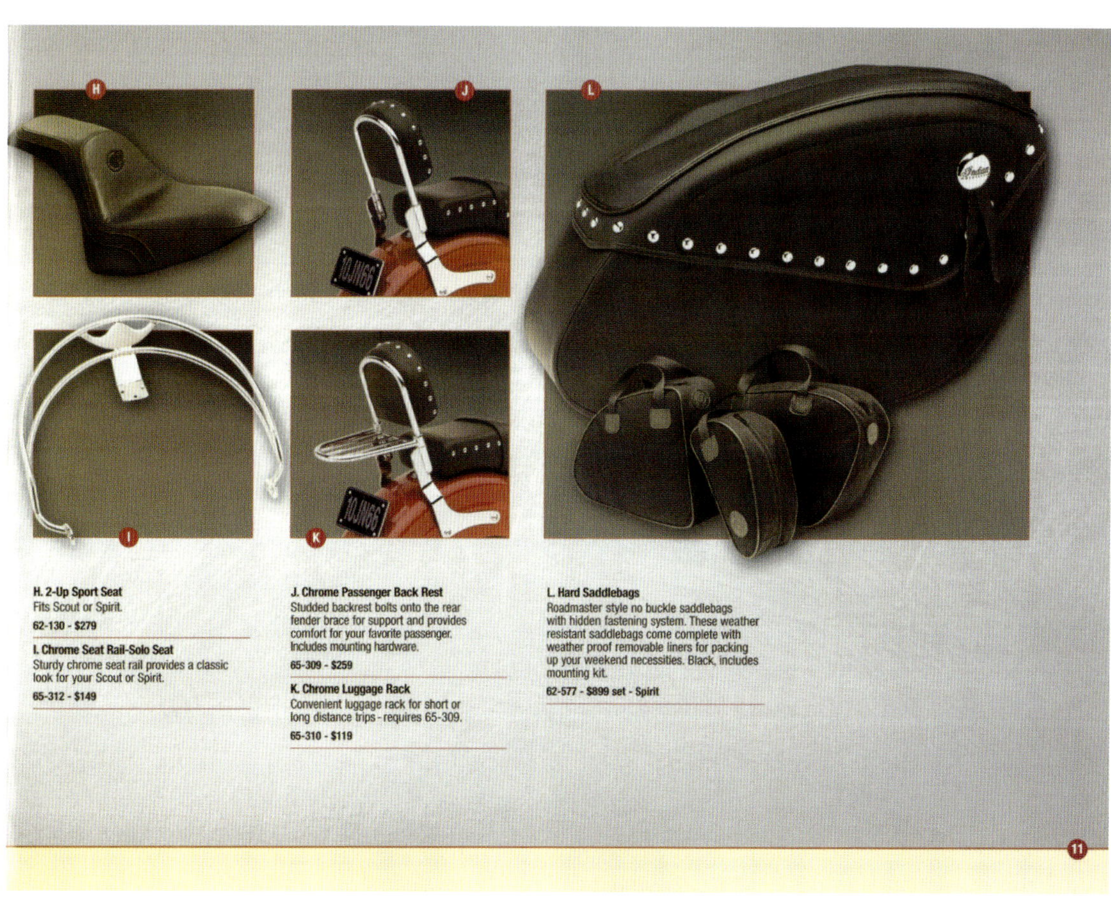

H. 2-Up Sport Seat
Fits Scout or Spirit.
62-130 - $279

I. Chrome Seat Rail-Solo Seat
Sturdy chrome seat rail provides a classic look for your Scout or Spirit.
65-312 - $149

J. Chrome Passenger Back Rest
Studded backrest bolts onto the rear fender brace for support and provides comfort for your favorite passenger. Includes mounting hardware.
65-309 - $259

K. Chrome Luggage Rack
Convenient luggage rack for short or long distance trips - requires 65-309.
65-310 - $119

L. Hard Saddlebags
Roadmaster style no buckle saddlebags with hidden fastening system. These weather resistant saddlebags come complete with weather proof removable liners for packing up your weekend necessities. Black, includes mounting kit.
62-577 - $899 set - Spirit

11

A. Highwayman Leather Jacket
Soft, supple Napa leather classic. Rear vents, snap-down collar, zippered sleeves and pockets. Warbonnet logo embossed on bottom front. (Actual logo may vary from picture). Black. Sizes: S-3XL.
88-391 $335
B. Powerplus™ 100 Leather Jacket
The ultimate collector's item with the Powerplus™ 100 leather logo on back, individually hand crafted and stitched. Featuring a snap-down collar, adjustable side laces, zippered cuffs and pockets.
Brown or Black Deerskin leather. Standard sizes: S-3XL. (Jacket is made to order, also available in custom sizes).
87-646 $850
Indian
MOTORCYCLE
POWERPLUS 100
Indian Motorcycle
AUTHORIZED DEALER
C. Distressed Vintage Biker Jacket
Distressed leather with adjustable side straps, one internal and three external pockets. Snap-down collar. Black. Sizes: S-3XL.
81-025 $465
12
MEN'S JACKETS & RIDING GEAR

D. Classic Heavy Leather Biker Jacket
Made with durable Napa leather, featuring a zip-out liner, adjustable side laces, snap-down collar and zippered pockets and cuffs. Indian Motorcycle logo embroidery on back. Black. Sizes: S-2XL.
81-115 $399
E. Retro Speed Leather Jacket
Napa leather jacket takes you back in time with a tapered fit. Double snap-down collar and zippered pockets. Warbonnet logo embossed on left shoulder sleeve. (Actual logo may vary from picture). Black. Sizes: S-3XL.
88-409 $330
F. Arrowhead Leather Jacket
Retro-styled, soft, supple Napa leather. Side ties, snap-down collar, zippered sleeves and pockets. Indian script logo embossed on back. Black. Sizes: S-3XL.
88-397 $330
G. Flight Star Leather Jacket
Napa leather and rugged styling. Snap-down pockets. Indian Motorcycle logo embossed on back. Black. Sizes: S-3XL.
88-403 $350
13

A
C. Distressed Leather Jacket
Handcrafted Indian and Indian Motorcycle logo leather patches on front and back in the perfect shade of brown. Your choice of "Chief", "Scout", "Spirit" or no patches on front of jacket. Standard sizes: S-3XL. (Jacket is made to order, also available in custom sizes).
86-741 $670
C
A. Streamliner Heated Vest
Excellent for cold riding conditions. Ultimate low bulk insulation. High-tech Dupont Conformax IB® snap-in vest for all Vanson jackets (compatible heater control unit/ bike adapter - sold separately). Vest also available without the electric heating option. Black. Sizes: S-2XL.
86-404 $315 (Electrified)
87-958 $255 (Non-electrified)
Heated Vest Control Unit
For use with the Streamliner Heated Vest. Plugs into your motorcycle and provides adjustable heat control.
87-926 $65
B
B. Dakota Heavy Leather Speed Jacket
Heavy-duty riding jacket by Vanson. Interior snaps for inserting the "Streamliner" snap-in vest to keep you warm. Indian script logo leather patch on back. Black with red and white stripes on arms. Sizes: S-2XL.
86-384 $740 (2XL-$799)
Indian
CHIEF
14
MEN'S JACKETS & RIDING GEAR

D
D. Classic Leather Biker Jacket
Top quality Napa cowhide leather with zippered cuffs and side lacing for a comfortable fit. Indian Motorcycle embroidery on back. Black. Sizes: S-3XL. Complementary women's version available (Pg. 26).
81-038 $365
E. Vintage Leather Flight Jacket
Top-quality Napa leather designed in the classic style with suede piping and suede Indian Motorcycle logo patch on back. Black with tan piping. Sizes: S-2XL.
81-100 $465
E
Indian Motorcycle
Indian MOTORCYCLE
G. Vented Leather Jacket
Cowhide leather vented jacket with zip-out liner. Indian script logo embossed on back. Black. Size S-5XL. Complementary women's version available (Pg. 26).
81-110 $499
(3XL-5XL-$599)
F
G
Indian
Indian
F. Deerskin Biker Jacket
Lightweight, soft deerskin leather. Snap-down collar, adjustable side laces for a custom fit and satin lining. Pockets for storage. Handcrafted Warbonnet leather patch on back. Dark Brown or Black. Standard sizes: S-3XL. (Jacket is made to order, also available in custom sizes).
86-736 $675
15

A
A. Combo Speed Jacket
Napa leather combined
with poly-coated nylon.
Snap-down collar
and front zipper.
Black. Sizes: S-3XL.
88-433 $170
B. Brando Leather Jacket
Boston Napa leather, classic style.
Full front zipper. Snap-down pockets
and zippered sleeves. Indian
script logo embossed on back.
Black. Sizes: S-3XL.
88-421 $235
B
C
C. Thunderbird Heavy Leather Biker Jacket
Rugged, heavy-duty leather jacket by Vanson.
Reinforced elbows, forearms, shoulders and extra
kidney support. Snap-down collar, zippered cuffs,
pockets and adjustable belt. Indian script logo
embroidery on back.
Black. Sizes: S-2XL (2XL-$699).
86-379 $645
Indian
16
MEN'S JACKETS & RIDING GEAR

D
D. Two-Tone Leather Jacket
The ultimate Indian riding jacket for
all your riding needs. With zip-out
lining, zipper air-vents and Indian
logo leather patch on back.
Black/Red. Sizes: S-3XL.
Complementary women's version
available (Pg 27).
87-619 $420
F. Canvas Twill Jacket
100% cotton twill with embroidered
Warbonnet on back and Indian script
logo embroidery on left front chest.
Black. Sizes: S-3XL.
87-921 $175
F
E
E. Twill Centennial Jacket
100% cotton twill jacket with embroidered
Indian Motorcycle logos and the
100-year centennial patches.
Available in Scout and
Spirit embroidered logos
on front of jacket.
Limited sizes and
quantity: L-3XL.
86-746 $170 - Spirit
87-637 $170 - Scout
Indian
SCOUT
100
G
G. Nylon Bomber Jacket
The ultimate cold weather
jacket with Dupont Thermolite
Plus™ insulation. With Indian
logo embroidery on back.
Black. Sizes: S-3XL.
Complementary women's
version available (Pg 27).
85-484 $165
Indian
MOTORCYCLE
17

A. Riding Shirt
High-tech Polyfin™ material keeps you warm and comfortable while riding.
Black with red Indian script logo embroidery.
Sizes: S-2XL.
86-412 $99
B. Hothead
Stay warm and comfortable with this under-helmet liner made from high-tech Polyfin™ material. Black with red Indian script logo embroidery. One size fits all.
86-410 $24
C. Headgator
Made from high-tech Polyfin™ material to keep you warm and comfortable. Fits under helmet. Black with red Indian script logo embroidery. One size fits all.
86-409 $24
D. Beanie
High-tech Polyfin™ material keeps you warm and comfortable. Fits under helmet. Black with red Indian script logo embroidery. One size fits all.
86-411 $20
E. Nylon Windbreaker with Indian Embroidery
Polyester and cotton mixed fabric with snap button collar. Indian script logo embroidery on left chest and Warbonnet logo embroidery on back. Black. Sizes: S-3XL.
88-465 $65
F. Nylon Jacket
Nylon jacket with Indian Motorcycle logo embroidery on left chest. Black. Sizes: S-3XL.
88-471 $60
G. Cap with Front Oval Felt Crest
The 100% cotton solution to helmet hair. Black. One size fits all.
87-844 $30
H. Full Zip Polar Fleece Vest
Full zip with red ultra-suede trim on collar. Black with red trim. Sizes: S-2XL.
86-358 $50
18
MEN'S JACKETS & RIDING GEAR

I. Full Zip Polar Fleece Jacket
Full zip with red ultra-suede trim on collar. Black with red trim. Sizes: S-2XL.
86-353 $50
J. Stone Wash Denim Jacket
Stylish denim jacket with Indian Motorcycle logo embroidery on back. Sizes: S-2XL. Complementary women's version available (Pg 26).
87-127 $98
K. Double Waxed Jacket
Double waxed cotton with leather yoke. Zippered sleeves for ventilation. Indian script logo embroidery on back (tone on tone). Folds into interior carrying bag. Black, Tan or Navy. Sizes: S-2XL.
87-764 $329
L. Two-Piece Lightweight Rain Suit
Keep dry in this stylish rain suit. Reflective hood and Indian Motorcycle script logo on back. Dark Charcoal. Sizes: M-3XL, jacket also 4XL.
82-004 $60 - Scout (Unlined)
82-014 $75 - Chief (Lined)
19

A. Leather Bandana
Help keep the wind off and stay warm. Indian script logo embossed on front. Black. One size fits all.
87-577 $30
C. Leather Skull Cap
Look cool without compromise. Indian script logo embossed on front. Black. One size fits all.
87-576 $34
D. Leather Vest with Adjustable Tie Sides
Adjustable lace-up sides allow a comfortable fit. Indian logo leather patch on back. Black. Sizes: S-3XL. Complementary women's version available (Pg 27).
87-628 $125
B. Leather Cargo Vest
Classic motorcycle vest. Full front zipper. Snap-down and zippered pockets provide plenty of storage space. Indian script logo embossed on bottom front. (Actual logo may vary from picture). Sizes: S-3XL.
88-427 $142 (3XL-$158)
20
MEN'S RIDING GEAR

E. Classic Suede Shirt
Front snap-down pockets and snap-down sleeves. Black. Sizes: S-3XL.
88-415 $225 (3XL-$250)
F. Embroidered Western Shirt
Authentic Western styling. Lightweight shirt for the summer or all year round. With polyester and cotton mixed fabric. Black. Sizes: S-3XL.
88-495 $45
I. Nubuck Gloves
Designed to provide comfortable warm protection. Snap wrist closure with embossed Warbonnet logo. Cotton lined only. Black. Sizes: S-XL.
85-472 $56
J. Deerskin Gloves
Deerskin leather with adjustable wrist snap closure. Black. Sizes: S-XL.
81-852 $52 - Unlined
81-856 $56 - Cotton lining
K. Brave Short Gauntlet Gloves
Durable black cowhide leather for rugged good looks. Available with Thinsulate™ lining. Black. Sizes: S-XL.
81-812 $52 - Unlined
81-816 $56 - Cotton lining
81-820 $59 - Thinsulate™ lining
G. Men's Leather Chaps
Strong and supple. Napa cowhide with built-in belt and heavy-duty zippered legs. Black. Sizes: S-2XL.
81-066 $195
H. Boot Cut Leather Pants
Durable Napa leather pants with 5 pockets. Black. Sizes: S-2XL.
81-071 $235
L. Fingerless Gloves
Durable deerskin leather with hook and loop fastener wrist closure for a comfortable fit. Unlined only. Black. Sizes: S-XL.
81-860 $50
21

A. Zipper Hooded Warbonnet Sweatshirt
Heavyweight polyester and cotton mixed fabric* Black. Sizes: S-3XL.
88-337 $45
B. Sweatshirt with Indian Embroidery
Heavyweight polyester and cotton mixed fabric. Black. Sizes: S-2XL.
88-511 $48
C. Circled Warbonnet Crew Sweatshirt
Stay warm after your ride in this 100% preshrunk cotton sweatshirt. Black. Sizes: S-3XL.
88-319 $32
D. Contrast Fleece Crew
100% polyester. Long sleeves for warmth and comfort. Taupe/Black. Sizes: S-2XL.
87-871 $39
E. V-Neck Sweater
Polyester and cotton mixed fabric.* Black/Cream only. Sizes: S-2XL.
88-531 $68
22
MEN'S SHIRTS & SWEATERS

G. Crew Sweater
Cotton and acrylic mixed fabric.* Contrast stitching and Indian Motorcycle logo on the front. Black. Sizes: S-2XL.
87-861 $55
H. Men's Twill Shirt - Est. 1901 Embroidery
100% cotton* twill. Durable lightweight. Stone, White or Denim. Sizes: S-2XL.
86-890 $60 (Stone, White)
86-495 $74 (Denim)
J. Combed Cotton Twill Long Sleeve Shirt
Lightweight 100% cotton.* Black, Stone or Denim. Sizes: S-3XL.
82-710 $70
K. Combed Cotton Twill Short Sleeve Shirt
Lightweight 100% cotton.* Black, Stone or Denim. Sizes: S-3XL.
82-728 $65
I. Denim Short Sleeve Shirt - Left Chest Embroidery
100% cotton* denim, lightweight yet durable. Black, White or Blue. Sizes: S-3XL.
82-776 $60
L. Denim Long Sleeve Shirt - Left Chest Embroidery
100% cotton* denim, rugged and durable. Black, White or Denim. Sizes: S-3XL.
82-752 $80
M. Denim Long Sleeve Shirt - Indian Logo
Pledge your allegiance in this 100% cotton* denim classic. Black or Blue. Sizes: S-3XL.
82-764 $85
N. Denim Long Sleeve Shirt - Warbonnet
100% cotton* denim. Classic comfort. Sizes: S-3XL.
87-661 $75
F. Heavy Sweater
100% cotton.* Indian script stitched across front chest with Chief (Black/Cream) or Scout (Black/Red) on sleeve. Sizes: S-XL.
88-523 $78 (Scout)
88-527 $78 (Chief)
*This product is made with 100% cotton, please note shrinkage may occur during wash and dry cycles.
23

E. Embroidered Henley
100% cotton* collarless, thermal Henley.
Black or Grey. Sizes: S-3XL.
88-441 $36
J. Classic Beret
The stylish solution to helmet hair.
100% brushed cotton.
Black. Sizes: S-XL.
81-195 $24
K. Powerplus™ 100 Long Sleeve T-shirt
100% preshrunk, lightweight cotton.
Black or Grey. Sizes: S-3XL.
88-379 $35
A. Embroidered Polo
100% cotton, classic polo shirt with Indian logo embroidery on the left chest.
Black or Charcoal.
Sizes: S-3XL.
88-453 $32 (3XL-$35)
F. Circled Warbonnet Short Sleeve T-shirt
100% preshrunk cotton.
Black, Blue or Grey.
Sizes: S-3XL.
88-301 $25
B. Indian 2003 Short Sleeve T-shirt
100% preshrunk cotton.
Black, Blue or Grey. Sizes: S-3XL.
White shirts are offered at a promotional price of $15.
88-057 $25
G. "Established 1901" Pocket T-shirt
100% preshrunk cotton.
Black or Grey.
Sizes: S-3XL.
88-367 $25
C. Men's Tank Top
100% preshrunk cotton.
Black or Grey. Sizes: S-3XL.
88-325 $20
H. "World's Finest" Short Sleeve T-shirt
100% preshrunk cotton.
Black, Blue or Grey. Sizes: S-3XL.
88-081 $30
D. Indian 2003 Pocket T-shirt
100% preshrunk cotton.
Black or Grey. Sizes: S-3XL.
88-355 $25
I. "Vintage World's Finest" Short Sleeve T-shirt
100% preshrunk cotton.
Black, Blue or Grey.
Sizes: S-3XL.
88-540 $25
24
MEN'S SHIRTS & HEAD WEAR

L. Warbonnet Long Sleeve T-shirt
100% preshrunk, lightweight cotton.
Black or Grey.
Sizes: S-3XL.
88-343 $35
N. Cap with Front Felt Patch
100% brushed cotton.
Black. One size fits all.
81-183 $24
O. Cap with 3-D Indian Embroidery
100% brushed cotton.
Black. One size fits all.
87-085 $24
P. Cap with Powerplus™ 100 Embroidery
100% brushed cotton.
Black, Navy or Stone. One size fits all.
87-770 $24
When ordered through the Indian Motorcycle website, the short and long sleeve t-shirts come with the standard back design as seen in item L (Pg. 25). To purchase t-shirts with specific city and state back print, please visit your nearest Indian Motorcycle dealership.
Q. Cap with Indian Embroidery
100% brushed cotton.
Black, Red, Navy or Stone. One size fits all.
81-169 $20
R. Pro Cap with Indian Embroidery
100% washed cotton.
Natural with Black rim. One size fits all.
88-188 $20
M. Bowling Shirt
Retro design with style to spare.
Polyester and Rayon mixed fabric.
Black. Sizes: S-XL.
87-097 $70
S. Embroidered Beanie
Keep your head warm during cold weather. Embroidered Warbonnet logo on front.
Black. One size fits all.
82-200 $12
U. & T. Embroidered Skull Cap with Tie Back
Stylish head wrap with Indian Motorcycle logo embroidery.
One size fits all.
U. 88-039 $16
T. 88-038 $14
V. Cotton Skull Cap with Indian Logo
100% cotton provides soft comfort.
Black. One size fits all.
87-769 $14
*This product is made with 100% cotton, please note shrinkage may occur during wash and dry cycles.
25

A. Napa Leather Jacket with Suede Piping
Styled to compliment a woman's figure with tapered princess seam. Small Indian Motorcycle embroidery on left chest. Black with tan piping. Sizes: S-3XL.
81-062 $310
D. Vented Leather Jacket
This soft leather jacket is perfect for those warm days on the bike and those cool nights out on the town. Cowhide vented jacket with zip-out liner. Indian logo embossed on back. Black. Size S-2XL.
81-130 $455
B. Classic Leather Biker Jacket
Top-quality Napa cowhide leather designed in the classic biker image. With snap-down collar, adjustable laced sides and zippered pockets and cuffs. Indian Motorcycle logo embossed on back. Black. Sizes: S-3XL.
81-058 $315
E. Stone Wash Denim Jacket
Cropped to the waist to give you the shape you want. Unique Indian Motorcycle script logo embroidery on back for added style. Light or Dark Denim. Sizes: S-XL.
87-160 $89
F. Napa Speed Jacket
Top quality Napa leather designed in the retro style. Mandarin collar and zippered pockets. Black with cream and red shoulder stripe with Indian Motorcycle block letter logo. Sizes: S-XL.
87-615 $335
C. Denim Style Leather Jacket
Napa leather with polyester lining. Flattering slim-fitting cut. Black. Sizes: S-XL.
87-595 $335
26
WOMEN'S JACKETS & RIDING GEAR

H. Nylon Bomber Jacket
This version of the classic "bomber" has unique Indian Motorcycle script logo embroidery that really stands out. Features Thermolite Plus™ insulation. Black. Sizes: S-XL.
85-480 $145
G. Two-Tone Leather Jacket
Leather jacket is perfect for those warm days and cool nights, with zip-out lining and zippered air-vents. Indian logo leather patch on back. Black/Red. Sizes: S-3XL.
87-624 $399
I. Zip Denim Vest
100% preshrunk cotton. Stylish and comfortable. Black. Sizes: S-2XL.
87-676 $49
J. Leather Vest with Adjustable Tie Sides
Adjustable lace-up sides allow a comfortable fit. Indian logo leather patch on back. Black. Sizes: S-3XL.
87-633 $99
K. Princess Gloves
Soft deerskin leather provides comfort and style. Hook and loop wrist closure for a secure fit. Comes in two lining options. Black. Sizes: S-L.
81-864 $54 - Unlined
81-867 $58 - Cotton lining
L. Cruiser Gloves
Stylish fringed gloves in soft deerskin. Get the adventurous look with added warmth and protection. Comes in two lining options. Black. Sizes: S-L.
81-876 $62 - Unlined
81-879 $66 - Cotton lining
27

A. Cap Sleeve T-shirt with Ruby Grommets
Diamonds may be a girl's best friend, but you can never go wrong with rubies. 100% preshrunk cotton. Black or White. Sizes: S-XL.
87-144 $38
D. Circled Warbonnet Tank
This top is designed to be figure flattering. 100% preshrunk cotton. Black or White. Sizes: S-XL.
88-574 $24
F. V-Neck Short Sleeve T-shirt
This 100% preshrunk cotton shirt is cut to fit just about everyone of all shapes and sizes. Black or White. Sizes: S-XL.
88-558 $22
B. Raglan Tank
This top shows just the right amount of skin. Show off that summer tan. 100% preshrunk cotton. Heather/Black or Black/Red. Sizes: S-XL.
88-582 $35
E. Indian Script Spaghetti Tank
You can never have enough glitter. 100% cotton.* Black or Red. Sizes: S-XL.
87-191 $24
C. Indian Wing Tank
Figure flattering top shows just the right amount of skin. 100% preshrunk cotton. Black or Red. Sizes: S-XL.
88-590 $26
28
WOMEN'S CASUAL WEAR

H. Indian Halter Top
This soft 100% cotton* top covers the bare necessities. Black or Red. Sizes: S-XL.
88-598 $24
K. Kid's Warbonnet Short Sleeve T-shirt
100% preshrunk cotton, sure to be a favorite. Blue or Heather. Sizes: S-L.
88-614 $18
L. Kid's Chief Crew Sweatshirt
100% preshrunk cotton. Stay warm and show your allegiance to the brand. Black. Sizes: S-L.
88-622 $25
G. Long Sleeve Crewneck T-shirt
Form fitting shape with front chest logo design. 100% preshrunk cotton. Heather or Red. Sizes: S-XL.
88-566 $29
I. Indian Chief Bandana
Classic biker head wrap. Small multiple Indian logo and Chief head designs. Black, Beige, Red or Burgundy. One size fits all.
87-267 $8
J. Embroidered Tye Shirt
Polyester and cotton mixed fabric gives you the comfort you need and the great style you want. Black, Stone or Red. Sizes: S-3XL.
88-477 $35
M. Kid's Chief Short Sleeve T-shirt
100% preshrunk cotton for your junior biker. Black or White. Sizes: S-L.
88-606 $18
*This product is made with 100% cotton, please note shrinkage may occur during wash and dry cycles.
29
KID'S CASUAL WEAR

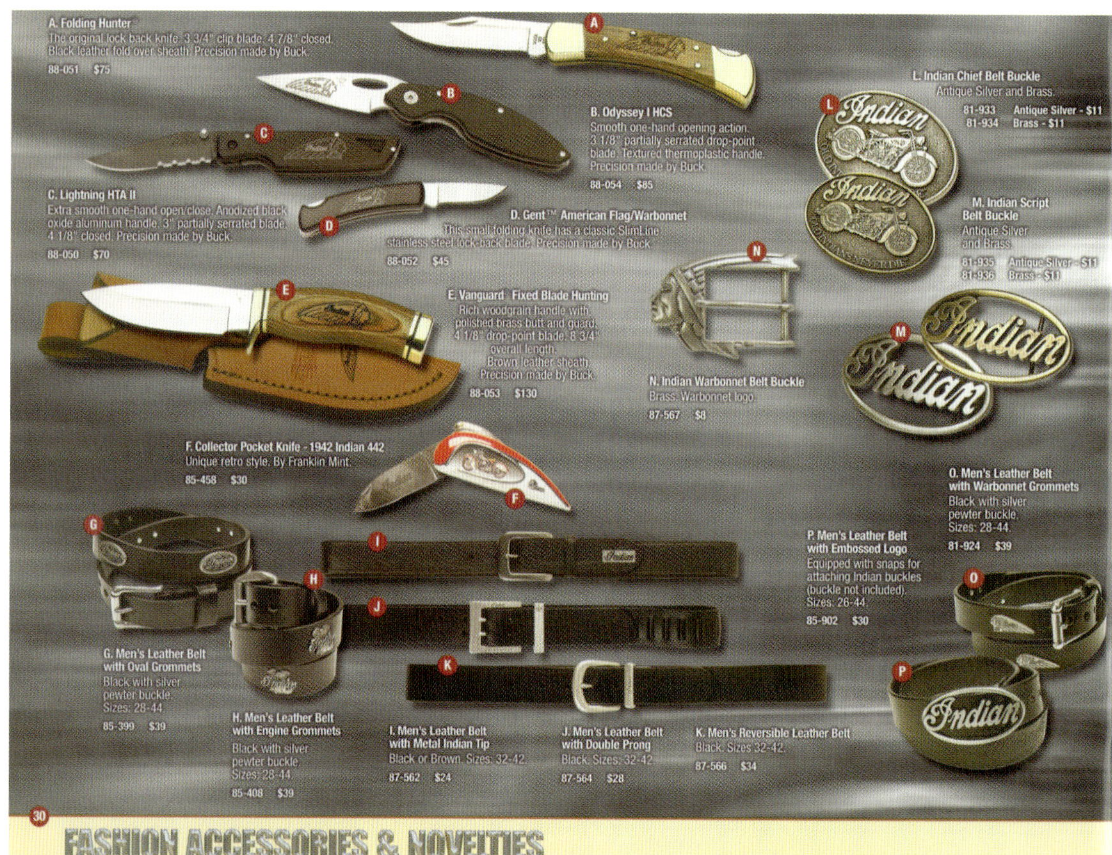
A. Folding Hunter
The original lock back knife. 3 3/4" clip blade. 4 7/8" closed. Black leather fold over sheath. Precision made by Buck.
88-051 $75
B. Odyssey I HCS
Smooth one-hand opening action. 3 1/8" partially serrated drop-point blade. Textured thermoplastic handle. Precision made by Buck.
88-054 $85
C. Lightning HTA II
Extra smooth one-hand open/close. Anodized black oxide aluminum handle. 3" partially serrated blade. 4 1/8" closed. Precision made by Buck.
88-050 $70
D. Gent™ American Flag/Warbonnet
This small folding knife has a classic SlimLine stainless steel lock-back blade. Precision made by Buck.
88-052 $45
E. Vanguard Fixed Blade Hunting
Rich woodgrain handle with polished brass butt and guard. 4 1/8" drop-point blade. 8 3/4" overall length. Brown leather sheath. Precision made by Buck.
88-053 $130
F. Collector Pocket Knife - 1942 Indian 442
Unique retro style. By Franklin Mint.
85-458 $30
L. Indian Chief Belt Buckle
Antique Silver and Brass.
81-933 Antique Silver - $11
81-934 Brass - $11
M. Indian Script Belt Buckle
Antique Silver and Brass.
81-935 Antique Silver - $11
81-936 Brass - $11
N. Indian Warbonnet Belt Buckle
Brass. Warbonnet logo.
87-567 $8
O. Men's Leather Belt with Warbonnet Grommets
Black with silver pewter buckle. Sizes: 28-44.
81-924 $39
P. Men's Leather Belt with Embossed Logo
Equipped with snaps for attaching Indian buckles (buckle not included). Sizes: 26-44.
85-902 $30
G. Men's Leather Belt with Oval Grommets
Black with silver pewter buckle. Sizes: 28-44.
85-399 $39
H. Men's Leather Belt with Engine Grommets
Black with silver pewter buckle. Sizes: 28-44.
85-408 $39
I. Men's Leather Belt with Metal Indian Tip
Black or Brown. Sizes: 32-42.
87-562 $24
J. Men's Leather Belt with Double Prong
Black. Sizes: 32-42.
87-564 $28
K. Men's Reversible Leather Belt
Black. Sizes 32-42.
87-566 $34
30
FASHION ACCESSORIES & NOVELTIES

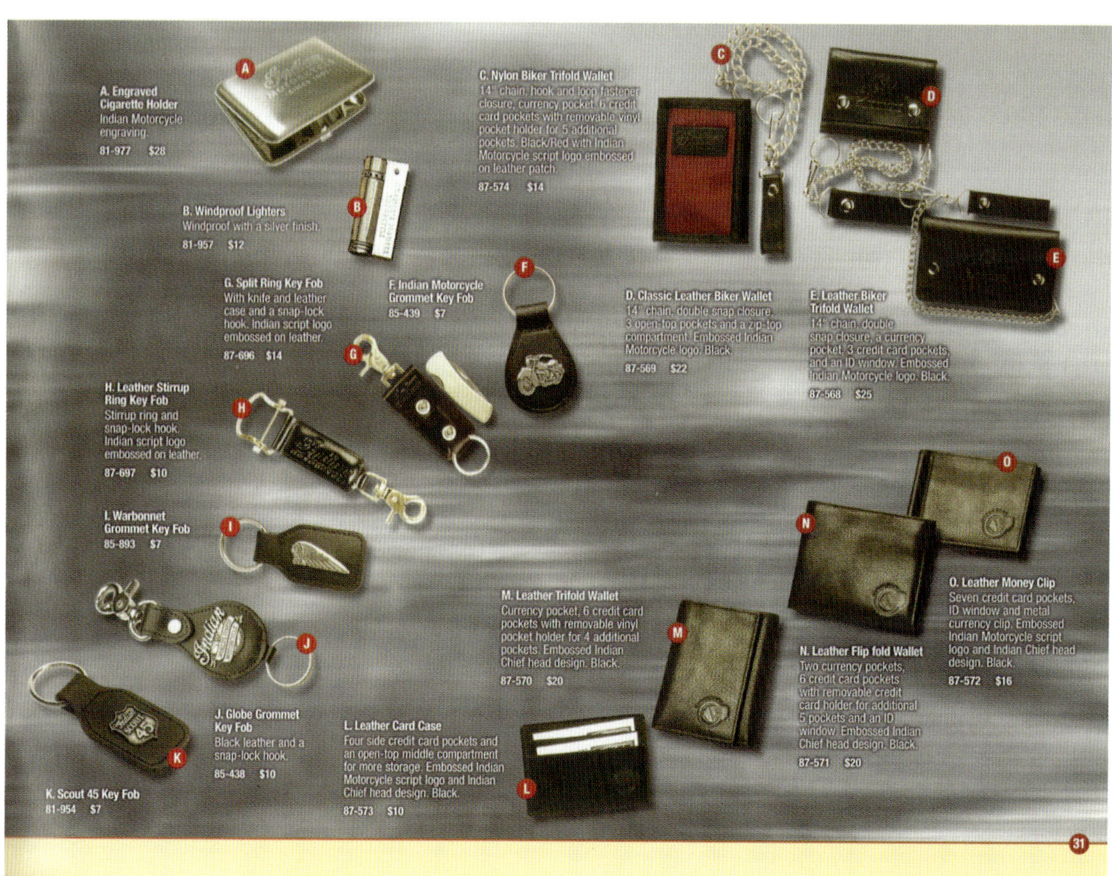
A. Engraved Cigarette Holder
Indian Motorcycle engraving.
81-977 $28
B. Windproof Lighters
Windproof with a silver finish.
81-957 $12
C. Nylon Biker Trifold Wallet
14" chain, hook and loop fastener closure, currency pocket, 6 credit card pockets with removable vinyl pocket holder for 5 additional pockets. Black/Red with Indian Motorcycle script logo embossed on leather patch.
87-574 $14
D. Classic Leather Biker Wallet
14" chain, double snap closure, 3 open-top pockets and a zip-top compartment. Embossed Indian Motorcycle logo. Black.
87-569 $22
E. Leather Biker Trifold Wallet
14" chain, double snap closure, a currency pocket, 3 credit card pockets, and an ID window. Embossed Indian Motorcycle logo. Black.
87-568 $25
G. Split Ring Key Fob
With knife and leather case and a snap-lock hook. Indian script logo embossed on leather.
87-696 $14
F. Indian Motorcycle Grommet Key Fob
85-439 $7
H. Leather Stirrup Ring Key Fob
Stirrup ring and snap-lock hook. Indian script logo embossed on leather.
87-697 $10
I. Warbonnet Grommet Key Fob
85-893 $7
J. Globe Grommet Key Fob
Black leather and a snap-lock hook.
85-438 $10
K. Scout 45 Key Fob
81-954 $7
L. Leather Card Case
Four side credit card pockets and an open-top middle compartment for more storage. Embossed Indian Motorcycle script logo and Indian Chief head design. Black.
87-573 $10
M. Leather Trifold Wallet
Currency pocket, 6 credit card pockets with removable vinyl pocket holder for 4 additional pockets. Embossed Indian Chief head design. Black.
87-570 $20
N. Leather Flip fold Wallet
Two currency pockets, 6 credit card pockets with removable credit card holder for additional 5 pockets and an ID window. Embossed Indian Chief head design. Black.
87-571 $20
O. Leather Money Clip
Seven credit card pockets, ID window and metal currency clip. Embossed Indian Motorcycle script logo and Indian Chief head design. Black.
87-572 $16
31

A. Leather Wallet with String Strap
Double snap closure and second single snap closure for extra security. 7 credit card pockets, 3 pockets, 2 ID windows, interior zip pocket, and fixed length string shoulder strap. Embossed Indian Motorcycle script logo. Black.
87-553 $26
D. Leather Zip Clutch
Double snap enclosure, 2 currency pockets, zippered currency divider, 4 credit card pockets, ID window, checkbook pocket, exterior zip-top currency and coin pockets. Embossed Indian Motorcycle script logo. Black.
87-546 $22
E. Leather Flap Bag
Front flip, single magnetic snap closure. Open-top side pockets, interior zip pocket, and removable shoulder strap. Embossed Indian Motorcycle script logo. Black.
87-552 $64
F. Leather Backpack
Bag with front flip, single magnetic snap closure. Front pocket with magnetic snap closure, back zip pocket, interior zip pocket, convenient loop grab handles, and adjustable shoulder straps. Embossed Indian Motorcycle script logo. Black.
87-549 $99
G. Leather Sling Bag
Zip-top main compartment, interior zip pocket, and fixed length shoulder straps. Embossed Indian Motorcycle script logo. Black.
87-550 $110
H. Leather Tote Bag
Two main open-top compartments, zip-top section, interior side zip pocket, and fixed length shoulder straps. Embossed Indian Motorcycle script logo. Black.
87-551 $87
B. Leather Change Purse
Single snap closure, currency pocket, 6 credit card pockets, zip-top compartment with key ring and an open side ID window. Embossed Indian Motorcycle script logo. Black.
87-548 $18
C. Leather Multi-Function Wallet
Double snap enclosure, currency pocket, 4 credit card pockets, ID window, 8 additional pockets, and an exterior zip pocket. Embossed Indian Motorcycle script logo. Black.
87-547 $18
I. Nylon Backpack
Front flip with zippered pocket, over top and secures in front. Interior zip pocket, full interior lining, two exterior side pockets, ID window, fully padded adjustable shoulder straps. Indian Motorcycle logo embroidered on front. Black/Red.
87-580 $60
J. Nylon Messenger Bag
Front flip with zippered pocket, opens to one compartment. Interior zip pocket, ID window, and fixed shoulder strap. Indian Motorcycle logo embroidered on front. Black/Red.
87-581 $56
K. Travel Shaving Kit
Nylon shaving kit that fits right into your saddlebag. Three zipper compartments and side pocket. Embossed Indian Motorcycle logo. Black.
87-575 $30
L. Travel Clock
Leather case with an interior pocket. Indian Motorcycle script logo embossed on front. Glow-in-the-dark hand for visibility.
87-578 $34
M. Manicure Set
Set includes small scissors, tweezers and metal nail file. Leather case with embossed Indian Motorcycle logo.
87-579 $14
32
FASHION ACCESSORIES & NOVELTIES

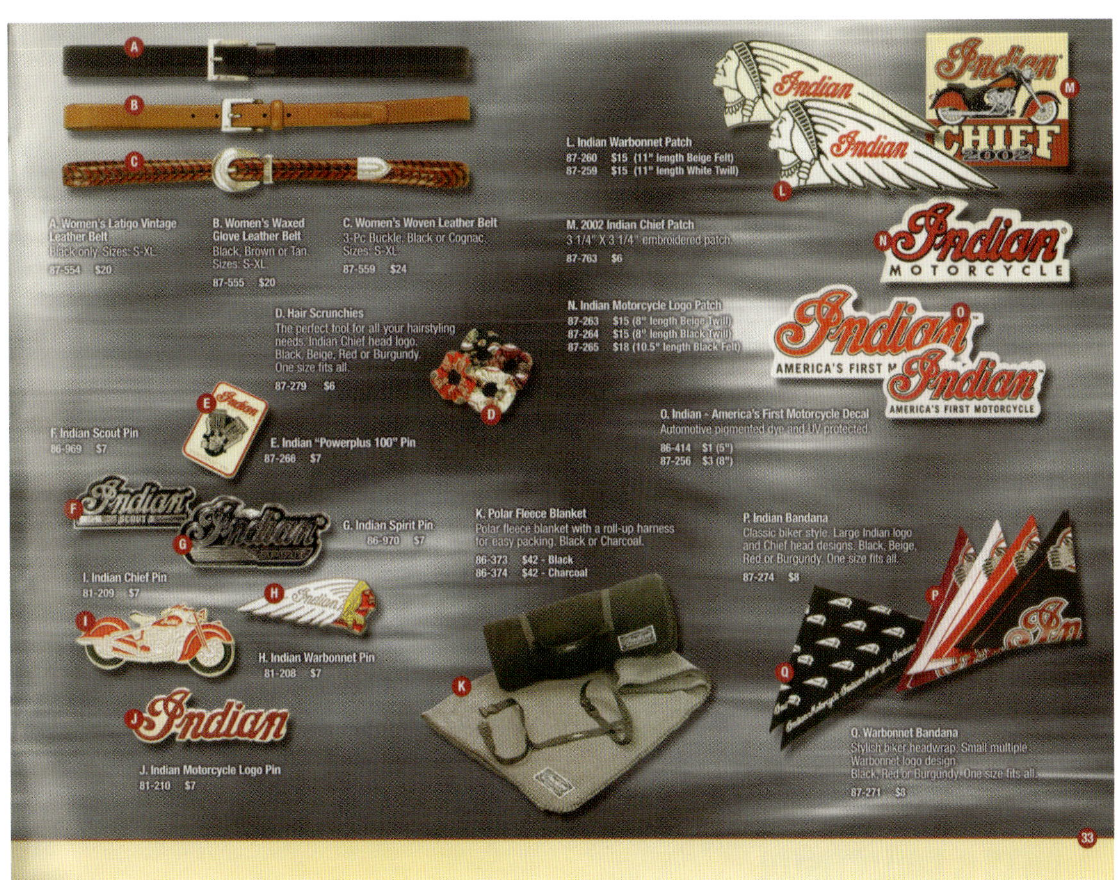
A. Women's Latigo Vintage Leather Belt
Black only. Sizes: S-XL.
87-554 $20
B. Women's Waxed Glove Leather Belt
Black, Brown or Tan. Sizes: S-XL.
87-555 $20
C. Women's Woven Leather Belt
3-Pc Buckle. Black or Cognac. Sizes: S-XL.
87-559 $24
D. Hair Scrunchies
The perfect tool for all your hairstyling needs. Indian Chief head logo. Black, Beige, Red or Burgundy. One size fits all.
87-279 $6
F. Indian Scout Pin
86-969 $7
E. Indian "Powerplus 100" Pin
87-266 $7
G. Indian Spirit Pin
86-970 $7
I. Indian Chief Pin
81-209 $7
H. Indian Warbonnet Pin
81-208 $7
J. Indian Motorcycle Logo Pin
81-210 $7
K. Polar Fleece Blanket
Polar fleece blanket with a roll-up harness for easy packing. Black or Charcoal.
86-373 $42 - Black
86-374 $42 - Charcoal
L. Indian Warbonnet Patch
87-260 $15 (11" length Beige Felt)
87-259 $15 (11" length White Twill)
M. 2002 Indian Chief Patch
3 1/4" X 3 1/4" embroidered patch.
87-763 $6
N. Indian Motorcycle Logo Patch
87-263 $15 (8" length Beige Twill)
87-264 $15 (8" length Black Twill)
87-265 $18 (10.5" length Black Felt)
O. Indian - America's First Motorcycle Decal
Automotive pigmented dye and UV protected.
86-414 $1 (5")
87-256 $3 (8")
P. Indian Bandana
Classic biker style. Large Indian logo and Chief head designs. Black, Beige, Red or Burgundy. One size fits all.
87-274 $8
Q. Warbonnet Bandana
Stylish biker headwrap. Small multiple Warbonnet logo design. Black, Red or Burgundy. One size fits all.
87-271 $8
Indian
CHIEF 2002
Indian MOTORCYCLE
AMERICA'S FIRST MOTORCYCLE
33

A. 1934 Indian Series 402
16.5" x 12.75" metal sign.
85-373 $12
3" x 2.25" magnet.
85-446 $4
B. Sales and Service
16.5" x 12.5" metal sign.
85-374 $12
3" x 2.25" magnet.
85-445 $4
C. Parts & Service - Springfield, Mass
16.5" x 10.25" metal sign.
85-375 $12
D. 1914 Indian V-Twin
16.5" x 11.75" metal sign.
85-376 $12
E. 1953 Roadmaster Chief
12.5" x 16.5" metal sign.
85-377 $12
2.25" x 3" magnet.
85-447 $4
F. 2000 Indian Chief
16.5" x 12.5" metal sign.
87-693 $12
G. Indian – American Muscle
11.5" x 16.5" metal sign.
85-381 $12
2.25" x 3" magnet.
85-448 $4
H. America's First Motorcycle
12.5" x 16.5" metal sign.
87-694 $12
I. Collector Plate - 1939 Indian 4
8" diameter collectable china plate.
85-453 $30
J. Collector Plate - 1942 Indian 442
8" diameter collectable china plate.
85-450 $30
K. The Indian: The History of a Classic American Motorcycle
Volume II by Todd Rafferty - Revised Edition. Read up on the history of America's first motorcycle from 1901-present.
87-850 $28
34
GIFTS & COLLECTIBLES

M. Salt & Pepper Shakers
Indian Motorcycle logo. Ceramic.
88-047 $12
L. Collector Plate - 1947 Indian Chief
8" diameter collectable china plate.
85-451 $30
N. Picture Frame
4" x 6" frame with Indian Motorcycle logo. Ceramic base holds two pictures within two glass slides.
88-046 $15
O. 385 Peterbilt Box Truck Die-Cast
Die-cast collectable bank.
87-852 $25
P. '32 Ford Street Rod Die-Cast
Die-cast collectable bank.
87-851 $30
Q. Playing Cards with Tin
Classic Indian playing cards with tin case.
80-096 $10
R. Small Tin Tote/Lunch Box
The classic Indian tin tote for kids of all ages.
80-097 $10
S. 20 oz. Decal Mug
Warbonnet logo.
80-098 $15
T. Business Card Holder
Ceramic business card holder with Indian Motorcycle script logo.
88-049 $15
U. Cookie Jar
Get this classic Indian Motorcycle jar and fill it up with all your favorites. Indian Motorcycle vintage art design. Ceramic top and base, tin can.
88-048 $25
V. Wall Clock
Indian Motorcycle logo.
80-099 $30
35

Although not an IMCOA-sold accessory, these Doss-designed teardrop spotlights/signals are occasionally found on Chiefs.

CHAPTER 4

IMCOA Corporate History

So these guys, these two venture capitalists, they show up at my doorstep and say, "Hey, we're Indian Motorcycle." I said, "Yeah, you and fifteen other guys . . ." They said, "We want you to build this bike," and they show me this picture of a Softail with Indian fenders on it. I said, "Yeah, I can build that." I said, "What are you going to do with it?"

—Rey Sotelo, former president and CEO of IMCOA

That initial meeting among Rey Sotelo, Murray Smith, and John Albright might well be considered the Indian Motorcycle Company of America's moment of conception. Sotelo agreed to build eight prototype Indian motorcycles to be available in time for showing at a Muscular Dystrophy Association charity event at Glendale, California, on November 7, 1998. By that time, Sotelo's California Motorcycle Company had been purchased by the consortium, which would soon establish the first company to manufacture Indian motorcycles in America since 1953.

But before that could happen, there was still one major loose end to be secured: the coveted rights to Indian trademarks and designs. There were dozens of complainants as part of the "Indian estate" who needed to be reimbursed for the losses incurred at the hands of flimflam artists and failed businessmen over the years (as described in chapter 1 and in the appendix). Among the contenders for next keeper of the Indian flame were the Eller group and the nine-company consortium (which, for the sake of clarity, we'll call the Gilroy group). The winner would have the dubious honor of making the Indian estate whole to the tune of nearly $20 million and, at that point, could figure out how to resurrect Indian motorcycles. Even so, the potential rewards were dazzling to investors, dealers, and customers.

The court-appointed receiver for the Indian estate, Rick Block, had originally supported the Eller group's bid for the Indian Intellectual Property (IP), but on November 6, 1998, Block obtained a restraining order preventing the Eller prototype from being displayed and prohibiting its images from being shown publicly. Block claimed that the Eller group had failed to meet its payment deadline—a claim that the head of the Eller group, Leonard Labriola, vehemently denied in public print. Meanwhile, Block threw his support to the Gilroy group.

On December 7, 1998, the matter of which group would satisfy the Indian estate was heard before Judge Zita Weinshienk of the US District Court for the District of Colorado. The Eller group had drawings of its nonrunning prototypes. However, two Gilroy prototypes were brought up to the courtroom in a freight elevator and, according to several accounts, were *ridden* into the courtroom. Judge Weinshienk was reportedly so impressed by this achievement that she descended from the bench and threw a leg over one of the Gilroy Chiefs. The day ended with Judge Weinshienk declaring IMCOA the contract purchaser of the Indian estate assets.

In March 1999, the Gilroy group was formally awarded the Indian IP, and Murray Smith wrote out a check to the Colorado Federal Claims Court to satisfy the members of the Indian estate. Not since 1949 (when the old Indian Motocycle Company had been split into the Indian Sales Corporation and the Indian Division of the Titeflex Corporation) had the Indian IP been held by a single corporate entity. Before building a single motorcycle, IMCOA had pulled off arguably its greatest achievement. The iconic brand had been saved. But the court—perhaps a bit *too* impressed by the running prototypes—ordered the Gilroy group to have its new Indian motorcycles available within only one year. Judge Weinshienk was all too cognizant of the earlier failures to resurrect Indian and was determined that her ruling would not add another blemish to the storied motorcycle brand name.

Those who invested in the Indian Motorcycle Company of America were less interested in saving America's oldest motorcycle brand than seeing a return on their investment. Having new Indian motorcycles rolling out of the Gilroy factory as soon as possible sounded fine to them. Much of the original financing came from Katama Capital and the J. L. Albright Venture Fund, plus Henry Schinburg (CEO) and Summerfield Johnston (chairman of the board) of Coca-Cola. By mid-2000, Indian's investors had burned through $100 million, with no sign of slowing expenditures, much less a return.

Meanwhile, Rey Sotelo grew restless in the board meetings. A biker and experienced builder, Sotelo knew that, as he put it, "slapping Indian tin on a Harley" was not going to satisfy the motorcycle community for long. In a little-known footnote of IMCOA history, Sotelo early on investigated the possibility of having an Indian engine supplied by an outside source:

> We needed a proprietary engine, and someone over at Yamaha had designed a 98-cubic-inch pushrod V-twin. Now everything metric back then was using overhead cams, but they came up with this pushrod engine which was pushing something like 100 horses. I mean, Harleys were doing 50 or 60 horses out of the box. And they [Yamaha] were willing to private-label this for us. It would have been a great short-term solution for our own engine, but Summerfield [Johnston] and Henry [Schinburg] killed it."
>
> —*Rey Sotelo, former president and CEO of IMCOA*

In the fall of 2000, Frank O'Connell was secured as a consultant. O'Connell was the former president of Reebok Brands North America and HBO Video. Additionally, he was the former chairman and CEO of Gibson Greetings, Inc., and Skybox International, and the founder of Fox Video Games. Perhaps most importantly, O'Connell was a lifelong motorcycle enthusiast with a deep respect for Indian. After many days of examining the books, the production area, and the warehouses, he generated a report outlining the problems he observed at the Gilroy plant. At this point, Indian was essentially bankrupt, with Summerfield Johnston writing weekly checks to keep the operation going. O'Connell's report and its recommendations made sense to the investors, and O'Connell was asked to become the president and interim CEO of IMCOA, with the primary responsibility of raising capital. To attract additional big-money investors, it would be necessary to rebuild the management team and trim expenses. At that point, the Gilroy workforce employed 610 workers. Major layoffs occurred in late 2000 / early 2001 and were later recalled by one disillusioned worker this way: "The blue jeans all left and the suits came to stay."

There was talk in the IMCOA boardrooms about taking the corporation public, but some preferred to wait until sales and profits were such that the stock price could be maximized. It was also thought expedient to wait until Indian had introduced its own engine before going public. The bursting of the dot-com bubble in 2000 was adversely affecting the stock market, so in light of all this, it was decided to wait until 2001 to take Indian Motorcycle public. However, due to new Audax investment that year, the IPO never happened. Years later, Rey Sotelo would claim, "Had they gone public in 2000 / early 2001, we'd probably still be in business."

On June 25, 2001, Audax, a newly launched private equity firm, bought $45 million worth of IMCOA preferred stock for a controlling interest. The company also announced that Frank O'Connell, the current interim chief executive officer, would assume full-time duties as CEO effective immediately. O'Connell later distilled the major problems of IMCOA as

> having gotten started on the wrong foot. Much of [the invested one hundred million] was wasted in building the wrong foundation. They did a good job of capturing the Indian DNA in the external design of the bike. However, it would have been easier to start from scratch and redesign the internal guts of the bikes for cost and quality manufacturability, as well as outsourcing the manufacturing of entire systems to enhance the ease of assembly. —*Frank O'Connell, former president and CEO of IMCOA*

Obviously, the fallout (i.e., insufficient time for R&D) from the court-ordered requirement to offer new Indian motorcycles within a year continued to haunt the enterprise. Meanwhile, Audax, as reported by O'Connell, was interested in putting a "world-class management team in place and establishing a solid strategic plan." But he added,

> Private-equity firms are typically not good at running companies. They are transaction people who don't have much operating experience.

Rey Sotelo, at that time traveling extensively with Henry Schinburg and Frank O'Connell to find additional investors, recalls that R&D funding for the PP100 dried up after the Audax buy-in:

> We still needed an Indian engine. We had a design and even set up a foundry down in Indio [California]. We were going to build the PP100 down there. But before we had the prototype, they pulled the plug.

Still, Audax made a serious run at saving the corporation. O'Connell later recalled,

> Indian needed a deeper, more professional management skill base. Key areas included design, engineering, product development, marketing, sales/dealer relations, licensing, sourcing, and operations.

Darrin Caddes, with a résumé that included BMW and Fiat, was brought in as head of design. Chick Ramsey, having worked at Autobytel, Toyota, and Lexus, was put in charge of sales and developing the dealer network. This focused on established car dealerships, which were solidly capitalized to support motorcycle inventory. Fran O'Hagan, former vice president of Jaguar Land Rover of North America and in charge of sales at BMW of North America, was brought in as vice president of marketing. Engineers were brought in from England, including several from Lotus. Chip Foose, a well-known designer of automobiles, restorer of motorcycles, and a hot-rod builder, was contracted to do some designs, which, O'Connell believed, "stimulated our creative thinking." John Hagen had been in charge of the Porsche/Harley V-Rod JV project and was brought in as vice president of manufacturing and director of operations. It's clear that Audax did its best to source the right people to turn Indian around. Unfortunately, Audax's people were financial experts, not motorcycle people.

Conversely, it was motorcycle people who had launched the new Excelsior-Henderson project in the 1990s. As Rey Sotelo recalled years later, "They [Excelsior-Henderson] did everything right; they just didn't have the money." A few years later, IMCOA found itself in a similar fiscal position, but for different reasons. The financial gurus were in charge and, through no fault of their own, didn't understand the core market with which they were dealing (especially the urgent need for a proprietary engine). The few upper-management people who understood the motorcycle community (Sotelo and O'Connell in particular) were outvoted in matters of capital allocation. Ultimately, IMCOA was unable to achieve the delicate balance between the need for a proprietary motorcycle line and the need for profits. Neither deficiency could be ignored for long without bringing down the entire enterprise.

The situation was somewhat reminiscent of the events that took place from 1913 to 1916, when Indian's founders (George Hendee and Oscar Hedstrom) left the company after financial control had been assumed by a board of directors / investors. That board was replaced in 1916 by a group led by John Alvord, followed by major management reorganization. Three years later, that group was in turn supplanted by a new board, followed by another new board in 1927 and again in 1929. In April 1930, E. Paul du Pont was elected to Indian's board, eventually assuming control of the company. Du Pont was a motorcycle man, trained as an engineer, and had very deep pockets. He was just the man Indian needed to save the enterprise. IMCOA would not be so fortunate.

Eventually, the financial spigot was carefully cracked open for development of the Indian Powerplus 100 engine. Unfortunately, the desperate need to generate income subordinated the need for sufficient R&D of the new engine. The investors' idea from the first had been to "sell the sizzle, not the steak." Now that Indian was preparing to offer an honest-to-goodness proprietary engine, frame, suspension, primary, and tins on its product, too many in upper management and Audax persisted in their tragic belief that the motorcycling community would be satisfied indefinitely with "the sizzle." The new engine was an Indian and *looked* great—and that would need to be enough for the moment.

In 2002, Audax brought in Louis Terhar as the new president and CEO, moving O'Connell to chairman, and tasked him with finding either a buyer for the corporation or additional investors. A number of other motorcycle companies (including Harley-Davidson and Polaris/Victory) were approached for various partnership or buyout opportunities, but without success. Management was shifting its emphasis from selling motorcycles to selling the company. Frank O'Connell later recalled that

> our dealer network was building momentum. Quality was improving day by day. Design improved significantly. And sales were steadily increasing. However, our cash burn was high, and we still had some distance from being cash flow positive, given

our cost structure. Warranty claims remained high and kept the company diverting cash and allocating manpower to repairing bikes manufactured several years earlier. —*Frank J. O'Connell, former president and CEO of IMCOA*

Rey Sotelo was approached by IMCOA management to assist in promoting the new Powerplus 100. Fully aware of the impending problems inherent in the partially gestated engine, he refused, further widening the gulf between him and upper management. Indian Chiefs equipped with the new Powerplus 100 began appearing in dealerships in the spring of 2002. It didn't take long for problems to emerge. In July 2002, Rey Sotelo left Indian.

The months passed by, and IMCOA continued to hemorrhage money. In 2003, Bob Stark toured the Gilroy plant and was told that production needed to be seventy units per day to break even. At that time, production was approximately twenty-five per day. May 2003 was Indian's top sales month yet, and September was looking even better. But it just wasn't enough.

Friday, September 19, 2003, seemed at first like a typical workday at the Gilroy factory. One assembly-line worker reported, "They handed out our paychecks at lunchtime, and everything seemed fine." Then, around 2:15 that afternoon, IMCOA president and CEO Louis Terhar called the Indian workforce to the parking lot. "What they told us was, we were doing fine, we were doing a hell of a good job, but they couldn't find anyone to give us money." Audax had finally thrown in the towel. No more funds would be forthcoming to keep Indian afloat. There was shocked silence, punctuated by stifled sobs and muttering. Virtually no one had seen it coming. Indian's first issue of its online newsletter, *The Legend*, had been sent out only the day before.

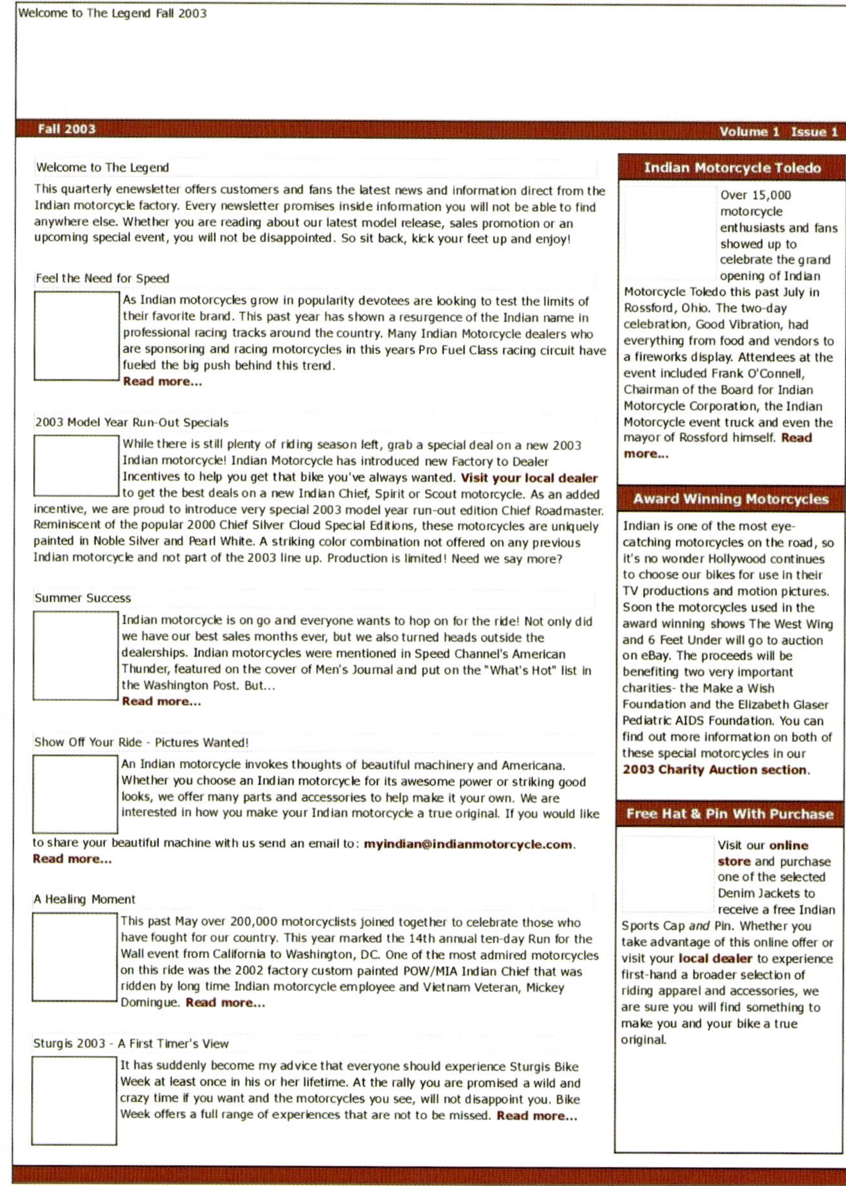

Welcome to The Legend Fall 2003

Fall 2003 **Volume 1 Issue 1**

Welcome to The Legend

This quarterly enewsletter offers customers and fans the latest news and information direct from the Indian motorcycle factory. Every newsletter promises inside information you will not be able to find anywhere else. Whether you are reading about our latest model release, sales promotion or an upcoming special event, you will not be disappointed. So sit back, kick your feet up and enjoy!

Feel the Need for Speed

As Indian motorcycles grow in popularity devotees are looking to test the limits of their favorite brand. This past year has shown a resurgence of the Indian name in professional racing tracks around the country. Many Indian Motorcycle dealers who are sponsoring and racing motorcycles in this years Pro Fuel Class racing circuit have fueled the big push behind this trend. **Read more...**

2003 Model Year Run-Out Specials

While there is still plenty of riding season left, grab a special deal on a new 2003 Indian motorcycle! Indian Motorcycle has introduced new Factory to Dealer Incentives to help you get that bike you've always wanted. **Visit your local dealer** to get the best deals on a new Indian Chief, Spirit or Scout motorcycle. As an added incentive, we are proud to introduce very special 2003 model year run-out edition Chief Roadmaster. Reminiscent of the popular 2000 Chief Silver Cloud Special Editions, these motorcycles are uniquely painted in Noble Silver and Pearl White. A striking color combination not offered on any previous Indian motorcycle and not part of the 2003 line up. Production is limited! Need we say more?

Summer Success

Indian motorcycle is on go and everyone wants to hop on for the ride! Not only did we have our best sales months ever, but we also turned heads outside the dealerships. Indian motorcycles were mentioned in Speed Channel's American Thunder, featured on the cover of Men's Journal and put on the "What's Hot" list in the Washington Post. But... **Read more...**

Show Off Your Ride - Pictures Wanted!

An Indian motorcycle invokes thoughts of beautiful machinery and Americana. Whether you choose an Indian motorcycle for its awesome power or striking good looks, we offer many parts and accessories to help make it your own. We are interested in how you make your Indian motorcycle a true original. If you would like to share your beautiful machine with us send an email to: **myindian@indianmotorcycle.com**. **Read more...**

A Healing Moment

This past May over 200,000 motorcyclists joined together to celebrate those who have fought for our country. This year marked the 14th annual ten-day Run for the Wall event from California to Washington, DC. One of the most admired motorcycles on this ride was the 2002 factory custom painted POW/MIA Indian Chief that was ridden by long time Indian motorcycle employee and Vietnam Veteran, Mickey Domingue. **Read more...**

Sturgis 2003 - A First Timer's View

It has suddenly become my advice that everyone should experience Sturgis Bike Week at least once in his or her lifetime. At the rally you are promised a wild and crazy time if you want and the motorcycles you see, will not disappoint you. Bike Week offers a full range of experiences that are not to be missed. **Read more...**

Indian Motorcycle Toledo

Over 15,000 motorcycle enthusiasts and fans showed up to celebrate the grand opening of Indian Motorcycle Toledo this past July in Rossford, Ohio. The two-day celebration, Good Vibration, had everything from food and vendors to a fireworks display. Attendees at the event included Frank O'Connell, Chairman of the Board for Indian Motorcycle Corporation, the Indian Motorcycle event truck and even the mayor of Rossford himself. **Read more...**

Award Winning Motorcycles

Indian is one of the most eye-catching motorcycles on the road, so it's no wonder Hollywood continues to choose our bikes for use in their TV productions and motion pictures. Soon the motorcycles used in the award winning shows The West Wing and 6 Feet Under will go to auction on eBay. The proceeds will be benefiting two very important charities- the Make a Wish Foundation and the Elizabeth Glaser Pediatric AIDS Foundation. You can find out more information on both of these special motorcycles in our **2003 Charity Auction section.**

Free Hat & Pin With Purchase

Visit our **online store** and purchase one of the selected Denim Jackets to receive a free Indian Sports Cap *and* Pin. Whether you take advantage of this online offer or visit your **local dealer** to experience first-hand a broader selection of riding apparel and accessories, we are sure you will find something to make you and your bike a true original.

You are receiving this email because you have expressed an interest in receiving Indian Motorcycle informational material.
If you would prefer not to receive future newsletters please **click here**

Indian's short-lived online newsletter, released the day before the factory closure. *Courtesy of Norm Zabala, founder, the Gilroy Era of Indian Motorcycles*

Executive vice president Fran O'Hagan stated,

> It came as a complete surprise to everybody, including the top management. . . . The motorcycle industry is not for the faint of heart. [It] takes an awful lot of capital to succeed. . . . In the end, the company didn't have the money. On the other hand, our 380 employees and 200 dealers have something to be proud of, and that's 13,000 beautiful Indian motorcycles driving around the country.

Frank O'Connell, like many others, was hit hard by the closure:

> This meant the loss of jobs to hundreds of employees in Gilroy. Also, dealers had invested a good deal of money building their dealerships with inventory of bikes and accessories, showrooms, and maintenance shops. Both groups were angry and blamed Audax for stopping funding. I guess you couldn't expect the employees to see that Audax had invested and lost $100 million and underwritten their jobs for four years. I felt bad for those dealers who had invested heavily in their dealerships. It was not how I had hoped things would go."

Geoff Rehnert, co-CEO and cofounder of the Audax Group, recalled in 2016:

> We tried to do too much, too quick . . . [Indian Motorcycle] was the single worst investment of my entire career, probably the most painful business experience of my career. . . . When it was clear that Indian was not gonna make it, that was very, very painful. I think I threw up every night for about a week straight.

Audax had lost fully one-fifth of its initial capital on a single investment.

A cofounder of the failed Excelsior-Henderson Motorcycle Company, Dan Hanlon, had written two years earlier that

> for those that continue to criticize the effort, let them try it. . . . Only those that were there will ever understand fully the individual and family sacrifices, and the moments of glory. There will forever be a bond.

IMCOA never filed for bankruptcy but, rather, was disbursed through the California Receivership Liquidation Process. The firm elected to be liquidated through an "assignment for the benefit of creditors" process, managed by CMA (Credit Managers Association) in Burbank, California. Initially, all tangible assets and the Indian intellectual property were offered as a single lot, with a hoped-for price of approximately $50 million. There were no takers, so assets were eventually offered in three lots: (1) parts inventory / machinery / tooling / completed bikes / two prototypes, (2) buildings and property, and (3) trademarks and all IP.

Bill Melvin, CEO of NREL (National Retail Equipment Liquidators), purchased the inventory of IMCOA on January 14, 2004, and remembered the following:

> Just before I bought Gilroy Indian, Rey [Sotelo] and I had a few discussions about joining forces to reopen the Gilroy factory; both of us were searching for the deep-pocket investors who could finance major go forward expenses.
>
> A hundred million won't even get the job done. It's just a start. So we knew at [that] point . . . that neither of us had found that link to the future yet. Buying the company would have been cheap, but reviving it a huge expense. . . . It had been my dream to restart Indian, but it couldn't be done. And the State of California was not helpful at all. Overregulation there was a nightmare.

In the period between the factory's shutdown and the sale of company assets, some product began to disappear. Former employees are naturally hesitant to divulge details, but it has been reliably reported that certain Indian treasure was surreptitiously appropriated "out the back door." While this activity would not have pleased Indian's creditors or owners at the time, today such stories only add to the legend.

Melvin scheduled a sale through the "assignment for benefit of creditors" process. He later recalled,

> Our sale at Gilroy lasted about four months. Hours 9 to 5. But we worked around the clock to organize, price, and discover what was there.

On January 21, 2004, Melvin opened the Gilroy plant to buyers, who bought tools, storage items, and miscellaneous motorcycle parts. Eighty-six Indian motorcycles (including the 2004 models) were offered separately to the motorcycling community, which included museums and collectors. CMA held back three 2004 Indians from Melvin's sale: a red Chief CST and both Scout Two-Tens. On February 11, 2004, a discounted liquidation sale commenced at the factory. The Gilroy factory itself was later (on March 18, 2004) sold to Ken Gimelli for $3.35 million.

On July 26, 2004, Stellican Ltd., a London-based private-equity firm, announced its acquisition of Indian's trademarks and intellectual property. Stellican's press release of the same day noted,

> Stellican Limited is an unusual private[-]equity firm in that it specializes in acquiring and reviving distressed companies, almost all with heritage brands, mainly in the recreational[-]products area. Even more unusually, its capital is provided by its own principals[,] who actively manage its portfolio companies directly. Most recently, in addition to

INDIAN

FACTORY ASSETS LIQUIDATION

HUGE DISCOUNTS! BUY IN BULK & $AVE!

Asset Liquidation Sale Starts WEDNESDAY, 2-11-04, 9am–5pm.
LIQUIDATION SALE continues DAILY until EVERTHING IS SOLD!
SALE LOCATION: Indian Motorcycle Factory in GILROY, CA.

ATTN: MOTORCYCLE DEALERS & ENTHUSIASTS!
HURRY IN FOR DEEP LIQUIDATION DISCOUNTS
ON HUGE QUANTITIES! EVERYTHING MUST GO:

- MOTORCYCLE PARTS (Power Plus Motors, S&S Parts, Frames, MORE – HUGE inventory, too much to list).
- POSTERS, MEMORABILIA & INDIAN FACTORY SIGNS.
- "INDIAN" LOGO APPAREL.
- TRUCKS & TRAILERS and SEMI-TRAILER.
- OFFICE FURNITURE & EQUIPMENT (Office Panels in "Like-New" condition, Computers, Printers & Fax Machines).
- FORKLIFTS & MATERIAL HANDLING EQUIPMENT.
- LARGE COMMERCIAL AIR COMPRESSOR (brand NEW).
- COMPLETE POWDER COAT LINE.
- ROBOTIC FRAMES & GAS TANK WELDERS.
- LG. QUANTITY OF ALUMINUM, STEEL AND STAINLESS raw material for building motorcycles.
- EMBROIDERY MACHINE & SEWING ROOM EQUIPMENT.
- ENGINE STANDS, BIKE LIFTS & HAND TOOLS.
- LG QTY of GAS TANKS & FENDERS (painted or raw).
- PALLET RACK, CARTS, FIXTURES & MORE!

SALE LOCATION:

Indian Motorcycle Factory, 200 E. 10th St. GILROY, CALIFORNIA
Call NREL (800) 613-6865 ■ Email sales@nrel.com ■ Visit www.nrel.com

TERMS OF SALE: Payment for purchases must be made by Cash, Cashier's Check, VISA or MasterCard. A 10% Buyer's Premium is added to all purchases.

CONDITIONS: Every item is being sold "As Is-Where Is" without warranty or guarantee intended or implied of any kind, including merchant-ability or fitness for particular purposes. Prices are subject to change at any time. The seller or its agents assumes no liability for accuracy, errors or omissions in this brochure. All items are subject to prior sale or deletion from the sale. Although most items are available, they may not be available at all locations.

Build Your Own Bike CHEAP!

Liquidation Prices on Apparel, Posters and Memorabilia

FACTORY Equipment Auction Coming SOON!

FACTORY MACHINERY & EQUIPMENT AUCTION COMING SOON!
■INSPECTION: March 16-17, 2004, 8am-4pm ■AUCTION: March 18, 2004, starting at 10:30 am

The final stage of Bill Melvin's liquidation sale. Note the box at the lower left: "Build Your Own Bike Cheap!" These were "kits" for building complete Indian motorcycles. Melvin later recalled selling about a hundred of these "kits," which did not include titles.

Chris-Craft boats, Stephen Julius, through Stellican Limited, acquired and turned around the iconic Italian yacht manufacturer Riva, and the Italian Premier League soccer team Vicenza.

E. Paul and Francis du Pont had lost $260,000 during their ownership of Indian from 1930 to 1945, but their stewardship undoubtedly saved Indian during the Great Depression. IMCOA lost over $100 million of its investors' funds from 1999 to 2003, but through this sacrifice the Indian brand was again saved.

Thus, resurrected by a company that died in the process, the iconic Indian brand survived to eventually be manufactured and marketed by two other firms. "The Legend Lives."

It's a damn good thing we failed, because we could never have done what you did. Our failure led to your success. *—Rey Sotelo to Steve Menneto, at the 2014 rollout of new Polaris Indian Motorcycles*

That's as much a compliment to you as it is to me. *—Steven Menneto, vice president, motorcycles (Indian), Polaris Inc., to Rey Sotelo*

Public Webcast Auction
COMPLETE MODERN MOTORCYCLE
MANUFACTURING FACILITY
IN THE MATTER OF
Indian®
AMERICA'S FIRST MOTORCYCLE
Thursday, March 18
Sale starts at 10:30 a.m.
Live Bidding Location:
200 East Tenth St., Gilroy, CA
Inspection: Tuesday & Wednesday, March 16 & 17,
8:00 a.m.-4:00 p.m. and morning of the sale
GREAT AMERICAN GROUP
WHOLESALE & INDUSTRIAL SERVICES

CHAPTER 5

Stillborn: The 2004 Indian Motorcycles

Inside the Gilroy factory during the liquidation of its contents

It is fortunate that Bill Melvin, former CEO of National Retail Equipment Liquidators, took a special interest in the remaining hard assets of the Indian Motorcycle Corporation of America and their dispersal. Among these assets were approximately forty-three 2004 model year Indian motorcycles that had never left the factory. Liquidating failed companies was routine, but this job was special for Bill. He was a lifelong motorcycle aficionado with a private museum, and the Indian brand was sacred to him. After exhausting the possibility of reviving the company, Bill set about documenting the last days of the IMCOA factory. In doing so, he interviewed a number of employees, including Lea Legnon (who was in charge of order entry, production records, and VIN records), Joe Leon (head of research and development), Bill Johnson (who built many of the 2004s on the production line), Chris Curon (a technical supervisor in charge of testing and final production), and Robert Jimenez (an R&D technician who, along with Joe Leon and Bill Johnson, performed final testing and setup of the 2004 motorcycles).

On September 19, 2003 (the day of the factory closure), there were approximately fifteen completed 2004 Indian motorcycles in the factory. During the following weeks, the remaining 2004 bikes were assembled and tested by a skeleton crew that included Chris Curon and Bill Johnson. Joe Leon hand-built the fat-tire Scout Two-Tens and checked/test-rode every completed 2004 Indian motorcycle.

During this process, Bill Melvin observed their completion, took photographs, and maintained a count. He asserts that the total number of 2004 Indian motorcycles he sold or kept was forty-three. However, Melvin believes that a few 2004s were taken from the factory by executives or employees of Indian or Credit Managers Association (CMA). This situation was mentioned in the April 16, 2004, issue of *The Gilroy Dispatch*:

> Melvin may not have the complete collection [of 2004s] for sale. This could be because Indian executives or board members took some 2004s before Melvin bought them, as was speculated at the time. It could also be that some of the 2004s cannot legally be sold because they have prototype parts—cheaper versions that don't meet safety standards—as [Fran] O'Hagan said in September.

A number of Gilroy Indians were assembled by private parties from leftover parts obtained at the factory sale, some of which used 2004 parts. When examining a 2003–04 Indian, the silver frame data tag should indicate if it was a factory build, but it has been reliably reported that one of the frame data tag printers was stolen at the time of the factory closure. This may have resulted in fraudulent 2004 data tags on some machines. The original 2004 sales data are condensed in this chapter, which should help verify the authenticity of most 2004 Indians.

The 2004 Indian Motorcycles

The following are the specification sheets for the 2004 Chiefs, sent to dealers in anticipation of the 2004 Indian motorcycles being shipped. Note the warning that this information was not to be made public until October 1, 2003.

All 2004 Powerplus 100 engines featured a breather at the back of the cam chest, an improved oil pump, and properly tapered flywheels (all improvements originally designed and implemented by Blackhawk and P&P Powertrain for the 2002–03 Chiefs). The rocker boxes were distinguished by a raised lip around the upper edge. Rocker arm shaft supports were machined into the lower rocker box, rather than the previous design of two separate supports bolted in place.

A 2004 Chief Vintage. *Courtesy of Motorcyclepedia Museum*

Courtesy of Motorcyclepedia Museum

INFORMATION EMBARGOED UNTIL OCTOBER 1, 2003

2004 INDIAN® CHIEF®

New Chief® CST and Impressive Refinements Lead the Way
Attractive Lower Pricing Makes the Chief More Affordable Than Ever

As the pinnacle of the Indian Motorcycle lineup, the 2004 Indian® Chief® is a rolling declaration of what Indian Motorcycle stands for—and a testament to our commitment to never stand still.

Under every 2004 Chief's beautiful skin are more than 170 improvements. Its all-American, all-Indian Powerplus™ 100 engine has been completely reengineered, from its tuned intake and high-performance valve train, to its redesigned cases and crankshaft, to its high-volume, low back-pressure 2-into-1 exhaust. The result is a smoother, quieter, even more durable powerplant, with easier starting, quicker throttle response and dramatically improved mileage. Not to mention stronger roll-on acceleration from a 14% boost in peak torque and a 7% increase in peak horsepower.

The improvements don't stop at the revised Powerplus 100 engine. From its refined, higher-quality hand and foot controls, to its smoother, lighter clutch, to its re-contoured, lowered seats, every 2004 Chief feels just as sophisticated as it looks. And from its upgraded, all-Brembo braking system to its new 41mm Paoli fork, every Chief motorcycle is equipped to stop and turn just as well as it accelerates.

MORE

Courtesy of Mark Peterson

2004 INDIAN CHIEF MOTORCYCLES, PAGE 2

Choose the classic Chief® Springfield, inspired by the birthplace of Indian Motorcycles in Springfield, Massachusetts. The new Chief® CST, with its sleek look, contemporary 20-spoke alloy wheels and standard two-up seating. The built-for-the-open-road Chief® Roadmaster, for riders who simply don't want to stop. Or the legendary Chief® Vintage, which celebrates the golden age of American design. All are offered with new pricing that makes owning an Indian Chief motorcycle more affordable than ever.

Performance

The heart of the Chief line is the Powerplus™ 100 cubic-inch (1638cc) 45-degree, V-twin engine designed and developed by Indian. Key refinements in 2004 enhance low-end and mid-range torque, sharpen throttle response and increase fuel mileage.

Key refinements for 2004 include:

Forged One-Piece Rocker Boxes: Towers and support rocker arm shaft are integrated into the base to provide added strength and durability of the valve train while reducing upper-end engine noise.

New Camshaft: Designed using computer dynamic analysis of the valve train, the camshaft is optimized to enhance low-end and mid-range torque without compromising top-end performance while reducing engine noise.

Valve Springs Optimized for New Camshaft: Adds to the reduction of valve train loads, enhancing engine starting performance while reducing engine noise.

New Cylinder Head Casting: Revised compression ratio (9.0:1) increases engine durability while reducing starting torque.

Vacuum-Advance Ignition System: Load-sensitive, this system senses engine load and adjusts engine timing enhancing engine response at lower RPMs.

New Internal Bypass Oiling System: Internal bypass design with internal pressure release provides improved bottom-end lubrication enhancing durability.

MORE

Courtesy of Mark Peterson

2004 INDIAN CHIEF MOTORCYCLES, PAGE 3

Newly Designed Exhaust: Two-into-one with a 4 ½" diameter high-flow muffler increases internal volume by 65% and reduces backpressure by 50%. Catalytic muffler on CA models reduces exhaust emissions without compromising performance.

Flywheel Assembly/Crankshaft: Crank pin and sprocket shaft engineered for greater assembly torque (increased 80% and 30% respectively), improves powertrain smoothness.

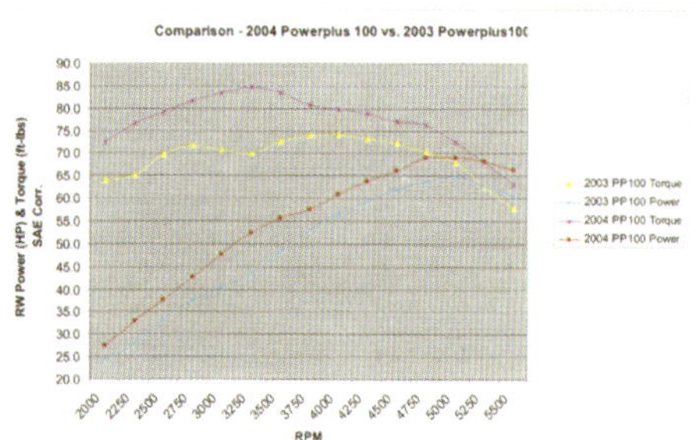

Suspension and Braking

The Chief® line features Paoli 41mm hydraulic, dual-damping forks and a nitrogen-charged, KW hydraulic rear shock absorber with adjustable preload for all-day comfort and responsive handling.

Key refinements for 2004 include:

Brembo Brake System: Brembo front and rear master cylinders (optimized 14mm bore size) and Brembo 4-piston front and rear calipers improve stopping power.

Newly Designed Foot Controls: Forged, polished aluminum shift and brake levers with contoured, elliptical rubber lever cushions add comfort while a newly designed, splined shifter delivers smooth, low-effort shifting.

MORE

Courtesy of Mark Peterson

2004 INDIAN CHIEF MOTORCYCLES, PAGE 4

Comfort and Styling

Key refinements for 2004 include:

New Hand Controls: New high-quality switch cubes deliver excellent durability and feel while new rubber grips with stainless-steel end caps add comfort and reduce vibration.

Newly Designed Floorboards: All-new spring-loaded, retractable floorboards with replaceable wear strip come with vibration-absorbing rubber cushions embossed with Indian Motorcycle script.

Lower, Re-contoured Seat: Re-contoured, ergonomically enhanced seat brings seat height down to 27.5" (1" lower than 2003).

MORE

Courtesy of Mark Peterson

2004 INDIAN CHIEF MOTORCYCLES, PAGE 5

Indian® Chief® Springfield

The Indian® Chief® Springfield is designed for the enthusiast who appreciates the classic style of early Indian motorcycles and the machines that first put America on two wheels.

The Chief Springfield wears the classic large Indian script logo originally seen on the 1917 Indian Powerplus model. The logo appears in rich gold, surrounded by double gold pinstriping. The 2004 Indian Chief Springfield comes with a hand-stitched solo seat, newly designed Fiamm horn and horn cover, 16-inch, 60-spoke chrome wheels and Michelin blackwall tires.

The Chief Springfield is offered in two solid colors: Jet Black and Deep Red. Manufacturer's suggested retail price is $19,995 (U.S.).

MORE

Courtesy of Mark Peterson

2004 INDIAN CHIEF MOTORCYCLES, PAGE 6

Indian® Chief® CST

The 2004 Indian® Chief® CST is designed for the motorcycle enthusiast who appreciates the classic lines and styling of early Indian motorcycles in a more contemporary looking package.

The Indian Chief CST is a seamless meeting of retro and current style with elegant, 20-spoke forged chrome wheels and Michelin blackwall tires. The Chief CST comes with a studded, dual gunfighter seat and newly designed Fiamm horn and horn cover.

The 2004 Chief CST is offered in three solid colors: Jet Black, Volcano Red Metallic and Cobalt Blue Metallic. Manufacturer's suggested retail price is $20,995 (U.S.).

MORE

Courtesy of Mark Peterson

2004 INDIAN CHIEF MOTORCYCLES, PAGE 7

Indian® Chief® Roadmaster

The 2004 Indian® Chief® Roadmaster celebrates the appeal and the freedom of the open road and is designed with long distance and weekend touring in mind.

The Indian Chief Roadmaster features a fringed dual seat, newly designed Fiamm horn and horn cover, new Metzeler whitewall tires, 60-spoke chrome wheels, fender graphics and saddlebags emblazoned with the Roadmaster logo. For long-distance comfort, the Chief Roadmaster features an integrated windshield and passenger backrest.

The 2004 Chief Roadmaster is offered in three solid colors and four two-tone color combinations respectively: Jet Black, Volcano Red Metallic, Cobalt Blue Metallic, Charcoal Metallic/Jet Black, Jet Black/Vanilla Cream, Blackberry Metallic/Jet Black, and Oakleaf Metallic/Pearl White. Manufacturer's suggested retail price is $22,495 (U.S.).

MORE

Courtesy of Mark Peterson

2004 INDIAN CHIEF MOTORCYCLES, PAGE 8

Indian® Chief® Vintage

The Indian® Chief® Vintage is a full-bodied, fully-dressed American cruiser, fully-loaded with chrome and leather accoutrements. It is designed for the enthusiast who is seeking the ultimate in classic styling.

The 2004 Indian Chief Vintage features a fringed leather solo seat, new Metzeler whitewall tires, 60-spoke chrome wheels, a luggage rack, engine guards and fringed saddlebags embossed with the Indian script logo. For long-distance comfort, the Chief Vintage is equipped with an integrated windshield. Also new for 2004 is a breathtaking Deep Turquoise/White Sand two-tone paint option.

The 2004 Indian Chief Vintage is offered in two solid colors and one two-tone color respectively: Century Red, Jet Black and Deep Turquoise/White Sand. Manufacturer's suggested retail price is $23,995 (U.S.).

Motorcycles are to be used only on the road by a licensed rider. Obey all local laws and regulations. We recommend that you always wear a helmet, protective clothing and eyewear, and that your passengers do the same. Never ride under the influence of alcohol or drugs. Ride with your headlight on at all times and ride safely. Read you owner's manual thoroughly. We recommend that all riders complete a recognized training program prior to operating a motorcycle.

Specifications, availability and prices subject to change without notice. California version differs slightly due to emissions equipment. All prices shown are the Manufacturer's Suggested Retail Price (MSRP). California models priced slightly higher, actual dealer prices may vary.

Indian, Chief, Scout, Indian Spirit, Powerplus, script Indian, Indian Motorcycle, Indian Riders Group, the skirted fender and war bonnet lamp designs and the logos are trademarks and registered trademarks of IMCOA Licensing America, Inc. in the U.S. and Foreign countries. © 2003 Indian Motorcycle Corporation.

Courtesy of Mark Peterson

2004 Indian® Chief® Springfield/Chief CST/ Chief Roadmaster/Chief Vintage Specifications

Engine:	Powerplus™ 100, 45-degree V-twin, black finish, polished fins
Displacement:	100 cubic inches (1638cc)
Bore X Stroke:	3.875" x 4.25"
Compression Ratio:	9.0:1
Valve System:	Two, push rod activated with hydraulic lifters, intake diameter 1.94", exhaust diameter 1.615"
Carburetor:	Mikuni HSR 42mm flat-slide
Exhaust System:	2-into-1
Ignition:	Electronic, computer-controlled
Transmission:	Constant-mesh, five-speed
Primary Drive:	Chain drive, wet clutch, reduction ratio 1.54:1
Final Drive:	Aramid-reinforced belt, reduction ratio 2.03:1
Frame:	High-tensile steel, powder-coated, black
Rake:	34 degrees
Trail:	5.92"
Front Suspension:	Paoli 41mm, dual-damping conventional style, 5.4" travel
Rear Suspension:	Rising-rate, KW single shock with adjustable preload, 4.25" travel
Front Brake:	Brembo, differential bore, 4-piston caliper, 11.5" rotor
Rear Brake:	Brembo, differential bore, 4-piston caliper, 11.5" rotor
Front Wheel:	60-spoke, chrome, 16" x 3.5", (Springfield, Roadmaster, Vintage) Forged, polished, 16" x 3.5", (CST)
Rear Wheel:	60-spoke, chrome, 16" x 3.5", (Springfield, Roadmaster, Vintage) Forged, polished, 16" x 3.5", (CST)
Front Tire:	Michelin, blackwall, 130/90-16 (Springfield, CST) Metzeler, whitewall, 130/90-16 (Roadmaster, Vintage)
Rear Tire:	Michelin, blackwall, 130/90-16 (Springfield, CST) Metzeler, whitewall, 130/90-16 (Roadmaster, Vintage)
Wheelbase:	68.4"
Seat Height:	27.5"
Dry Weight:	Chief Springfield: 687 lbs. Chief CST: 690 lbs. Chief Roadmaster: 716 lbs. Chief Vintage: 733 lbs.
Fuel Capacity:	5.5 gal including 1.2 gal reserve
Warranty:	12 months/unlimited mileage
Instruments:	Speedometer with digital odometer & tripmeter
MSRP:	Chief Springfield: $19,995 (U.S.) Chief CST: $20,995 (U.S.) Chief Roadmaster: $22,495 (U.S.) Chief Vintage: $23,995 (U.S.)

Prices and specifications subject to change without notice.

Courtesy of Mark Peterson

The 2004 Indian inner primaries and inner cam covers were powder-coated black. A new two-into-one exhaust for the Chiefs was enlarged to 4.5 inches in diameter (Spirits and Scouts were equipped with a 3-inch-diameter two-into-one exhaust). The rear brake pedal was elliptical in cross section and featured a one-piece rubber sheath rather than the multiple rubber rings of earlier years. The heel shifters underwent a similar redesign.

Hand controls were a mix of chrome and black, including black Brembo master cylinders for front and rear brakes. The distinctive Gilroy headlight nacelle was one piece. Brake rotors and rear pulleys featured a new pattern, and the swing arms and rear-wheel adjusters were redesigned. Most (but not all) 2004 Indians featured a new pattern of rubber floorboard mat. Forged chrome wheels were standard on the new Chief CST.

Courtesy of Motorcyclepedia Museum

Courtesy of Motorcyclepedia Museum

Courtesy of Motorcyclepedia Museum

A 2004 Chief (Springfield) with its new 4.5-inch exhaust. The elliptical brake pedal can be seen. *Courtesy of Mark Peterson*

2004 Indian Chief rear-wheel adjusters. *Courtesy of Mark Peterson*

The Aurora taillight/signal assembly was retained only on the 2004 Chief Vintage. *Courtesy of Motorcyclepedia Museum*

Other 2004 Chief models received a new taillight design. *Courtesy of Mark Peterson*

The unloved plastic air box somehow survived into the 2004 models. *Courtesy of Motorcyclepedia Museum*

The 2004 Scouts and Spirits featured the long-awaited new Indian Powerplus 92 engine. This development (described in detail in the Spirit/Scout spec sheets below) finally made IMCOA's motorcycle lineup all Indian.

The following are the specification sheets for the 2004 Scouts, sent to dealers in anticipation of the 2004 Indian motorcycles being shipped. Note the warning that this information was not to be made public until October 1, 2003.

INFORMATION EMBARGOED UNTIL OCTOBER 1, 2003

2004 INDIAN® SCOUT™

Revolutionary "Wide-tire" Scout, New Powerplus™ 92 Engine and $15,995 Starting Price Energize the Scout Line

Eighty years ago, Indian® motorcycles revolutionized the early motorcycle status quo with the long, lean, and powerful Scout™ model that was unlike anything the world had seen before. Today, Indian Motorcycle Corporation embraces that revolutionary spirit and captures the style and excitement of the contemporary, custom motorcycle scene in the all-new Indian® Scout Two-Ten.

The Indian Scout line, known for its low seat, light weight and agile feel, features a long list of key refinements and the addition of the all-new Indian Powerplus™ 92 engine. The "92" engine boasts a 25 percent increase in overall power and a 26 percent increase in torque compared to the 2003 powerplant.

The new Scout Two-Ten delivers contemporary, custom "wide-tire" styling with no compromises in handling, ride quality or performance. Customers receive all of the style of a "custom" machine with none of the performance or reliability drawbacks. And the Two-Ten is available at a surprisingly low price, only $17,995. (Note: Scout Two-Ten shown in photo on this page is equipped with some optional accessories).

MORE

Courtesy of Mark Peterson

2004 INDIAN SCOUT MOTORCYCLES, PAGE 2

Performance

The heart of the Scout™ line is the all-new Powerplus™ 92 cubic-inch (1498cc) 45-degree, V-twin engine. Black powdercoated with high-contrast machined finish fins on rounded cylinder barrels, the "92" is similar in style to the Chief's Powerplus™ 100 and historic Indian engines. This engine boasts a 25 percent increase in overall power and a 26 percent increase in torque compared to the 2003 powerplant.

Key features of the Powerplus™ 92 engine include:

"Square" Bore and Stroke: New engine design features 3.875" x 3.875" bore and stroke for a broad torque curve throughout the RPM range.

Proven Pushrod Design: Two-valve, push rod actuated with hydraulic lifters, intake diameter 1.94", exhaust diameter 1.575", with 9.1:1 compression ratio.

Torque and Horsepower: Engine produces more than 65 lb./ft. of torque from 2000-5250 RPM with a peak of 74.6 lb./ft. @ 3750 RPM. Maximum horsepower is 64.2 @ 4750 RPM. Measurements taken at the rear wheel.

New Exhaust System: Optimized headers and a new two-into-one system with a 3" diameter muffler provide increased flow and better sound quality.

Revised Airbox: Low-noise, high-flow intake design increases air flow to the carburetor for increased performance.

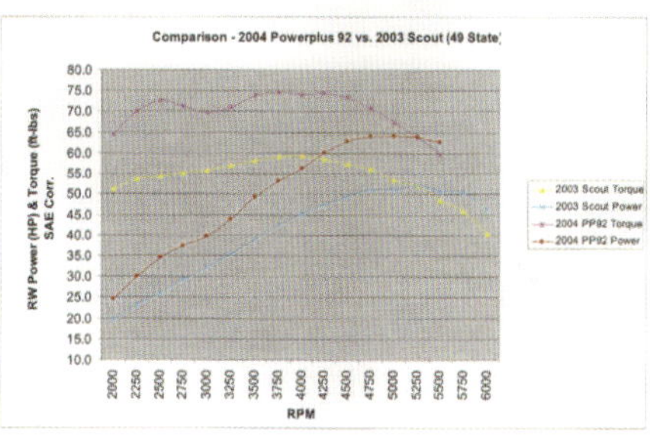

MORE

Courtesy of Mark Peterson

2004 INDIAN SCOUT MOTORCYCLES, PAGE 3

Suspension and Braking
Key refinements for 2004 include:

All-new Brembo Brake System: Brembo front and rear master cylinders (optimized 14mm bore size) and Brembo 4-piston front and rear calipers improve stopping power.

New Front Suspension: Paoli 41mm hydraulic, dual-damping forks with new triple clamps for improved ride quality and handling.

New Wheels: Scout features a new 60-spoke chrome wheel (vs. 40-spoke in 2003). The Scout Two-Ten has 5-spoke forged, machined, polished aluminum wheels with a 6.25" wide rear to accommodate the 210mm rear tire.

Comfort and Styling
Key refinements for 2004 include:

New Hand Controls: New high-quality switch cubes deliver excellent durability and feel while new rubber grips with stainless-steel end caps add comfort and reduce vibration.

Newly Designed Foot Controls: Forged, polished aluminum shift and brake levers with contoured, elliptical rubber lever cushions add comfort while a newly designed, splined shifter delivers smooth, low-effort shifting.

Horn/Horn Cover: Fiamm horn and horn cover adorned with Indian Motorcycle logo.

MORE

Courtesy of Mark Peterson

2004 INDIAN SCOUT MOTORCYCLES, PAGE 4

Indian® Scout Two-Ten
The all-new Indian® Scout Two-Ten combines the freedom, performance and styling long attributed to Indian motorcycles with the muscle, excitement and raw individuality of the contemporary custom motorcycle scene.

The Scout Two-Ten delivers "fat-tire" styling with no compromises in handling, ride quality or performance. Customers receive all of the style of a "custom" machine with none of the performance or reliability drawbacks. In fact, with the addition of the all-new Powerplus™ 92 engine, performance will be taken to a new level.

The Scout Two-Ten features eye-catching five-spoke forged aluminum wheels and an extra-wide, meaty 210mm Metzeler blackwall rear tire. A newly designed extra wide fender and sporty, hand-stitched solo seat complete the look of this aggressive machine. The new swingarm is designed to accommodate the wide 210mm rear tire as well as offering full suspension travel for excellent comfort.

The Scout Two-Ten also features a polished stainless steel belt guard, sporty new front fender design, color-matched frame and new Fiamm horn and horn cover.

The Scout Two-Ten is offered in four solid colors: Red Rock, Citrus Yellow, Aspen White and Jet Black. And it is available at a surprisingly low manufacturer's suggested retail price of only $17,995 (U.S.).

MORE

Courtesy of Mark Peterson

2004 INDIAN SCOUT MOTORCYCLES, PAGE 5

Indian® Scout™

The 2004 Indian® Scout™ is designed for the motorcycle enthusiast looking for classic retro style and a sporty feel in a motorcycle that doesn't sacrifice on performance.

The 2004 Indian Scout combines power, precise handling, rock-solid stability and comfort in a package suited for riders of all sizes and levels. It features a newly designed sporty front fender, 16-inch chrome wheels with Michelin blackwall tires, a new horn and horn cover, black frame and polished, stainless steel belt guard.

The Indian Scout is offered in two solid colors: Cobalt Blue Metallic and Jet Black. Manufacturer's suggested retail price is $15,995 (U.S.).

Motorcycles are to be used only on the road by a licensed rider. Obey all local laws and regulations. We recommend that you always wear a helmet, protective clothing and eyewear, and that your passengers do the same. Never ride under the influence of alcohol or drugs. Ride with your headlight on at all times and ride safely. Read you owner's manual thoroughly. We recommend that all riders complete a recognized training program prior to operating a motorcycle.

Specifications, availability and prices subject to change without notice. California version differs slightly due to emissions equipment. All prices shown are the Manufacturer's Suggested Retail Price (MSRP). California models priced slightly higher, actual dealer prices may vary.

Indian, Chief, Scout, Indian Spirit, Powerplus, script Indian, Indian Motorcycle, Indian Riders Group, the skirted fender and war bonnet lamp designs and the logos are trademarks and registered trademarks of IMCOA Licensing America, Inc. in the U.S. and Foreign countries. © 2003 Indian Motorcycle Corporation.

Courtesy of Mark Peterson

2004 Indian® Scout™/Indian Scout Two-Ten
Specifications

Engine:	Powerplus™ 92, 45-degree V-twin, black finish, machined fins
Displacement:	91.4 cubic inches (1498cc)
Bore X Stroke:	3.875" x 3.875"
Compression Ratio:	9.1:1
Valve System:	Two, push rod actuated with hydraulic lifters, intake diameter 1.94", exhaust diameter 1.575"
Carburetor:	1 7/8" venturi, four-pattern
Exhaust System:	Chrome, 2-into-1
Ignition:	Electronic, computer-controlled
Transmission:	Constant-mesh, five-speed
Primary Drive:	Chain, wet clutch
Final Drive:	Aramid-reinforced belt
Frame:	High-tensile steel, powder-coated, black
Rake:	32 degrees
Trail:	5.25"
Front Suspension:	Paoli 41mm, hydraulic compression and rebound damping, 5.4" travel
Rear Suspension:	Nitrogen-charged hydraulic dampers, coil springs with adjustable preload
Front Brake:	Brembo, differential bore, 4-piston caliper, 11.5" rotor
Rear Brake:	Brembo, differential bore, 4-piston caliper, 11.5" rotor
Front Wheel:	40-spoke, chrome, 19" x 2.15" (Scout) 5-spoke forged aluminum, polished, 19" x 2.15" (Scout Two-Ten)
Rear Wheel:	60-spoke, chrome, 16" x 3.5" (Scout) 5-spoke forged aluminum, polished, 17" x 6.25" (Scout Two-Ten)
Front Tire:	Michelin, blackwall, 100/90-19 (Scout) Metzeler, blackwall, 100/90-19 (Scout Two-Ten)
Rear Tire:	Michelin, blackwall, 130/90-16 (Scout) Metzeler, blackwall, 210/50-17 (Scout Two-Ten)
Wheelbase:	67"
Seat Height:	26.5" (Scout), 25.5" (Scout Two-Ten)
Dry Weight:	Scout: 606 lbs. Scout Two-Ten: 616 lbs.
Fuel Capacity:	5.5 US gallons including 1.2 gallon reserve
Warranty:	12 months/unlimited mileage
Instruments:	Speedometer with digital odometer & tripmeter
MSRP:	Scout: $15,995 (U.S.) Scout Two-Ten: $17,995 (U.S.)

Prices and specifications subject to change without notice.

Courtesy of Mark Peterson

One of two completed 2004 Indian Two-Ten Motorcycles (the second is in the background) featuring the new Indian 92-cubic-inch engine. *Courtesy of Mark Peterson*

Courtesy of Mark Peterson

Courtesy of Mark Peterson

Courtesy of Mark Peterson

The following are the specification sheets for the 2004 Spirits, sent to dealers in anticipation of the 2004 Indian motorcycles being shipped. Note the warning that this information was not to be made public until October 1, 2003.

INFORMATION EMBARGOED UNTIL OCTOBER 1, 2003

2004 INDIAN SPIRIT™

All-new Powerplus™ 92 Engine Boosts Performance

Lower Pricing Makes the Indian Spirit™ Line More Affordable Than Ever

With its unmistakable profile, robust design and focus on performance, the 2004 Indian Spirit™ embodies the enduring appeal and mystique of Indian® motorcycles and encourages riders to follow their own road.

The Indian Spirit motorcycle continues to evolve as one of the finest cruisers on the road today with the addition of the all-new Indian Powerplus™ 92 engine and a long list of styling and performance refinements. The "92" engine boasts a 25 percent increase in overall power and a 26 percent increase in torque compared to the 2003 powerplant.

Making up the Indian Spirit line are the Spirit Springfield, the new Spirit CST and the Spirit Roadmaster. They offer Indian enthusiasts a wider range of styling options, from the classic retro style of the Spirit Springfield to the powerful, elegant look of the Spirit CST with its 20-spoke forged wheels, to the built-for-the-open-road features of the Spirit Roadmaster. All are offered with new pricing that makes owning an Indian motorcycle more affordable than ever.

MORE

Courtesy of Mark Peterson

2004 INDIAN SPIRIT MOTORCYCLES, PAGE 2

Performance

The heart of the Indian Spirit™ line is the all-new Powerplus™ 92 cubic-inch (1498cc) 45-degree, V-twin engine. Black powdercoated with high-contrast machined finish fins on rounded cylinder barrels, the "92" is similar in style to the Chief's Powerplus™ 100 and historic Indian engines. This engine boasts a 25 percent increase in overall power and a 26 percent increase in torque compared to the 2003 powerplant.

Key features of the Powerplus™ 92 engine include:

"Square" Bore and Stroke: New engine design features 3.875" x 3.875" bore and stroke for a broad torque curve throughout the RPM range.

Proven Pushrod Design: Two-valve, push rod actuated with hydraulic lifters, intake diameter 1.94", exhaust diameter 1.575", with 9.1:1 compression ratio.

Torque and Horsepower: Engine produces more than 65 lb./ft. of torque from 2000-5250 RPM with a peak of 74.6 lb./ft. @ 3750 RPM. Maximum horsepower is 64.2 @ 4750 RPM. Measurements taken at the rear wheel.

New Exhaust System: Optimized headers and a new two-into-one system with a 3" diameter muffler provide increased flow and better sound quality.

Revised Airbox: Low-noise, high-flow intake design increases air flow to the carburetor for increased performance.

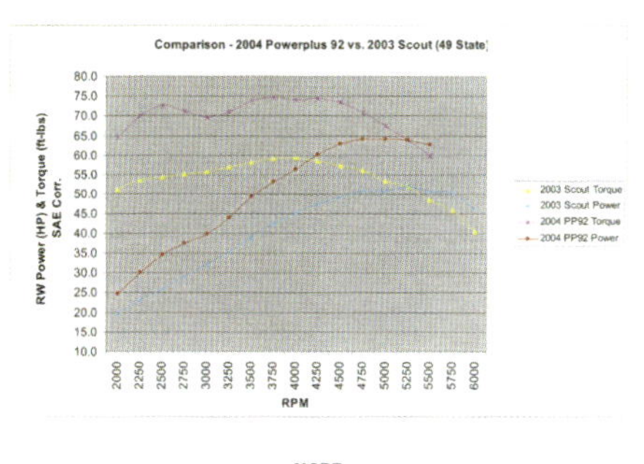

MORE

Courtesy of Mark Peterson

2004 INDIAN SPIRIT MOTORCYCLES, PAGE 3

Suspension and Braking

Key refinements for 2004 include:

All-new Brembo Brake System: Brembo front and rear master cylinders (optimized 14mm bore size) and Brembo 4-piston front and rear calipers improve stopping power.

New Front Suspension: Paoli 41mm hydraulic, dual-damping forks with new triple clamps for improved ride quality and handling.

Comfort and Styling

Key refinements for 2004 include:

New Hand Controls: New high-quality switch cubes deliver excellent durability and feel while new rubber grips with stainless-steel end caps add comfort and reduce vibration.

Newly Designed Foot Controls: Forged, polished aluminum shift and brake levers with contoured, elliptical rubber lever cushions add comfort while a newly designed, splined shifter delivers smooth, low-effort shifting.

Newly Designed Floorboards: All-new spring-loaded, retractable floorboards with replaceable wear strip come with vibration-absorbing rubber cushions embossed with Indian Motorcycle script.

Horn/Horn Cover: Fiamm horn and horn cover adorned with Indian Motorcycle logo.

Front Fender Ornament: New contemporary fender ornament cast in aluminum with a triple-chrome finish.

MORE

Courtesy of Mark Peterson

2004 INDIAN SPIRIT MOTORCYCLES, PAGE 4

Indian Spirit™ Springfield

The Indian Spirit™ Springfield, a classic-looking motorcycle with a long, low chassis, is designed for the enthusiast who appreciates the classic style of early Indian® motorcycles, the machines that first put America on two wheels.

The look of the Indian Spirit Springfield harkens back to the 1917 Indian Powerplus model, with its classic, large Indian script logo. The logo appears in rich gold, surrounded by double gold pinstriping. The 2004 Indian Spirit Springfield comes with a hand-stitched solo seat, all-new contemporary front fender ornament with a chrome finish, 16-inch, 60-spoke chrome wheels and Michelin blackwall tires.

The Indian Spirit Springfield is offered in two solid colors: Jet Black and Deep Red. Manufacturer's suggested retail price is $17,795 (U.S.).

MORE

Courtesy of Mark Peterson

2004 INDIAN SPIRIT MOTORCYCLES, PAGE 5

Indian Spirit™ CST

The 2004 Indian Spirit™ CST is designed for the motorcycle enthusiast who appreciates the classic lines and styling of early Indian motorcycles in a more contemporary looking package.

The Indian Spirit CST is a seamless merging of retro and current style with elegant, 20-spoke forged aluminum wheels and Michelin blackwall tires. The Spirit CST comes with a sleek dual gunfighter seat, all-new contemporary front fender ornament with a chrome finish and newly designed Fiamm horn and horn cover.

The 2004 Indian Spirit CST is offered in three solid colors: Volcano Red Metallic, Noble Silver and Jet Black. Manufacturer's suggested retail price is $18,795 (U.S.).

MORE

Courtesy of Mark Peterson

2004 INDIAN SPIRIT MOTORCYCLES, PAGE 6

Indian Spirit™ Roadmaster

The 2004 Indian Spirit™ Roadmaster is designed to heed the call of the open road and quench any enthusiast's quest for adventure. An integrated windshield, passenger backrest and leather saddlebags couple with a long, low chassis to provide the agility riders need to cruise around town and the stability they seek for the long haul.

The Indian Spirit Roadmaster features a studded dual seat, all-new contemporary front fender ornament with a chrome finish, newly designed Fiamm horn and horn cover, Metzeler whitewall tires, 60-spoke chrome wheels, fender graphics and saddlebags emblazoned with the Roadmaster logo. The Roadmaster also features new spring-loaded, retractable floorboards with replaceable wear strip and vibration-absorbing rubber cushions embossed with Indian Motorcycle script.

The 2004 Spirit Roadmaster is offered in one solid color and five two-tone color combinations respectively: Jet Black, Jet Black/Volcano Red Metallic, Charcoal Metallic/Jet Black, Blackberry Metallic/Jet Black, and Oakleaf Metallic/Pearl White. Manufacturer's suggested retail is $18,995 (U.S.).

Motorcycles are to be used only on the road by a licensed rider. Obey all local laws and regula tions. We recommend that you always wear a helmet, protective clothing and eyewear, and that your passengers do the same. Never ride under the influence of alcohol or drugs. Ride with your headlight on at all times and ride safely. Read you owner's manual thoroughly. We recommend that all riders complete a recognized training program prior to operating a motorcycle.

Specifications, availability and prices subject to change without notice. California version differs slightly due to emissions equipment. All prices shown are the Manufacturer's Suggested Retail Price (MSRP). California models priced slightly higher, actual dealer prices may vary.

Courtesy of Mark Peterson

**2004 Indian® Spirit™ Springfield/
Indian Spirit CST/Indian Spirit Roadmaster
Specifications**

Engine:	Powerplus™ 92, 45-degree V-twin, black finish, machined fins
Displacement:	91.4 cubic inches (1498cc)
Bore X Stroke:	3.875" x 3.875"
Compression Ratio:	9.1:1
Valve System:	Two, push rod actuated with hydraulic lifters, intake diameter 1.94", exhaust diameter 1.575"
Carburetor:	1 7/8" venturi, four-pattern
Exhaust System:	Chrome, 2-into-1
Ignition:	Electronic, computer-controlled
Transmission:	Constant-mesh, five-speed
Primary Drive:	Chain, wet clutch
Final Drive:	Aramid-reinforced belt
Frame:	High-tensile steel, powder-coated black
Rake:	32 degrees
Trail:	5.25"
Front Suspension:	Paoli 41mm, hydraulic compression and rebound damping, 5.4" travel
Rear Suspension:	Nitrogen-charged hydraulic dampers, coil springs with adjustable preload
Front Brake:	Brembo, differential bore, 4-piston caliper, 11.5" rotor
Rear Brake:	Brembo, differential bore, 4-piston caliper, 11.5" rotor
Front Wheel:	60-spoke, chrome, 16" x 3.5" (Springfield, Roadmaster) Forged, polished, 16" x 3.5" (CST)
Rear Wheel:	60-spoke, chrome, 16" x 3.5" (Springfield, Roadmaster) Forged, polished, 16" x 3.5" (CST)
Front Tire:	Michelin, blackwall, 130/90-16 (Springfield, CST) Metzeler, whitewall, 130/90-16 (Roadmaster)
Rear Tire:	Michelin, blackwall, 130/90-16 (Springfield, CST) Metzeler, whitewall, 130/90-16 (Roadmaster)
Wheelbase:	67"
Seat Height:	28"
Dry Weight:	Spirit Springfield: 624 lbs. Spirit CST: 636 lbs. Spirit Roadmaster: 644 lbs.
Fuel Capacity:	5.5 US gallons including 1.2 gallon reserve
Instruments:	Speedometer with digital odometer & tripmeter
Warranty:	12 months/unlimited mileage
MSRP:	Spirit Springfield: $17,795.00 (U.S.) Spirit CST: $18,795.00 (U.S.) Spirit Roadmaster: $18,995.00 (U.S.)

Prices and specifications subject to change without notice.

Courtesy of Mark Peterson

The Thirty-Nine Documented 2004 Indian Motorcycles Sold by National Retail Equipment Liquidators

The following 2004 Indian motorcycles were offered for sale by NREL in 2004. Credit Managers Association of California reportedly held back three 2004 Indians from the sale: a red Chief CST and both Scout Two-Tens. In addition, Bill Melvin kept a Chief for himself, which was not included in this sale. These four machines, plus the thirty-nine described below, compose the forty-three 2004 Indian motorcycles known to Bill Melvin at the time of the factory liquidation. The following descriptions and VINs are compiled here as they appeared in the NREL sales listings.

Chief, Charcoal/Black; VIN # 5CDNRCAJ74G014083
Chief Roadmaster, White; VIN # 5CDNRCAJ24G014086
Chief Roadmaster, Pearl White; VIN # 5CDNRCAJ34G014016
Chief Roadmaster, White/Gold; VIN # 5CDNRCAJ04G014085
Chief Vintage, Century Red; VIN # 5CDNVCAJ24G000734
Chief Vintage, Turquoise/White; VIN # 5CDNVCAJ44G000735
Spirit Roadmaster/ Black / Metallic Gray, VIN # 5CDM5B5134G014206
Chief Vintage, Turquoise/White; VIN # 5CDNVCAJ74G000731
Chief Roadmaster, Blackberry; VIN # 5CDNRCAJ94G014084
Chief Roadmaster, Black/Gray; VIN # 5CDNRCAJ14G014080
Chief Roadmaster, Blue; VIN # 5CDNRCAJ54G014082
Spirit, Silver; VIN # 5CDM5B5144G014022
Spirit, Deep Red; VIN # 5CDM5B5114G014205
Spirit, Volcano Red; VIN # 5CDM5B5144G014019
Chief Springfield, Black; VIN # 5CDNNCAJ74G014032
Chief Springfield, Black; VIN # 5CDNNCAJ34G014030
Chief Springfield, Black; VIN # 5CDNNCAJ34G014013
Chief Custom, Red; VIN # 5CDNNCAJ24G014035
Chief Custom, Jet Black; VIN # 5CDNNCAJ84G014038
Chief, Jet Black; VIN # 5CDNNCAJ04G014034
Chief Roadmaster, Red; VIN # 5CDNRCAJ34G014081
Chief Roadmaster, Blue/Blue; VIN # 5CDNRCAJ14G014015
Chief, Cobalt Blue; VIN # 5CDNNCAJ44G014036
Chief, Cobalt Blue; VIN # 5CDNNCAJ14G014012
Chief Custom, Cobalt Blue; VIN # 5CDNNCAJ64G014037
Chief Springfield, Deep Red; VIN # 5CDNNCAJ54G014031
Chief Springfield, Red; VIN # 5CDNMCAJ74G014029
Spirit Springfield, Deep Red; VIN # 5CDM5B5124G014018
Spirit, Jet Black; VIN # 5CDM5B5144G014201
Spirit, Jet Black; VIN # 5CDM5B5104G014017
Spirit, Gray/White; VIN # 5CDM5B5104G014020
Spirit, Jet Black; VIN # 5CDMTB5194G014023
Scout, Jet Black; VIN # 5CDMTB5124G014204
Scout, Blue with Tan Seat; VIN # 5CDMTB5194G014202
Scout, Black; VIN # 5CDMTB5184G014028
Scout, Cobalt Blue; VIN # 5CDMTB5144G014026
Chief Vintage, Jet Black; VIN # 5CDNVCAJ94G000732
Spirit Roadmaster, Blackberry/Black; VIN # 5CDM5B5124G024021
Chief Deluxe, Blue; VIN # 5CDNNCAJ84G014203

At the time the 2004 Indians were being assembled, there was hope that a new investor(s) might step up to save the company. In light of the initial problems associated with the 1999–2003 Gilroy Indians, the 2004s would be IMCOA's redemption: proof that the company had prevailed and was finally building motorcycles whose warranty repairs would not haunt the enterprise. It was important to broadcast a message to potential investors: Gilroy was building world-class Indian motorcycles. Those forty-three 2004 machines would be the tangible proof.

In the end, it was a heartbreaking might-have-been. IMCOA had finally achieved the dream of an all-Indian line of high-quality motorcycles, but it came too late to save the company.

Powerplus 100 engines sit forlornly on the factory floor after the closure. One engine's intact oil lines and lack of a cam chest breather suggest that some of these units may have been warranty returns.

CHAPTER 6

Facts, Figures, Lists, and Legacy

The Indian brand cast an aura that was more powerful than money or any individual. It truly felt like you were working toward the second coming of some mythological god.

—Frank O'Connell, former president and CEO of IMCOA

Those of us who are attracted to Gilroy Indians have many and various reasons. Of course, appearance plays a major role, and one can imagine the impact made in 1999 when skirted fenders, the war bonnet on fuel tanks, war bonnet fender lamps, and the classic Indian script made their legitimate reappearance after nearly a half century. The S&S 88-cubic-inch V-twins were high-powered engines for their time, and the 2002–03 Powerplus 100 was the largest OEM motorcycle engine in America. Mated to their large primary drives and separate five-speed transmissions, these machines were quintessential American cruisers at the turn of the twenty-first century. Over two decades later, Gilroy Indians are an appealing amalgam of 1940s art deco and Y2K pre-unit technology. Unlike today's motorcycles, packed with electronic whirligigs, a Gilroy Indian takes you back to motorcycling as it once was—fundamental seat-of-the-pants adventure with few "guardrails." No gas gauge. You'll know you need gas when you hit the reserve. No illuminated gear indicator. You'll know what gear you're in by the sound of your engine and the speed you're traveling. The "instrument panel" consists of a speedometer/odometer and little lights to indicate high beam, neutral, oil, and signals. Catalytic converters? Electric windshields? Heated grips and seats? Navigation? Tire pressure indicators? Get real. Gilroy Indians embody the essence of motorcycling as it used to be, wrapped in a stylish carbureted package. They're not for everyone, but that's a good thing because they're rare machines. As the IMCOA advertising suggested, "Take your own road."

Gilroy Vehicle Identification Numbers

Many owners of IMCOA Indians are interested in the significance of vehicle identification numbers (VINs) stamped on their bikes. But like so much that occurred at Gilroy, VINs on these motorcycles are confusing. An authoritative explanation was provided by Bill Melvin, former CEO of NREL, Inc., shortly after he liquidated IMCOA:

This sometimes-haphazard VIN distribution—as well as skipped blocks of numbers—may be why the reported annual production figures total 15,759 plus 676 special models (Millennium, Silver Cloud, Neiman Marcus, T3, 9/11 Spirit). From these numbers, one might surmise that over 16,000 Gilroy Indians had been built, but my research shows (with only a handful of exceptions) Gilroy VINs trailing off in the mid-12,000 range. Accordingly, I have chosen to credit the 13,000 figure cited by IMCOA executive vice president Fran O'Hagan at the time of closure.

According to all factory employees at Indian, there was never any continuity of VIN numbers or engine numbers on production machines. To explain this further, there was not a match between frame numbers and engine numbers, nor was there a systematic sequence between the engine or frame numbers. They were put together at random . . . VIN numbers were stamped [on the frames] at the beginning of the production line, which started at the south end [of the factory]. Engines were installed a few stations to the north . . .

Frames were used as they were built or needed, and a new model or a different model would just get the next frame in line. Also, some frames may have been stamped and then discarded or used for some other purpose than the production at hand. In some cases, certain numbers were just skipped.

As to why, I'm not sure. But there was little order to the application of numbers at the factory. Many . . . questions will arise about the order in which certain machines were built. The truth is that even though a machine might have a lower VIN number than its partner, a machine that was started down the line at a later date may have been finished earlier. If . . . a certain machine needed more attention or a mistake was made, it would be removed from the line, corrected, and put back on. There was never any guarantee that a low-numbered machine was the first off the line, unless it was a special event and recorded as such. For example . . . the first Scout has a frame number ending in 21!

Gilroy VIN Code

As noted in the "Gilroy Vehicle Identification Numbers" section, numerous IMCOA employees have reported that there were unused blocks of serial numbers, and that they were not always issued sequentially. There was no strict continuity between the VIN and engine number, although there was of course a general trajectory toward higher numbers over time. For these reasons, determining a Gilroy Indian's production sequence by its VIN is impossible. At times, a higher VIN would leave the assembly line before a lower number, depending on parts availability or problems encountered on a particular build. Be aware that a number of Gilroy Indians were assembled by private parties from leftover parts obtained at the factory sale. When considering a 2003–04 Indian, check the Mylar certification label on the frame to determine if it was a factory build. (It has been reliably reported that one of the frame certification label printers was stolen at the time of the factory closure, which may have resulted in fraudulent 2004 labels on some machines. The original sales sheets exist, which can verify the authenticity of most 2004 Indians. A list of documented 2004 Indian Motorcycles is included in chapter 5.)

As printed in the IMCOA service manuals, "The VIN is stamped into a plate welded to the front frame tube on the right side near the fork pivot [steering neck]. It is also printed on the mylar certification label affixed to the frame tube just below the VIN plate." There are seventeen characters in an IMCOA vehicle identification number:

The first three characters (5CD) indicate an IMCOA product.

The fourth character indicates the frame style:
C = stretched/raked smoothtail (Chief, 1999–2001).
N = single down-tube monoshock (Chief, 2002–04).
M = single down-tube smoothtail (Scout/Spirit, 2001–04).

The fifth character indicates the model:
N = Chief
3 = Centennial Chief
X = Chief Deluxe
R = Chief Roadmaster
V = Chief Vintage
T = Scout
C = Centennial Scout
5 = Spirit

The sixth character indicates the engine:
B = 88 cubic inches
C = 100 cubic inches

The seventh character indicates the horsepower:
5 = 85 hp (S&S 88)
A = 75 hp (PP 100)
(Reported horsepower specs for these two engines vary widely. Original Indian certificates of origin list the PP100 at only 65 hp! Installing the optional war bonnet billet chrome air cleaner with its included carburetor jets boosted horsepower, but the PP100's real forte was torque—nearly 92 ft.-lbs. in stock form.)

The eighth character indicates the engine manufacturer:
1 = S&S
J = Indian

The ninth character is a checksum error detection variable. It can be ignored.

The tenth character indicates the model year:
X = 1999
Y = 2000
1 = 2001
2 = 2002
3 = 2003
4 = 2004

The eleventh character indicates the IMCOA factory:
G = Gilroy, California
The remaining six numbers are the serial sequencing.

Reported Annual IMCOA Production Numbers

For many years, the following Gilroy production numbers have been widely posted on the internet. These numbers have not been verified and should be regarded as estimates. No one seems to know the exact source of these figures ("They came from the factory") or whether they reflect production for calendar years, fiscal years, or model years. The production numbers for special models are believed to be accurate.

1999 total (Chiefs): 1,109
2000 total (Chiefs): 3,616
2001 total (Chiefs, Spirits, and Scouts): 3,856
2002 total (Chiefs, Spirits, and Scouts): 3,278
2003 total (Chiefs, Spirits, and Scouts): 3,900–4,000
Special models:
Millennium Chief: 252
Silver Cloud Chief: 226
Centennial Chief: 215
Neiman Marcus Chief: Advertised as seventy-five but has been reliably reported that only approximately forty were manufactured.
9/11 Spirit with flag: 70
T3 Chief: 52
Chief Vintage: 655
An interesting comparison: Reported Harley-Davidson production during the IMCOA years
1999: 184,954
2000: 209,635
2001: 240,416
2002: 273,233
2003: 301,000
Total reported H-D production during the Gilroy era (1999–2003): 1,209,238

PP 100 Engine Numbers

Each Indian Powerplus 100 installed in a production Chief carried a six-digit serial number stamped into a boss located on the left-hand side of the crank case, just above the primary housing, at the base of the rear cylinder. The first four digits were the actual engine serial number. The final two digits corresponded to the calendar year in which the engine was manufactured. In January 2003 the serial numbers were reset to "0001," and the final two digits were changed from "02" to "03."

The author conducted research to determine whether enough correlation existed between Chief production dates and their sequentially numbered Powerplus 100 engines, which might suggest production numbers for the 2002–03 Chiefs. Two different Facebook groups devoted to Gilroy Indians were canvassed, and three conclusions were reached.

(1) Although there certainly is no strict correlation of engine numbers / VINs / manufacture dates, there naturally is a general pattern of gradually higher PP 100 serial numbers as Chief manufacture progressed. (Note that the PP 100 was built and sequentially numbered by Performance Assembly Solutions in Livonia, Michigan—not IMCOA in Gilroy, California.)

(2) The PP 100 engine number year suffix indicates *calendar* year of manufacture, not IMCOA model year (which typically—but not always—began in September of the previous year). In the case of the 2002 Chiefs equipped with the new PP 100, the bikes were not available until the spring of 2002. Early-production 2003 model year Chiefs will be found with "02" suffixes on their PP 100 engine numbers.

(3) It was initially hoped that a rough estimate of Chief production for each calendar year (2002 and 2003) might be made through their PP 100 engine numbers. Since IMCOA was still working through inventoried 2002 PP 100s in early 2003, it's apparent that PAS engine production was exceeding IMCOA's motorcycle production (as noted in chapter 2). The haphazard order in which engines were installed in frames makes an accurate production estimate very difficult without a large sample of existing bikes. As a result, no reliable estimates of Chief production in 2002 and 2003 can presently be inferred from PP 100 engine numbers.

Powerplus 100 Engine Rebuilds

The Powerplus 100 often experienced failure in its original form (see chapter 2 for details). As a result, a cottage industry developed to rebuild these engines. Most (but not all) rebuilders marked the rebuilt engines in some manner. Here are commonly encountered rebuild markings:

(1) IMCOA-Subsidized Rebuilds

The Powerplus 100 has an engine number stamped on the left side of the crankcase, just above the primary housing and at the base of the rear cylinder. A stamped suffix (a capital "R") to the engine number is explained by Frank Aliano, Blackhawk Motor Works, Inc.:

> While Indian [Gilroy] was still in business and after upgrades and testing was completed by Posie and me [Frank Aliano] as consultants, Indian contracted both our businesses [Blackhawk, P&M Powertrain] to rebuild engines that had failed in the field to our new, approved specifications. Indian would ship the engines to us; we would rebuild them and send back in pallets of six. Each of our facilities was rebuilding ten engines per week. All engines rebuilt by our facilities were marked with an "R" at the end of the serial number, regardless of which facility did the rebuilding.

(2) Blackhawk Motor Works

As noted above, Frank Aliano (Blackhawk Motor Works) worked as a consultant at Gilroy from 2001 to 2003 and was on-site for the first eleven months. Aliano plus Posie & Mikey (P&M Powertrain, Ltd.) developed fixes for the PP100.

On early Blackhawk rebuilds with Falco cases, this engraving is seen:

Courtesy of Tom Borchardt

> After the closing of Gilroy Indian and upon Blackhawk and P&M rebuilding engines as independent builders, any engine that came in my shop with a loose pinion race insert was

remanufactured and machined for an oversize insert and also had the "Blackhawk" script machined into the front case boss. These were the Falco cases. When I started receiving engines with Mansfield cases, the script was discontinued due to the fact that the crankcase on a Mansfield is left in as-cast condition and not machined. That would have been somewhere around 2006.

—Frank Aliano, Blackhawk Motor Works, Inc.

Mansfield crank case rebuilds by Blackhawk show a stamped suffix to the engine number (RB): rebuilt by Blackhawk (Palm Bay, Florida) with a complete rebuild procedure.

Post-IMCOA PP 100 builds by Blackhawk exist. For example, one such engine is marked "BMW 70091." The "BMW" denotes "Blackhawk Motor Works"; the "7" denotes 2007; the "009" denotes the ninth engine built in 2007; the "1" denotes the engine model (PP100).

(3) P&M Powertrain Ltd.

A stamped suffix to the engine number (RP): rebuilt at P&M Powertrain Ltd. (Dilsburg, Pennsylvania) with a complete rebuild procedure (P&M Powertrain is no longer in operation).

(4) JAM Ltd.

An oval engraving encircling "JAM" indicates a rebuild at JAM Ltd. (Reno, Nevada) with a complete rebuild procedure. These markings can be found on the top of the cam case or on top of the cylinder head.

Courtesy of Paul Grice

JAM engraving on the cylinder head. *Courtesy of Gilbert Ruiz*

Celebrities and IMCOA Indians

Some recent accounts of the Gilroy Indians claim that customers weren't interested in Indian motorcycles powered by S&S engines, and even after the introduction of the Powerplus 100, the bikes never found a market. The fact is that IMCOA couldn't build the bikes fast enough, and demand (as well as production) increased each year during the firm's existence. The California Motorcycle Company (CMC) had made something of a specialty building motorcycles for celebrities. When CMC operations morphed into building Indian motorcycles, that trend continued. Gilroy Indians made quite a splash when they appeared, and were popular among actors, pro athletes, musicians, and others in the public eye. Celebrities who rode Gilroy Indians included Arnold Schwarzenegger, George Clooney, Dusty Baker (of the San Francisco Giants), Rich Gannon (of the Oakland Raiders), Tom Chambers, Ben Maccabee, Jeff Gordon, Dennis Hopper, Kenny Olson (lead guitarist for Kid Rock), Jeff Garcia and Bryant Young (both of the San Francisco 49ers), Laurence Fishburne, Mike Ditka, Billy Joel, Robert Wyland, Peter Fonda, Drew Carey, Dale Jarrett, Nicholas Hoult, Gerard Butler, Danny Trejo, drummer Mickey Jones, Arlo Guthrie, Steve McQueen, Dale Watson, Mark Wahlberg, Brad Pitt, Angelina Jolie, David Letterman, John Mellencamp, Branscombe Richmond, Dee Snider, Jon Bernthal, and Dan Aykroyd, among others.

Legacy

This one is pretty straightforward. IMCOA resurrected Indian motorcycles. Period. Would another company have done the same thing eventually? We'll never know, because it was IMCOA that coughed up twenty million 1999 dollars for the Indian IP. Every post-1998 Indian motorcycle owes its existence to IMCOA. Not a bad legacy.

> You guys are stupid—you never had to pay me. I'd have done all this for nothing, just to bring back Indian. —*Rey Sotelo, former IMCOA president and CEO, upon leaving the company in July 2002*

Interim Limbo

When IMCOA folded in 2003, the future of the legendary brand was once again in doubt. If any Indian motorcycles were to be built after 2003, they would be built by a different company. While many pondered the future of Indian, 13,000 owners of Gilroy-built Indians were facing a more pressing, personal problem. They had been left without factory/dealer support (this was particularly problematic for most owners of 2002–03 Chiefs with their Powerplus 100 engines). Some owners found qualified motorcycle mechanics to service their bikes. Others found mechanics of debatable talent, to the detriment of their Gilroy Indian motorcycles. Some became their own mechanics. Still others rode their Gilroys into the ground, eventually substituting a different bike for the deceased Indian. The failure of IMCOA immediately resulted in these bikes being exposed to maintenance of variable quality. Today, like any vintage bike, a Gilroy Indian's condition (and value) will depend on the care and skill of those who serviced and maintained it over the past decades.

IMCOA/Gilroy Indians experienced a brief production run, and it's open to question how many still exist. Much like 101 Scouts during the late 1930s / 1940s, Gilroy Indians are often regarded these days simply as "old bikes," and their value has probably reached bottom. However, as they approach "antique" status, interest in these machines will likely grow. If you have one, take care of it!

Final Thoughts

I'm aware of the current downward trajectory of the American heavyweight motorcycle industry, and the relative lack of interest among younger riders. Some doomsayers are convinced that IMCOA/Gilroy Indians will never be more than "old motorcycles." As an experienced collector and market watcher of other vintage/antique items for nearly sixty years, I firmly believe in the cyclical patterns inherent in generational interests. As a broad rule, children are usually disinterested in their parents' environment but are often attracted to their grandparents' or great-grandparents' worlds. Likewise, certain classes of goods experience an ebb and flow of popularity. Motorcycles, however, are something else again. Despite the changing styles and types demanded by riders, there has always been a fluctuating demand for motorcycles. This pattern has been observable for over a century.

The American motorcycling community has been notoriously loyal to visual designs that originated in the mid-twentieth century. As we have seen, this ultimately led to the revival of Indian, but in recent years many old-time riders have lamented the shift to smaller, "metric-looking" Indians. There are of course good reasons for this change in the market—not the least of which is the aging segment of riders who are no longer buying skirted fenders at the same rate as twenty-five years ago. If Indian is to survive as a brand (and I sincerely hope it does), it must provide what its current and future customers want.

> It's important to acknowledge where you're coming from in your heritage . . . but ultimately, you need to be relevant today, and tomorrow. So in order to do that, you know, you can't look back too much. You cannot repackage or offer again what's been offered before, just in a slightly modern way. That doesn't work.
>
> *—Massimo Frascella, director of Land Rover Creative Design*

As the passion cools for classic American cruisers, manufacturers will need to produce more of what riders demand, and on roadways populated by small, buzzing streaks of lightning, a Gilroy Indian is going to stand out. That, I believe, will ensure their long-term popularity despite the changeable tastes of the broader motorcycling community. But should some future Peter Fonda–like character appear in a feature film riding a distinctive old Gilroy Indian, who knows what might happen?

And So . . .

> The motorcycle industry is not for the faint of heart. [It] takes an awful lot of capital to succeed. . . . In the end, the company didn't have the money.
> *—Fran O'Hagan, executive vice president of IMCOA*

The Indian Motorcycle Corporation of America died with neither a bang nor a whimper. Most employees recall Friday, September 19, 2003, beginning as an ordinary day. At lunchtime, paychecks were distributed. Then, around 2:15 p.m., Lou Terhar (IMCOA's president and CEO) made the fatal announcement to his workforce. It was followed by stunned silence and some weeping. Over the next

One of the "might-have-beens" discovered in the IMCOA factory: a prototype 2005 bagger called the "Silver Arrow."
Courtesy of Mark Peterson

days and weeks, there was mourning and the usual stages of grief. It was as though a dream rather than a company had died. Over time, work-related belongings were stashed away, stories were occasionally shared, and the former IMCOA employees gradually got on with their lives. But they never forgot. Over the years, the memories of coworkers, their exploits, and the motorcycles they built became almost legendary. The company didn't survive, but the brand it resurrected persists to this day. The legend still lives and is a fitting eulogy for the Gilroy-based Indian Motorcycle Corporation of America.

APPENDIX

The Tortuous Trail of the Indian IP

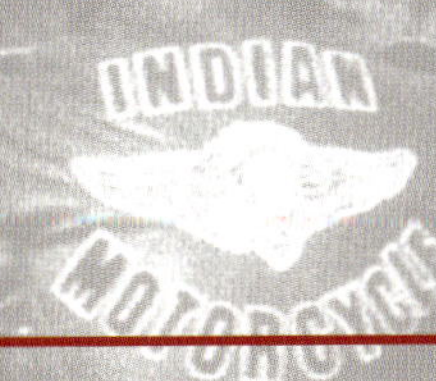

In 1949, Indian was divided into two separate companies: the Indian division of the Titeflex Corporation (itself a division of the Atlas Corporation), and the Indian Sales Corporation. Frederick B. Stote, president of the Sales Corporation, utilized part of the East Springfield factory for warehousing. The Sales Corporation also began importation and sales of the following British motorcycles: AJS, Douglas, Excelsior, Royal Enfield, Matchless, Norton, and Vincent-HRD. The Royal Enfield motorcycles were initially badged as "Indians" but later were sold under Americanized model names through Indian dealers.

In May 1953, the last American-made Indian motorcycles were assembled in Springfield, Massachusetts.

On December 2, 1953, a letter was sent to all Indian dealers, which read, in part,

> The management of the Indian Company has just completed a study of conditions adversely affecting motorcycle production in the United States. This has led to a decision to suspend assembly of complete motorcycles at Springfield during 1954. The sole purpose of this production holiday is to strengthen the position of the Company for future activities in the motorcycle manufacturing field. During this period, Indian manufacturing facilities will be engaged in parts fabrication and other revenue-producing operations.

Motorcycle manufacturing was never resumed.

After the 1955 sales season, the import rights to all British motorcycle brands except Royal Enfield were sold to individual US distributors.

On September 1, 1959, the Indian Sales Corporation was acquired by Associated Motorcycles, Ltd.

In 1962, with the failure of Associated Motorcycles, Ltd., the Indian Sales Corporation was acquired by the Berliner Motor Company of Hasbrouck Heights, New Jersey. It soon passed into the hands of Norton-Matchless Ltd., followed by a holding corporation called Metal Profiles Ltd.

In July 1962, "the Indian Company" of Chicopee Falls, Massachusetts, announced its liquidation. At roughly the same time, Sam Pierce unsuccessfully attempted to purchase the old Titeflex tooling. In 1968, Pierce built a few "Super Scout" Indian motorcycles, using vintage engines in new frames. Pierce claimed that the Indian name had been abandoned and was public domain. He eventually reorganized his business as "the American Indian Motocycle Company" and later sold it to Charles Mathre.

In the mid-1960s, Floyd Clymer registered Indian trademarks under the Clymer Publishing Company in Colorado and California. At the time, there was no Indian motorcycle manufacturer to protest.

In 1967, Floyd Clymer commissioned Friedl Münch to develop a modern Indian Scout in Germany. Clymer acquired the US distribution rights and operated the business, allowing Münch to focus on R&D. A factory was built in Ossenheim, West Germany, employing about twenty people.

In 1968 and 1969, Clymer marketed an "Indian" with a 500 cc single-cylinder Velocette Thruxton engine, in addition to 50 cc "Indian"-branded minibikes built by Italjet. Floyd Clymer died in January 1970. The train of events he set in motion would not be settled for nearly thirty years.

The insidious appropriation of the Indian trademarks begins.

CLYMER PAPOOSE

ENGINE

Type	single cylinder, two cycle
Bore and stroke	38.8mm x 42mm
Displacement	49.6cc
Compression ratio	10.0 to 1
Max. horsepower	4.9 at 8,000 rpm
Ignition	flywheel magneto
Carburetion	one 19mm U.A. Dell'Orto
Lubrication	oil in gas

DIMENSIONS

Length	60 inches
Seat height	25 inches
Wheelbase	45 inches
Ground clearance	6.2 inches
Dry weight	130 pounds

BRAKES

Front brake	single leading shoe
Rear brake	single leading shoe
Tires	choice of trail or street

TRANSMISSION

Type	4-speed, foot operated
Clutch	wet, multi plate
Primary drive	gear

PERFORMANCE

Indicated highest one-way speed	47 mph
Acceleration 0-60	none
Braking distance 30-0	31 feet

FRAME AND SUSPENSION

Front suspension	telehydraulic fork
Rear suspension	hydraulic shock
Frame type	tubular backbone

COLORS -- red, blue
PRICE AS TESTED -- $345.00

DISTRIBUTOR
Floyd Clymer, Motorcycle Division
222 N. Virgil Ave.
Los Angeles, Calif.

Indian The "Family" Line in Cycling

MINI MINI

An engineering jewel — a true miniaturized motorcycle. Only 18 inches high and weighing 57 pounds, the Mini Mini is perfect for the four to eight year old. Recommended for the youngest riders, its 50cc engine has been detuned to limit maximum speed to 10 m.p.h. but can easily be made to go 20 to 25 m.p.h. The Mini Mini starts with an easy kick, has an automatic "no shift" transmission, full front and rear suspension, safe dual brakes, chrome spoke wheels, Pirelli tires and a competition number plate. Sturdy spring-loaded training wheels are available as an option. Your choice of red, blue or yellow.

SCRAMBLER '50'

Just right for the young trail rider from eight to fourteen, this model fills the gap between a mini-bike and a full-size motorcycle. Full suspension, large 16-inch spoke wheels and superior brakes make for perfect handling. Excellent workmanship, attention to detail and a polished finish add up to an outstanding appearance. Skid plate, extra clearance fenders, a fully shielded exhaust and three competition-type number plates are all "plus items" included at no extra cost. This model is available with either a four-speed transmission or single-speed fully automatic and comes in red, blue and yellow.

BOBCAT

The finest mini-cycle ever built gives you superior performance in either the supersport '50' or enduro '100' model. It is equipped with chrome fenders, spoke wheels, upswept exhaust, four-speed transmission, telescopic forks with deep travel, kick-starter, large comfortable seat, full suspension and dual brakes. These features give this machine a real "big bike" feel and make it the ideal model for both Dad and son. Lighting equipment is optional.

COMPETITION SCRAMBLER '100'

The high performance Competition Scrambler '100' is for the serious rider who only wants the best. Housed in a light single-cradle frame, it features a race proven two-stroke engine. It is equipped with special motocross forks having a full 6½ inches of travel, adjustable rear shocks, high-volume air cleaner, expansion chamber, skid plate, quick action throttle and powerful brakes. This beauty is designed to be a winner right out of the box.

In 1971, Charles Manthos reported that Floyd Clymer's widow had agreed to sell him the Indian trademark rights for $10,000. Manthos leased a portion of the original East Springfield Indian factory, intending to build new engines/gearboxes for 1940s–'50s Chiefs. When Floyd Clymer's widow unexpectedly sold the Indian rights to Alan Newman, Manthos gave up the project.

In 1972, Alan Newman's "Indian" operation was launched in Taiwan, manufacturing mopeds until the late 1970s. The Indian trademarks were then offered for bid in the *Los Angeles Times* as part of the defunct company's assets.

On January 28, 1978, Carmen D. DeLeone purchased the Indian trademarks from Alan Newman (who had purchased them from Floyd Clymer's widow). He had the trademarks registered under his own name in 1983. DeLeone believed he had the right to manufacture clothing, motorcycle parts, hand luggage, and other retail items with the Indian trademark.

In 1984, Carmen DeLeone considered manufacturing replica Indian Chief motorcycles, but the high cost of tooling and lack of a dealership network prompted him to drop the project.

On June 4, 1990, Carmen DeLeone assigned one-half of the Indian trademark rights to Philip S. Zanghi. At about the same time, Zanghi announced that he was organizing a manufacturing company to revive the Indian motorcycle. He made these announcements in New York, Boston, and the home of the original Indian motorcycles, Springfield, Massachusetts, promising that motorcycle production would be underway by 1993. Licenses to use the Indian trademark on various products were sold, as well as dealership franchises. Zanghi negotiated a contract with Robert Stark to build an updated Indian Chief, but when Stark closely examined the contract, he discovered that by signing, he would have relinquished control of his entire restoration and parts sales to Zanghi.

In 1990, Wayne Baughman formed a company in Albuquerque, New Mexico (Indian Motorcycle Manufacturing Inc., or IMMI), for the revival of the Indian motorcycle. Baughman disputed DeLeone's and Zanghi's claims to the trademarks and began to offer dealership franchises.

This is what an "Indian Four" looked like in 1941.

This is what an "Indian Four" looked like in 1979. Oh, the humanity . . . !

In 1990, Philip Zanghi registered a new firm in Massachusetts as the American Indian Motorcycle Company. He began demanding royalties from firms and individuals who were using Indian trademarks.

In 1991, Carmen DeLeone filed legal action against Zanghi, claiming he had not been reimbursed for his share of dealer franchise income. Litigation was settled with Zanghi being awarded full ownership of the Indian trademark.

In May 1991, Wayne Baughman announced production of Indian Sport Scouts, adding that the project would require a $10 million outlay and the acquisition of a 30,000-square-foot factory, and that IMMI dealer franchises and stock were available.

During 1991–92, Philip Zanghi made arrangements with several engineering firms to design updated Indians but never paid for any work. Suspicion of Zanghi mounted, and he fled to Hartford, Connecticut, offering stock and dealer franchises.

In the fall of 1992, Wayne Baughman announced that production of new IMMI Sport Scouts was being postponed, with the focus on the all-new IMMI "Century Chief."

In 1993, Philip Zanghi, fleeing a class-action lawsuit, moved his operation to Raleigh, North Carolina. In August 1993, Zanghi closed his office on Avocado Street in Springfield. That same month, Zanghi's American Indian Motorcycle Company was forced into Chapter 7 involuntary bankruptcy by unpaid advertisers and engineering firms. Meanwhile, Zanghi was still offering dealerships and stock in Atlanta and Athens, Georgia. In October, it was reported that Zanghi had fled to Spain.

In the late fall of 1993, Wayne Baughman reported that prototype work had been completed on the "Century Chief."

In the early spring of 1994, Wayne Baughman placed public advertisements inviting all Indian enthusiasts to attend a June IMMI open house in Albuquerque. During this demonstration, the motorcycles could not be ridden, but rides were promised for a scheduled Las Vegas dealership opening in September. The promised rides did not occur, and in October all communication from Baughman ceased and IMMI phone lines were discovered to be disconnected.

In February 1995, an Albuquerque press release announced that the Indian Motorcycle Manufacturing Inc. (IMMI) had remaining liquid assets of only $22,000.

On April 7, 1995, a court complaint was filed by Eller Industries (an investor in Baughman's IMMI) to appoint a receiver for the failed enterprise. Sterling Consulting (Richard Block as president) was appointed receiver on April 10.

In early 1995, a group of Australian investors announced their intention to manufacture new Indian motorcycles. The group had purchased licensing and manufacturing rights from Zanghi's defunct American Indian Motorcycle Company and, in addition, had the support of Charles Mathre. The group was prepared to make whole Zanghi's creditors to the tune of $2 million.

Meanwhile, amid the chaos surrounding the contested Indian IP, the number of licensed 1901–53 Indian motorcycles rose to over 50,000 (from approximately 35,000 in the mid-1970s).

On September 7, 1995, Colorado-based First Entertainment Inc. claimed to assume control of Indian trademarks and logos from Zanghi's American Indian Motorcycle Manufacturing Company. The subsidiary would be called "Indian Motorcycle Classic Kit Company."

On March 7, 1996, David J. Noonan and Richard (Rick) A. Block appeared at the Klassic Museum at Daytona to answer questions concerning the possibility for a revival of Indian motorcycles. Noonan

Introducing
The New
Century V-Twin Chief
All American
Motorcycle!

Wherever They Go
The Crowds Gather!
Only A Limited
Number Of Chiefs
Will Be Produced
In 1995.

was trustee in bankruptcy action against Philip Zanghi's companies ("American Indian Motorcycle Manufacturing Company," "Indian Motorcycle Apparel Company," and "Indian Motorcycle Company, Inc."). Block was the receiver for Wayne Baughman's Indian Motorcycle Manufacturing, Inc. (IMMI). By September 1996, the trustee and the receiver had consolidated all material aspects of Indian, including all trademarks and partially developed prototypes. These assets, as well as the complainants who had lost their investments with Zanghi and Baughman, became known as the "Indian estate."

During late 1996–February 1997, First Entertainment was widely reported to be behind the consolidation of Indian IP, and the corporation continued to make public announcements that it held controlling interest in Indian IP and owned worldwide licensing rights for Indian logos and trademarks. First Entertainment had agreed to pay $2.3 million to Block & Noonan for arranging a sales transaction, but by February 1996, no payments had been made, so Block & Noonan canceled the agreement.

On August 13, 1997, Philip Zanghi was convicted of twelve counts of securities fraud, three counts of tax evasion, and six counts of money laundering. In December, he was sentenced to seven and a half years in federal prison.

In 1998, Eller Industries (Lonnie Labriola, president) raised several million dollars and announced plans to build a new line of Indian motorcycles. Eller secured several respected consultants and invested $1.5 million in developing a new Indian engine. Rick Block, the court-appointed receiver for Baughman's IMMI, and now acting for the Indian estate, expressed his support for the Eller group's bid to settle the claims of the Indian estate, and to eventually purchase the Indian trademarks and IP. The Eller group developed two prototype motorcycles, which attracted favorable attention from the motorcycle press.

In September–October 1998, Rey Sotelo's California Motorcycle Company was purchased by a consortium that would soon become the Indian Motorcycle Company of America (IMCOA; based in Gilroy, California).

In October 1998, Rick Block reported that the Eller group had missed one of its scheduled payments to the Indian estate, and declared the contract broken.

On November 6, 1998, Block obtained a restraining order that prohibited public display of the Eller prototypes or pictures of them, claiming that the Eller group had failed to act according to schedule, a claim that Lonnie Labriola vehemently denied. Block shifted his support to the Gilroy group (IMCOA).

On December 7, 1998, US District Court judge Zita L Weinshienk declared IMCOA to be the contract purchaser of Indian estate assets.

In March 1999, IMCOA was formally awarded ownership of all Indian IP, with the requirement that new Indian motorcycles be available within one year. After a half century, the Indian motorcycle designs, trademarks, and model names were once again under the legal ownership and protection of a single corporate entity: the Indian Motorcycle Company of America (IMCOA). In this way, the iconic Indian motorcycle brand was resurrected.

On September 19, 2003, IMCOA abruptly closed its factory and laid off its employees.

In July 2004, the Indian IP was purchased by Stellican Ltd., and in 2009 production of new Indian motorcycles commenced in Kings Mountain, North Carolina. The bikes—all Chiefs—were improved copies of the IMCOA Chiefs powered by the improved Powerplus engine, bored out to 105 cubic inches.

In April 2011, Polaris Inc. purchased the Stellican operation and transferred production of Chiefs to its plant in Spirit Lake, Iowa. For the next two years, Polaris manufactured and sold the Indian motorcycles, whose fundamental designs were developed by IMCOA in Gilroy, California.

SELECTED BIBLIOGRAPHY

There were countless newspaper and magazine accounts documenting the revival and subsequent struggles of the Indian Motorcycle brand in Gilroy. A comprehensive bibliography would consume dozens of pages and be largely repetitive. The following selected bibliography is a good representation of what was being published on the subject from 1999 through 2003 and also includes earlier source material.

Carroll, John. *The Classic Indian Motorcycle*. London: Salamander, 1996.

Cho, Joshua. "Events." *Indian Motorcycle Illustrated*, January 1995.

Chung, Dennis. "Polaris Says Indian Motorcycle Turned a Profit for the First Time." *Motorcycle.com*, February 1, 2024. https://www.motorcycle.com/bikes/news/polaris-says-indian-motorcycle-turned-a-profit-for-the-first-time-44598298.

Crowley, Peter. "Indian Motorcycle Brand Sold; Gilroy Considered for Plant." *Gilroy (CA) Dispatch*, July 27, 2004.

Crowley, Peter, and Eric Leins. "Indian Shuts Its Doors." *Gilroy (CA) Dispatch*, September 22, 2003.

Douglas, Clayton R. "Heart of the New Indian." *Indian Motorcycle Illustrated*, Summer 1994.

Friedman, Art. "Indian Motorcycle Company Goes Bankrupt." *Motorcycle Cruiser*, October 2003.

Friedman, Art. "Indian's Stillborn 2004 Motorcycles." *Motorcycle Cruiser*, September 2003.

Haefele, Fred. "The Lost Tribe of Indian." *American Heritage*, August/September 2005.

Hanson, Tom. "Letters." *Indian Motorcycle Illustrated*, Autumn 1994.

Hatfield, Jerry. *Indian Motorcycle Photographic History*. Osceola, WI: Motorbooks, 1993.

Holstrom, Darwin. *120 Years of America's First Motorcycle Company*. Beverly, MA: Motorbooks, 2020.

"Indian Motorcycle Roars Ahead with $45 Million in New Funding." *Auto Channel*, June 25, 2001. https://www.theautochannel.com/news/2001/06/25/023935.html.

"Indian Motorcycle Sells 45 Million of Preferred Stock to Audax." *Boston Business Journal*, June 25, 2001. https://www.bizjournals.com/boston/stories/2001/06/25/daily3.html.

"Indian Motorcycles Are Ready to Roar Back to Life." *San Jose Mercury News* (reprinted by *Orlando Sentinel* on August 19, 1999).

"Indian Shutdown: No Choice." *Gilroy (CA) Dispatch*, September 25, 2003.

Kanter, Buzz. "The Indian Saga, What's This All About?" *American Iron*, February 1999.

Kanter, Buzz. "The Indian Saga, Part II, Indian Giver." *American Iron*, March 1999.

"Last of Indian's Motorcycles for Sale." *Gilroy (CA) Dispatch*, April 16, 2004.

McCraw, Jim. "Revival of Indian Cycle Runs Into a New Barrier." *New York Times*, November 15, 1998.

McDermon, Daniel. "At Indian, One More Try at a Comeback." *New York Times*, October 1, 2009.

Meikle, Brad. "Audax Jumpstarts Indian Motorcycle." Buyoutinsider.com, July 16, 2001. https://www.buyoutsinsider.com/audax-jumpstarts-indian-motorcycle/.

Melvin, Bill. Reminiscences shared January–March 2023 on "Gilroy Indian Motorcycles" Facebook group (private). https://www.facebook.com/groups/1617550735224694.

Melvin, Bill. Unpublished essay.

Moriarty, Dave R. "Letters." *Indian Motorcycle Illustrated*, January 1995.

"Motorcycles—an Indian Uprising." *Los Angeles Business Journal*, September 10, 2000.

Nauman, Matt. "Remnants of a Ride."*Mercury News*, March 17, 2004.

O'Connell, Frank J. *Jump First, Think Fast*. New York: Worth Books, 2022.

"On the Indian Auction Block." *Gilroy (CA) Dispatch*, January 20, 2004.

Peacock, Nigel. "Before You Choke: Interview the Interviewer; Rey Sotelo." July 8, 2021. https://anchor.fm/nigel-peacock7/episodes/Interview-the-Interviewer---Rey-Sotelo-e144uk8.

Peterson, Mark. "On the Warpath." *Easyriders*, April 1999.

Placa, J. Joshua. "Indian Trademark Saga." *Indian Motorcycle Illustrated*, Spring 1993.

Placa, J. Joshua. "Return of the Indian." *Indian Motorcycle Illustrated*, Winter 1993.

Printz, Larry, "The Rise and Fall (and Rise Again) of Retro Car Design," *Ars Technica*, January 15, 2021.

Rafferty, Tod. *The Indian*. London: Salamander, 2001.

Sawyer, Christopher A. "An Honest Engine." *Manufacturing Marketer*, May 1, 2002.

Scott, Phil. "The Indian Rides Again." *Cigar Aficionado*, March/April 2003.

Seidel Ray. "Interview with Rey Sotelo." *Quick Throttle*, December 2016. https://www.facebook.com/photo/?fbid=10220809426159098&set=gm.4332103330146751.

Stellican. Press release: "Owners of Chris-Craft Boats Acquire Indian Motorcycle Brand." July 26, 2004. Sarasota, FL.

Sucher, Harry V. "Indian Sighting in Albuquerque." *Indian Motorcycle Illustrated*, Autumn 1994.

Sucher, Harry V. *The Iron Redskin*. Sparkford, UK: Haynes, 2010.

Sullivan, John. "Inside the New Indian Chief Motor." *Hot Rod Bikes*, April 2003.

Szczesny, Joseph. "Indian Cycles' Failure a Tale of Recalls." *Chicago Tribune*, July 11, 2004.

UMC Staff. "Indian Motorcycle . . . The Resurrection." *Ultimate Motorcycle*, November 4, 2009.

"Uneasy Rider." *Forbes*, September 17, 2001. https://www.forbes.com/forbes/2001/0917/124.html?sh=541f8c2a49fa.

Wilson, Marshall. "Indian Roars Back to Life; Gilroy Factory Builds First Motorcycles to Don Legendary Name Since 1953." *San Francisco Chronicle*, August 16, 1999.